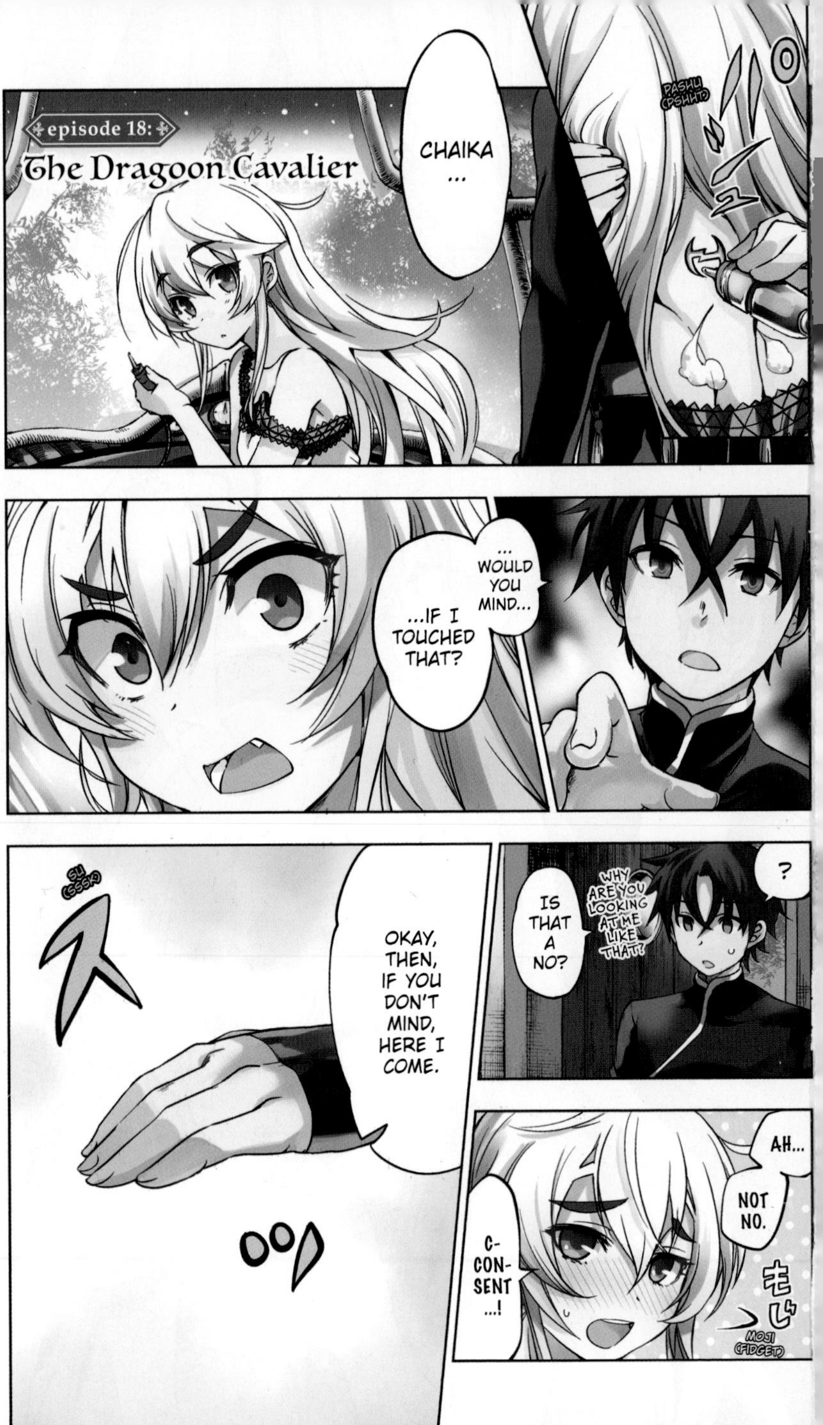
PASHU (PSHHT)
CHAIKA ...
episode 18:
The Dragoon Cavalier
... WOULD YOU MIND...
...IF I TOUCHED THAT?
?
IS THAT A NO?
WHY ARE YOU LOOKING AT ME LIKE THAT?
AH...
NOT NO.
MOJI (FIDGET)
C-CONSENT ...!
OKAY, THEN, IF YOU DON'T MIND, HERE I COME.
SU (SSSK)

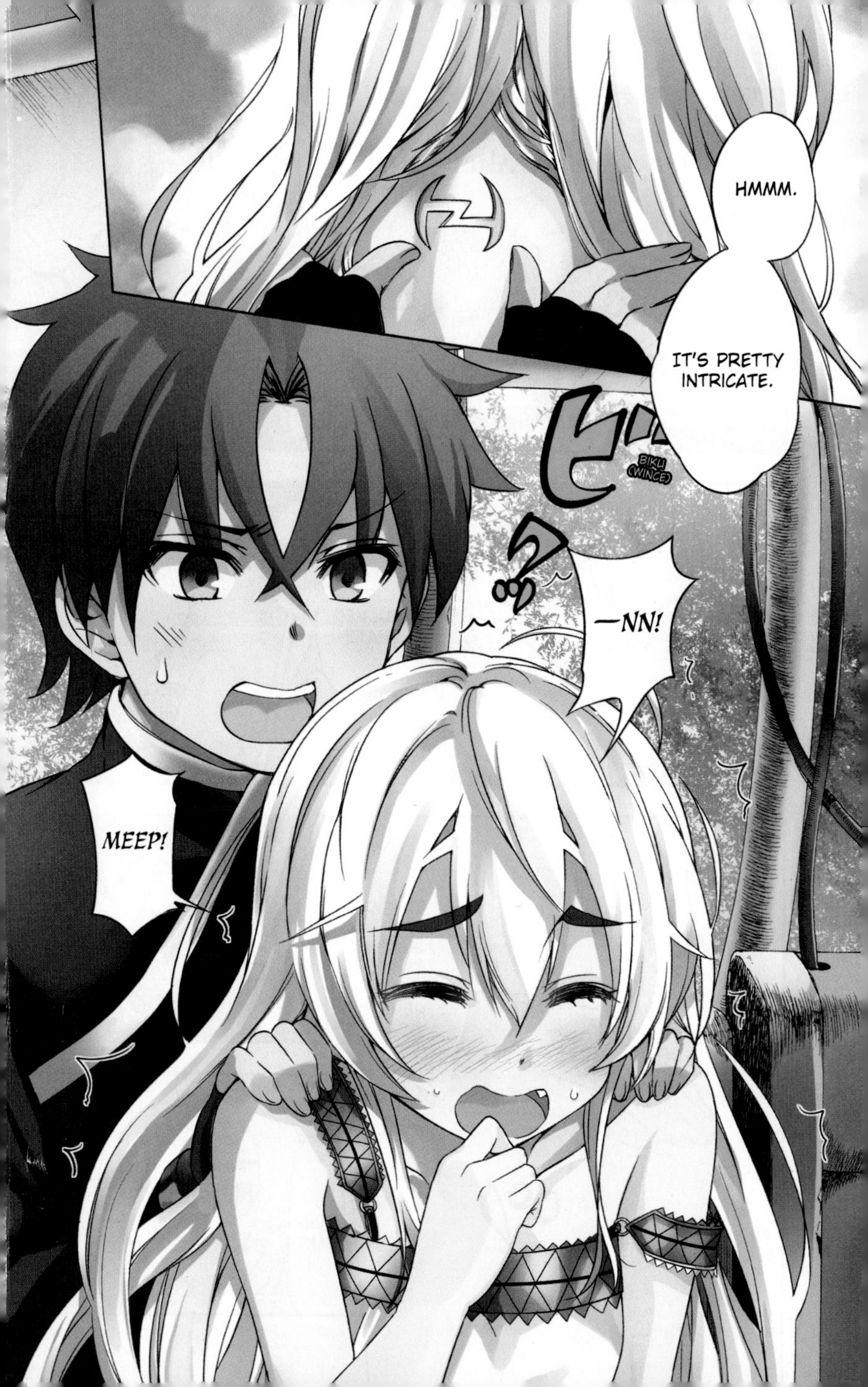
HMMM.
IT'S PRETTY INTRICATE.
BIKU (WINCE)
—NN!
MEEP!

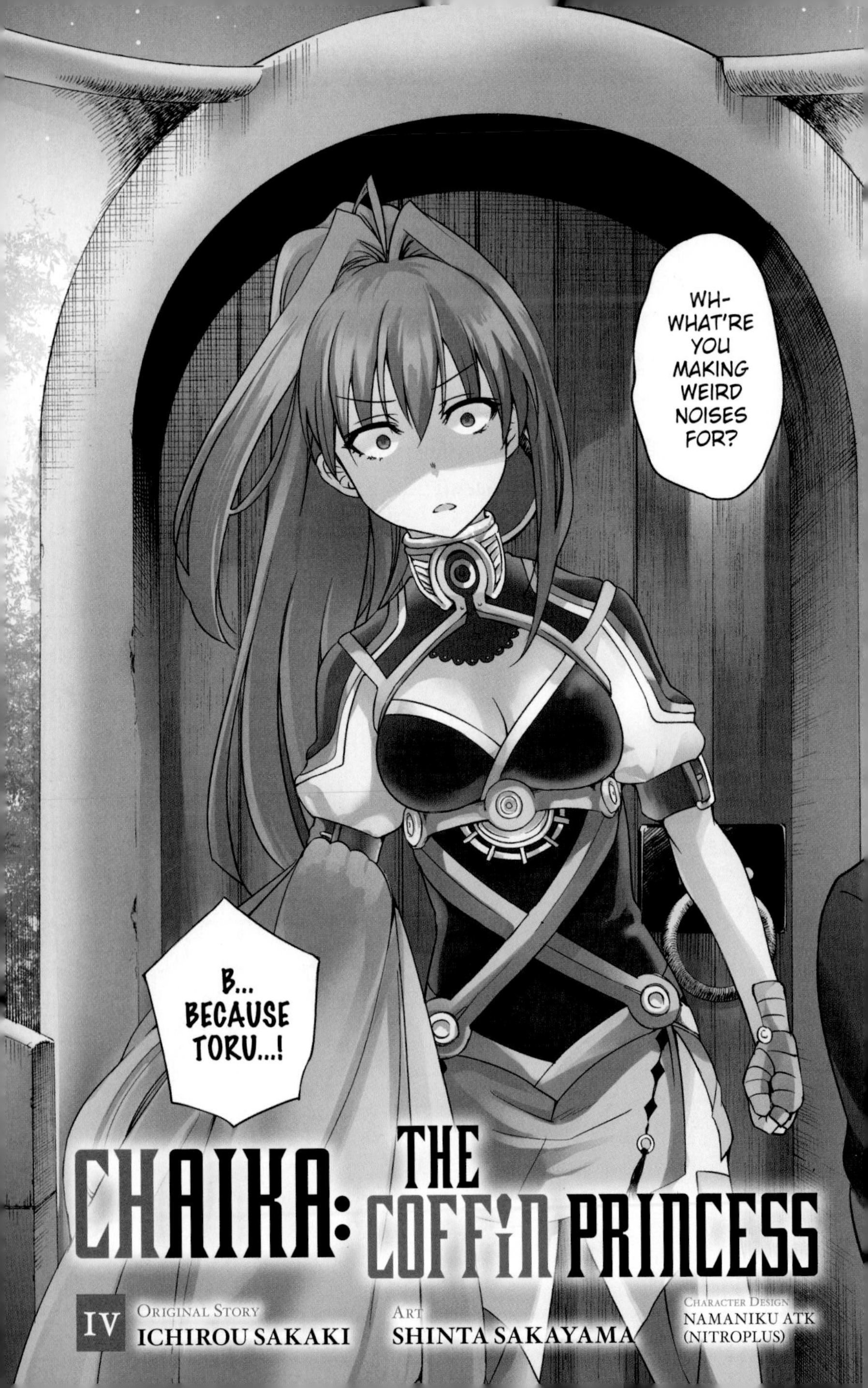
WH- WHAT'RE YOU MAKING WEIRD NOISES FOR?
B... BECAUSE TORU...!
CHAIKA: THE COFFIN PRINCESS
IV
ORIGINAL STORY ICHIROU SAKAKI
ART SHINTA SAKAYAMA
CHARACTER DESIGN NAMANIKU ATK (NITROPLUS)

CONTENTS

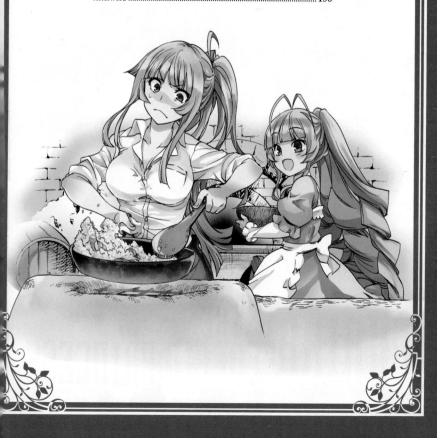

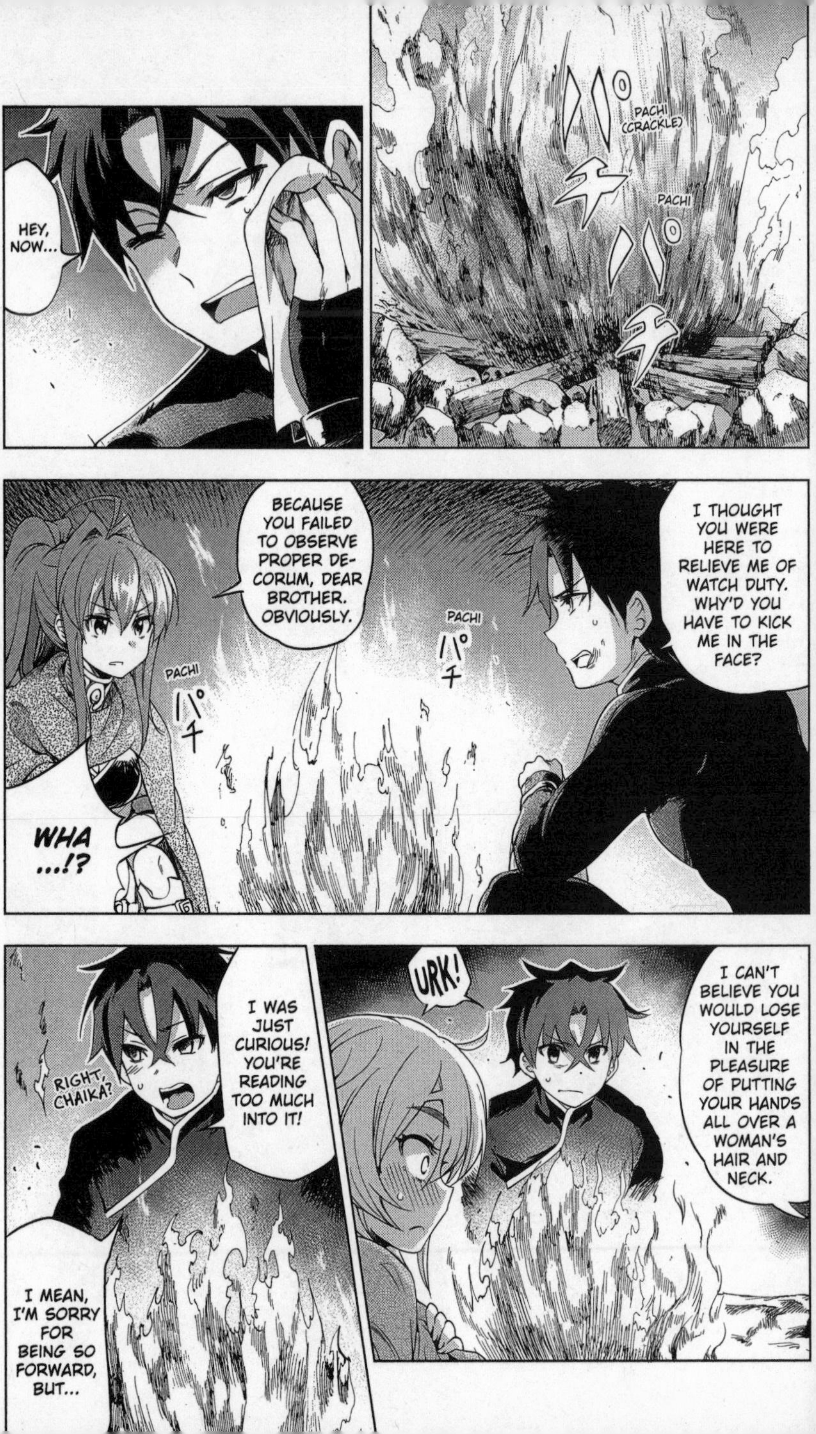
パチ
PACHI (CRACKLE)
パチ
PACHI
HEY, NOW...
I THOUGHT YOU WERE HERE TO RELIEVE ME OF WATCH DUTY. WHY'D YOU HAVE TO KICK ME IN THE FACE?
パチ
PACHI
BECAUSE YOU FAILED TO OBSERVE PROPER DE-CORUM, DEAR BROTHER. OBVIOUSLY.
パチ
PACHI
WHA ...!?
I CAN'T BELIEVE YOU WOULD LOSE YOURSELF IN THE PLEASURE OF PUTTING YOUR HANDS ALL OVER A WOMAN'S HAIR AND NECK.
URK!
I WAS JUST CURIOUS! YOU'RE READING TOO MUCH INTO IT!
RIGHT, CHAIKA?
I MEAN, I'M SORRY FOR BEING SO FORWARD, BUT...

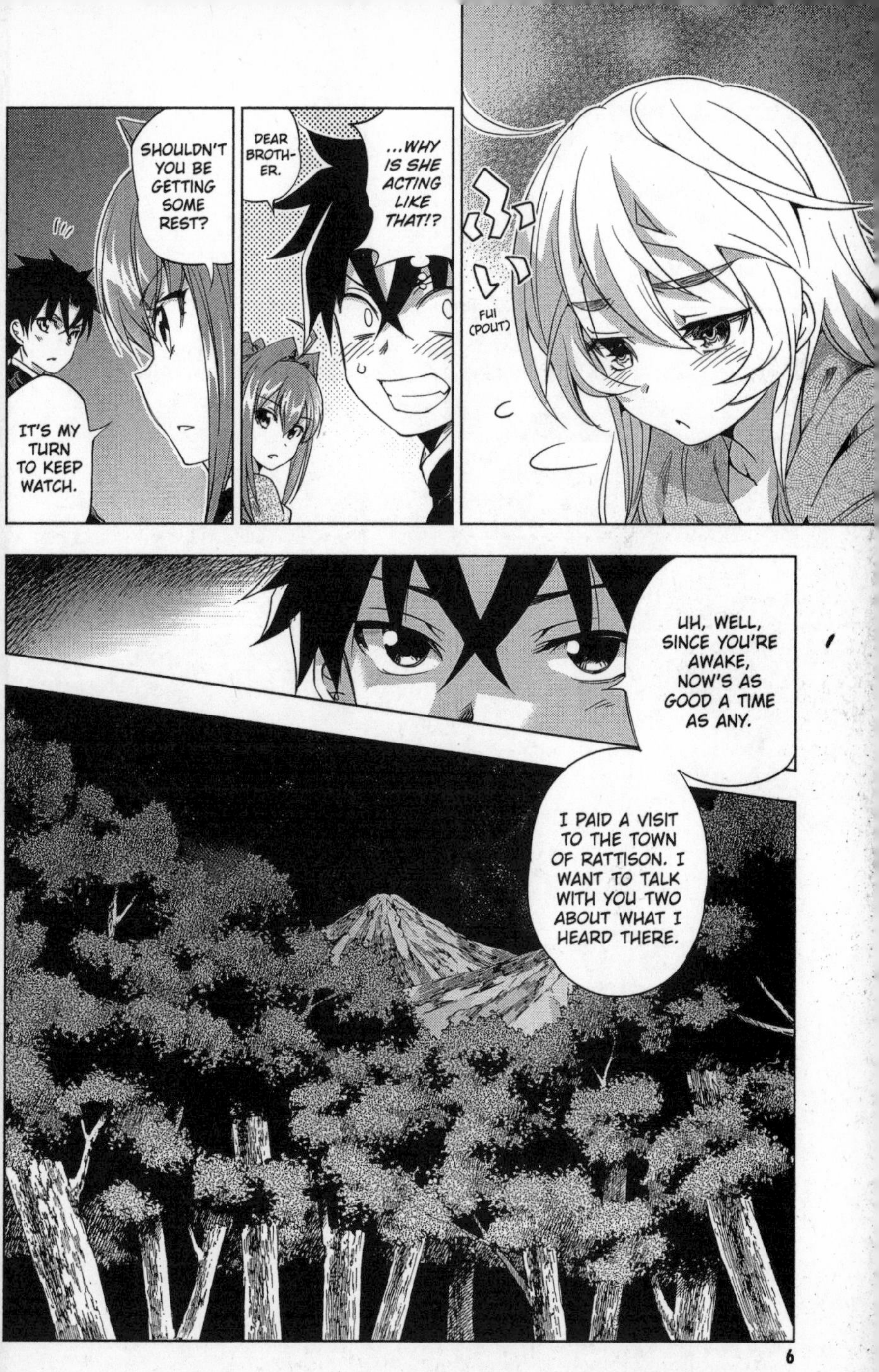
FUI (POUT)
DEAR BROTH-ER.
...WHY IS SHE ACTING LIKE THAT!?
SHOULDN'T YOU BE GETTING SOME REST?
IT'S MY TURN TO KEEP WATCH.
UH, WELL, SINCE YOU'RE AWAKE, NOW'S AS GOOD A TIME AS ANY.
I PAID A VISIT TO THE TOWN OF RATTISON. I WANT TO TALK WITH YOU TWO ABOUT WHAT I HEARD THERE.

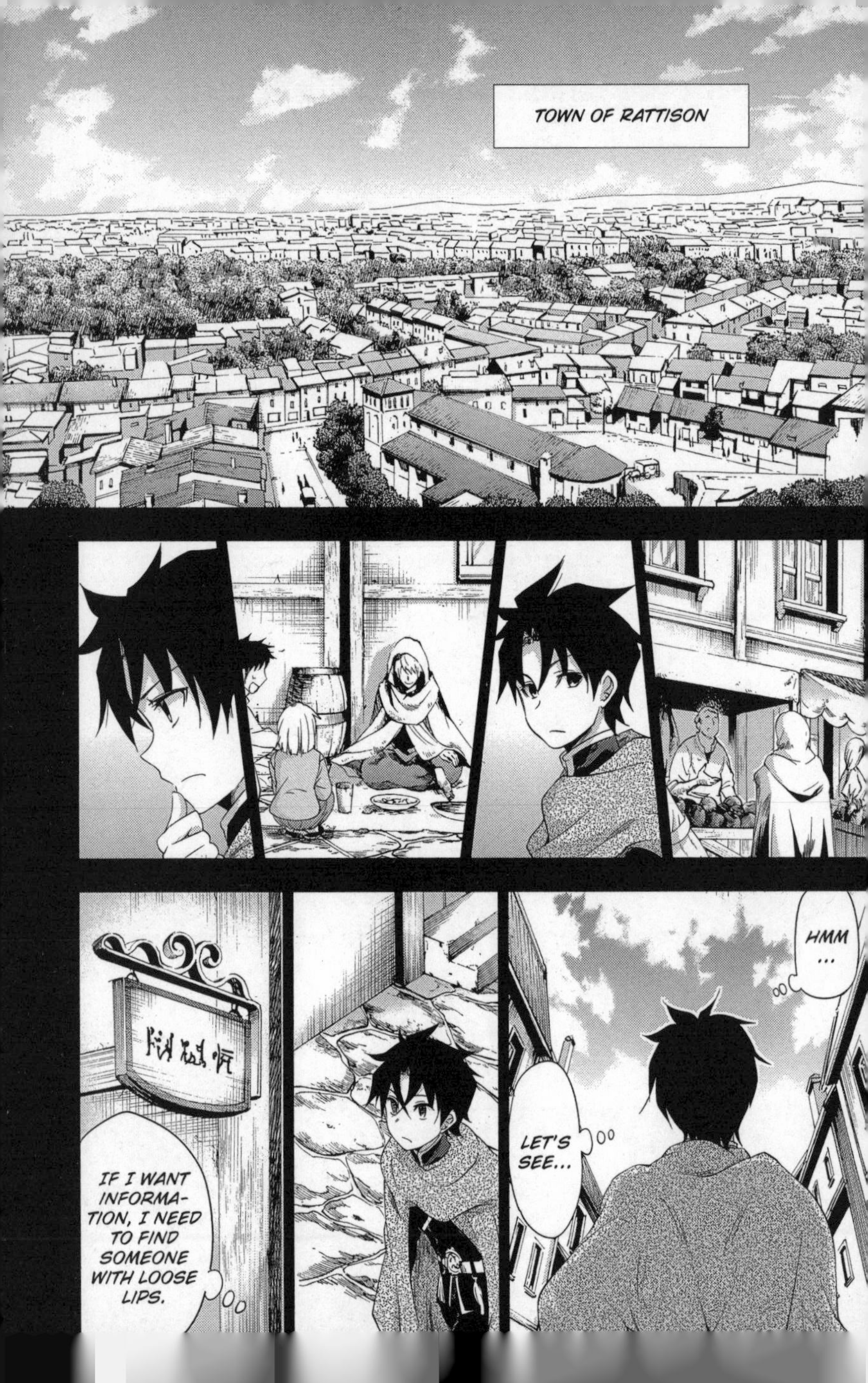
TOWN OF RATTISON
HMM...
LET'S SEE...
IF I WANT INFORMATION, I NEED TO FIND SOMEONE WITH LOOSE LIPS.

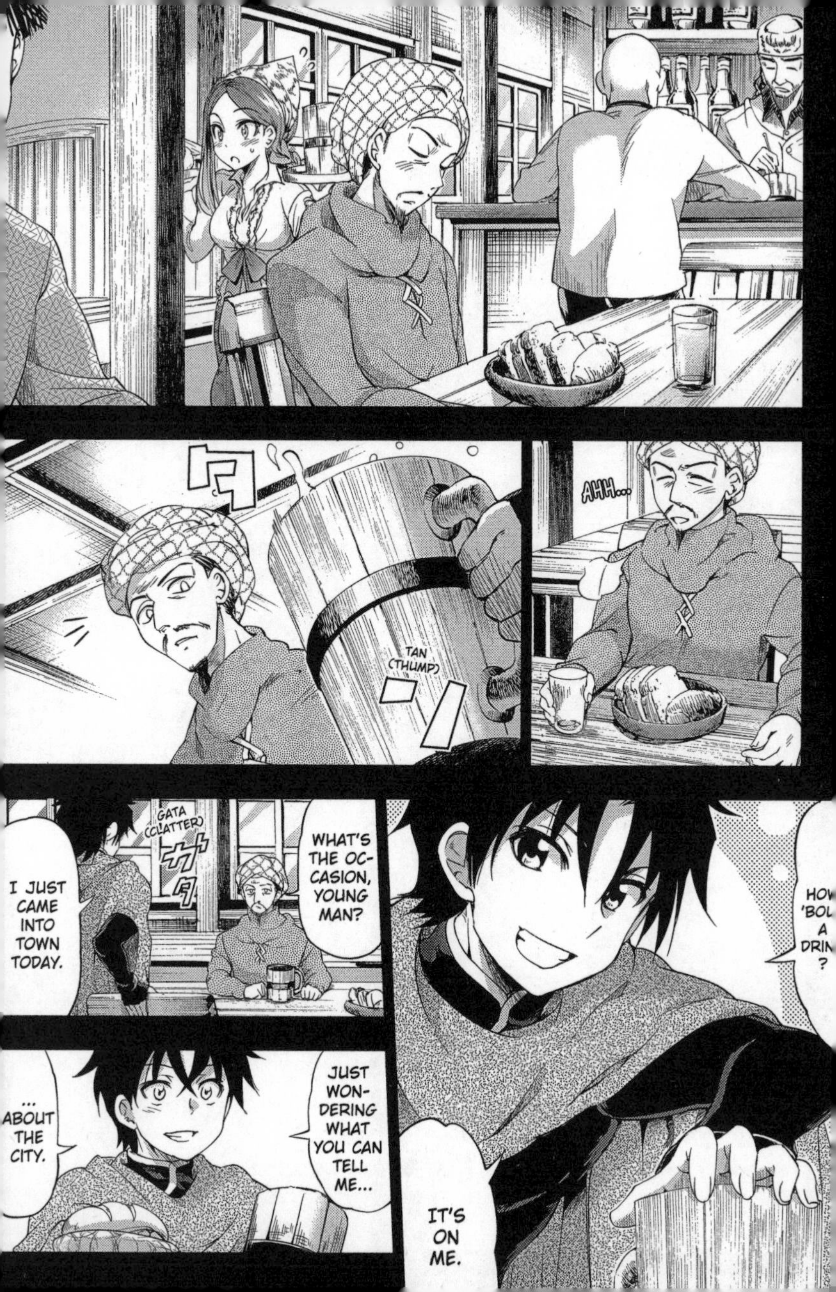
AHH...
TAN (THUMP)
HOW
'BOU
A
DRIN
?
IT'S ON ME.
WHAT'S THE OC-CASION, YOUNG MAN?
GATA (CLATTER)
I JUST CAME INTO TOWN TODAY.
JUST WON-DERING WHAT YOU CAN TELL ME...
...ABOUT THE CITY.

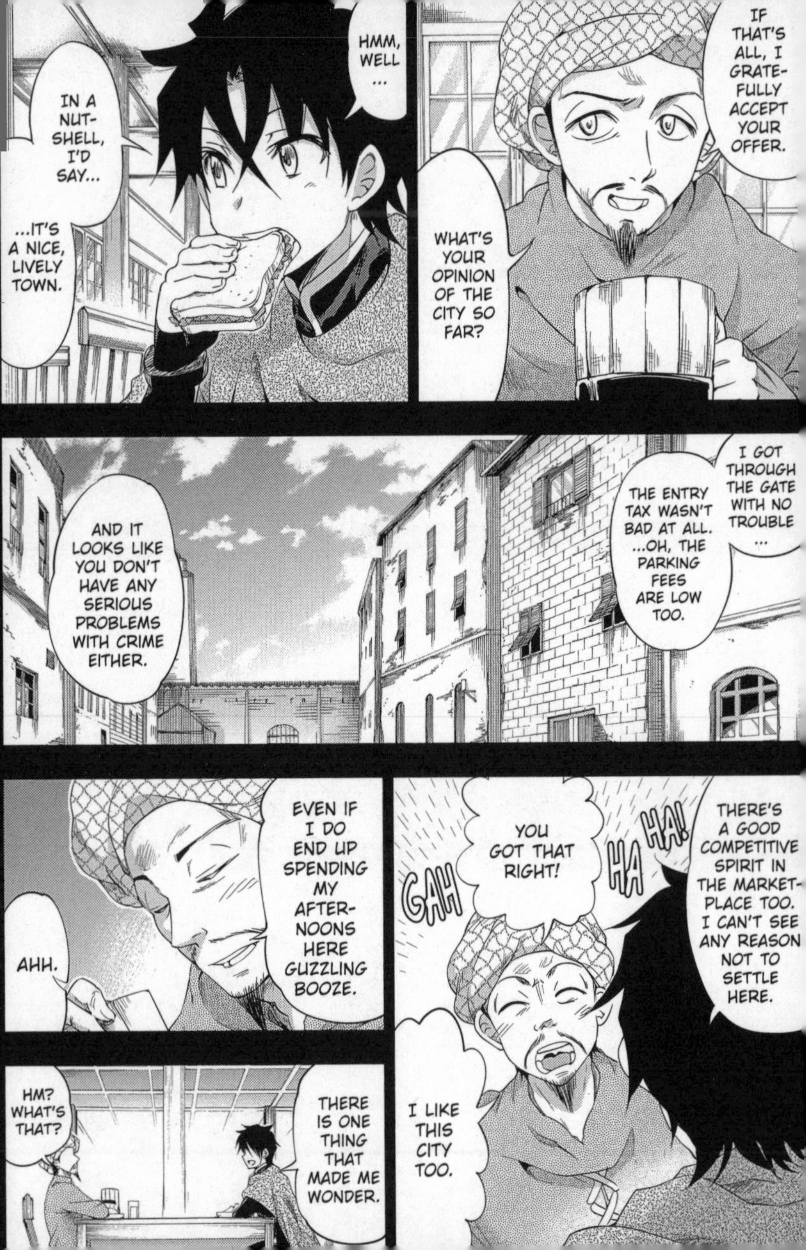
IF THAT'S ALL, I GRATEFULLY ACCEPT YOUR OFFER.
WHAT'S YOUR OPINION OF THE CITY SO FAR?
HMM, WELL ...
IN A NUTSHELL, I'D SAY...
...IT'S A NICE, LIVELY TOWN.
I GOT THROUGH THE GATE WITH NO TROUBLE ...
THE ENTRY TAX WASN'T BAD AT ALL. ...OH, THE PARKING FEES ARE LOW TOO.
AND IT LOOKS LIKE YOU DON'T HAVE ANY SERIOUS PROBLEMS WITH CRIME EITHER.
THERE'S A GOOD COMPETITIVE SPIRIT IN THE MARKETPLACE TOO. I CAN'T SEE ANY REASON NOT TO SETTLE HERE.
YOU GOT THAT RIGHT!
GAH HA HA!
I LIKE THIS CITY TOO.
EVEN IF I DO END UP SPENDING MY AFTERNOONS HERE GUZZLING BOOZE.
AHH.
THERE IS ONE THING THAT MADE ME WONDER.
HM? WHAT'S THAT?

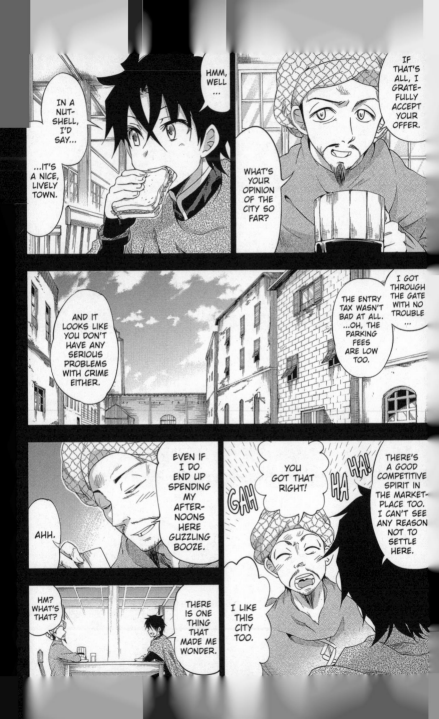

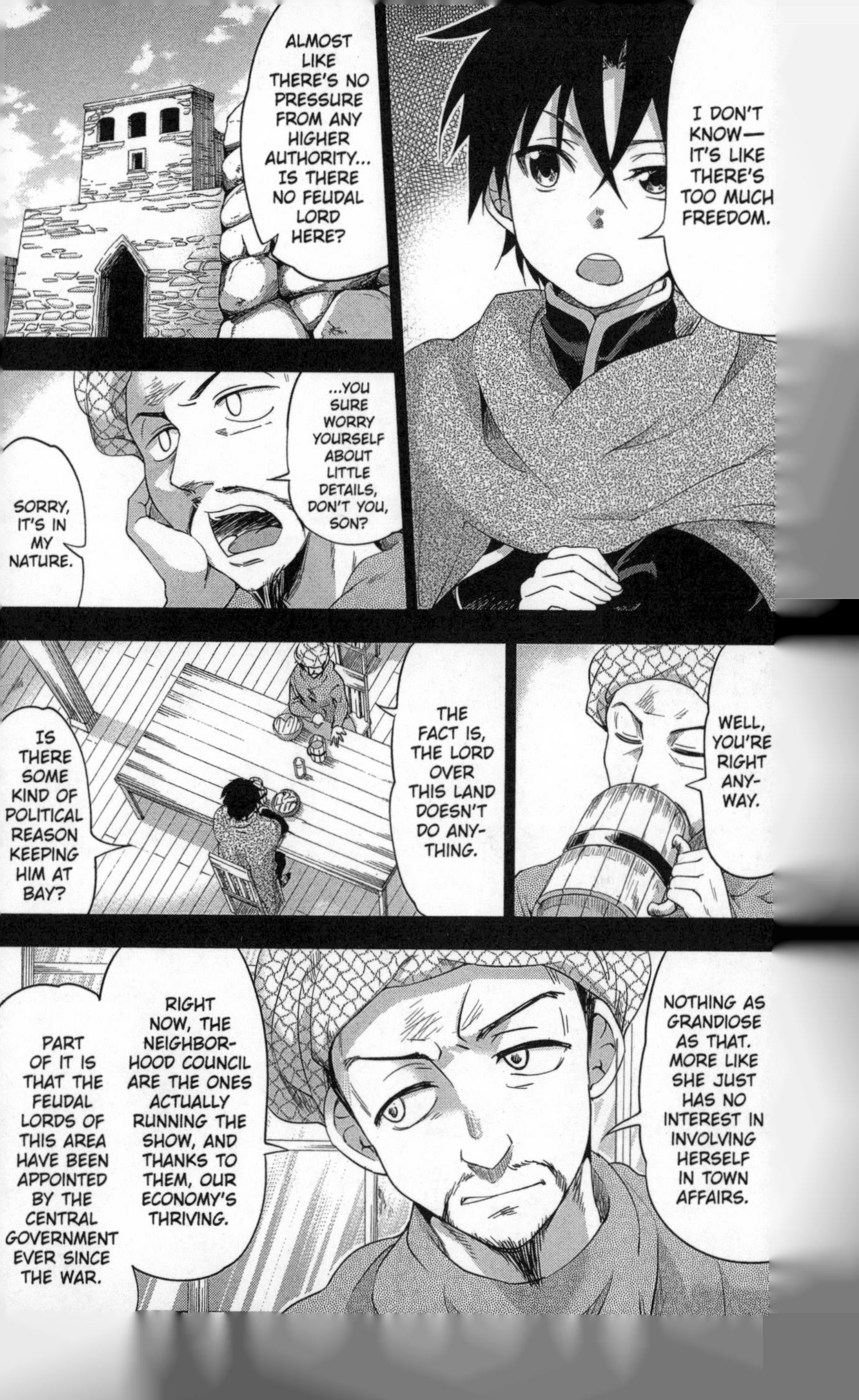
I DON'T KNOW—IT'S LIKE THERE'S TOO MUCH FREEDOM.
ALMOST LIKE THERE'S NO PRESSURE FROM ANY HIGHER AUTHORITY... IS THERE NO FEUDAL LORD HERE?
...YOU SURE WORRY YOURSELF ABOUT LITTLE DETAILS, DON'T YOU, SON?
SORRY, IT'S IN MY NATURE.
WELL, YOU'RE RIGHT ANYWAY.
THE FACT IS, THE LORD OVER THIS LAND DOESN'T DO ANYTHING.
IS THERE SOME KIND OF POLITICAL REASON KEEPING HIM AT BAY?
NOTHING AS GRANDIOSE AS THAT. MORE LIKE SHE JUST HAS NO INTEREST IN INVOLVING HERSELF IN TOWN AFFAIRS.
RIGHT NOW, THE NEIGHBORHOOD COUNCIL ARE THE ONES ACTUALLY RUNNING THE SHOW, AND THANKS TO THEM, OUR ECONOMY'S THRIVING.
PART OF IT IS THAT THE FEUDAL LORDS OF THIS AREA HAVE BEEN APPOINTED BY THE CENTRAL GOVERNMENT EVER SINCE THE WAR.

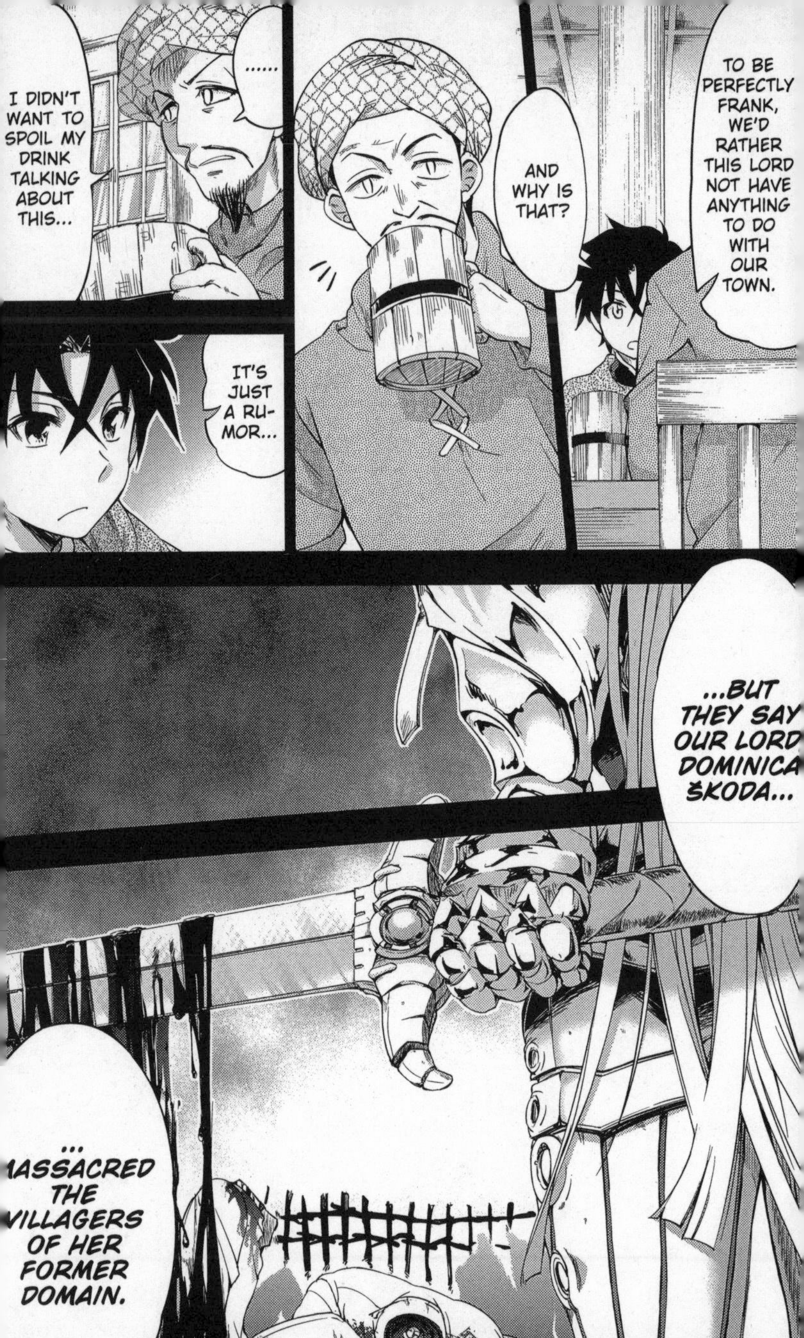
TO BE PERFECTLY FRANK, WE'D RATHER THIS LORD NOT HAVE ANYTHING TO DO WITH OUR TOWN.
AND WHY IS THAT?
......
I DIDN'T WANT TO SPOIL MY DRINK TALKING ABOUT THIS...
IT'S JUST A RU-MOR...
...BUT THEY SAY OUR LORD DOMINICA ŠKODA...
...MASSACRED THE VILLAGERS OF HER FORMER DOMAIN.

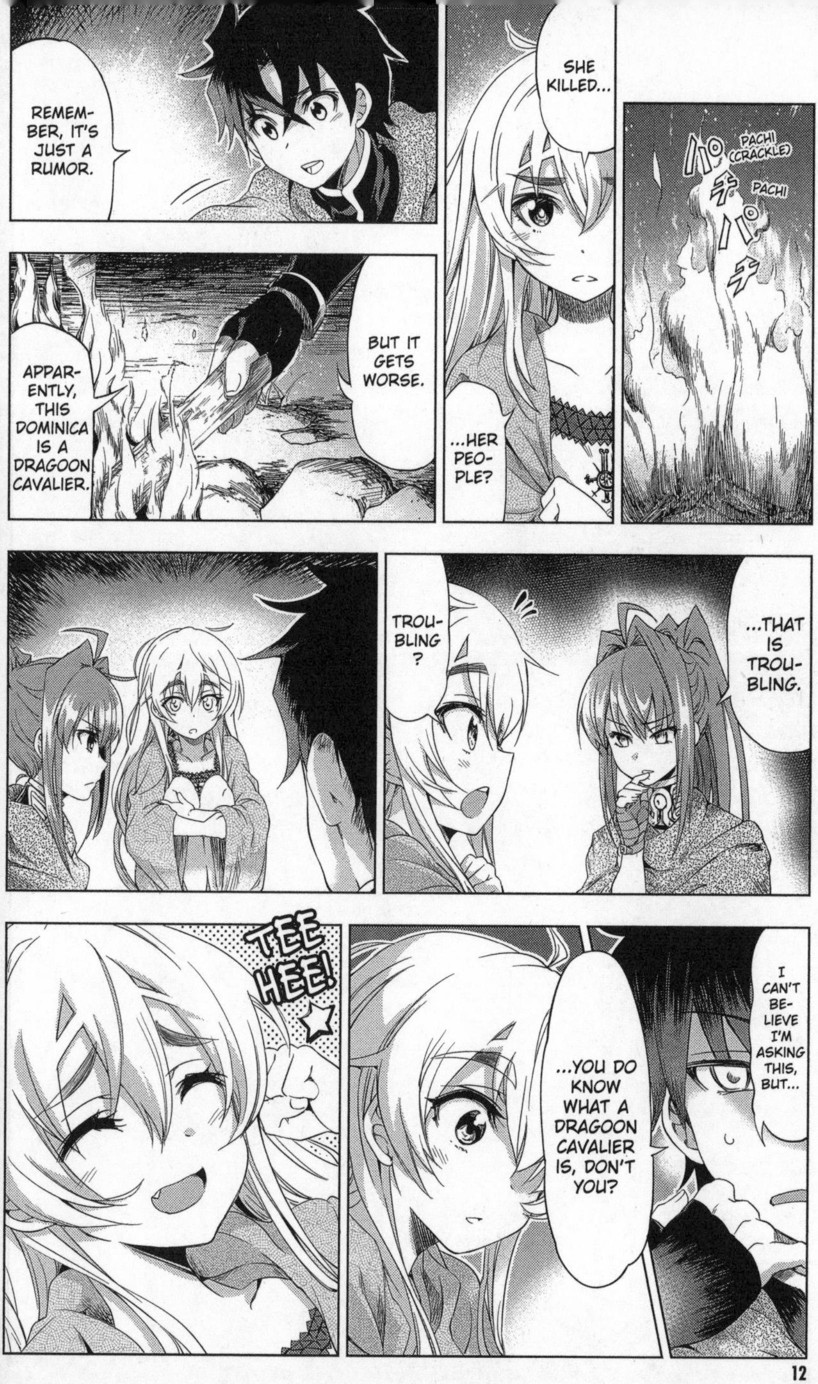
PACHI (CRACKLE)
PACHI
SHE KILLED...
...HER PEOPLE?
REMEMBER, IT'S JUST A RUMOR.
BUT IT GETS WORSE.
APPARENTLY, THIS DOMINICA IS A DRAGOON CAVALIER.
...THAT IS TROUBLING.
TROUBLING?
I CAN'T BELIEVE I'M ASKING THIS, BUT...
...YOU DO KNOW WHAT A DRAGOON CAVALIER IS, DON'T YOU?
TEE HEE!

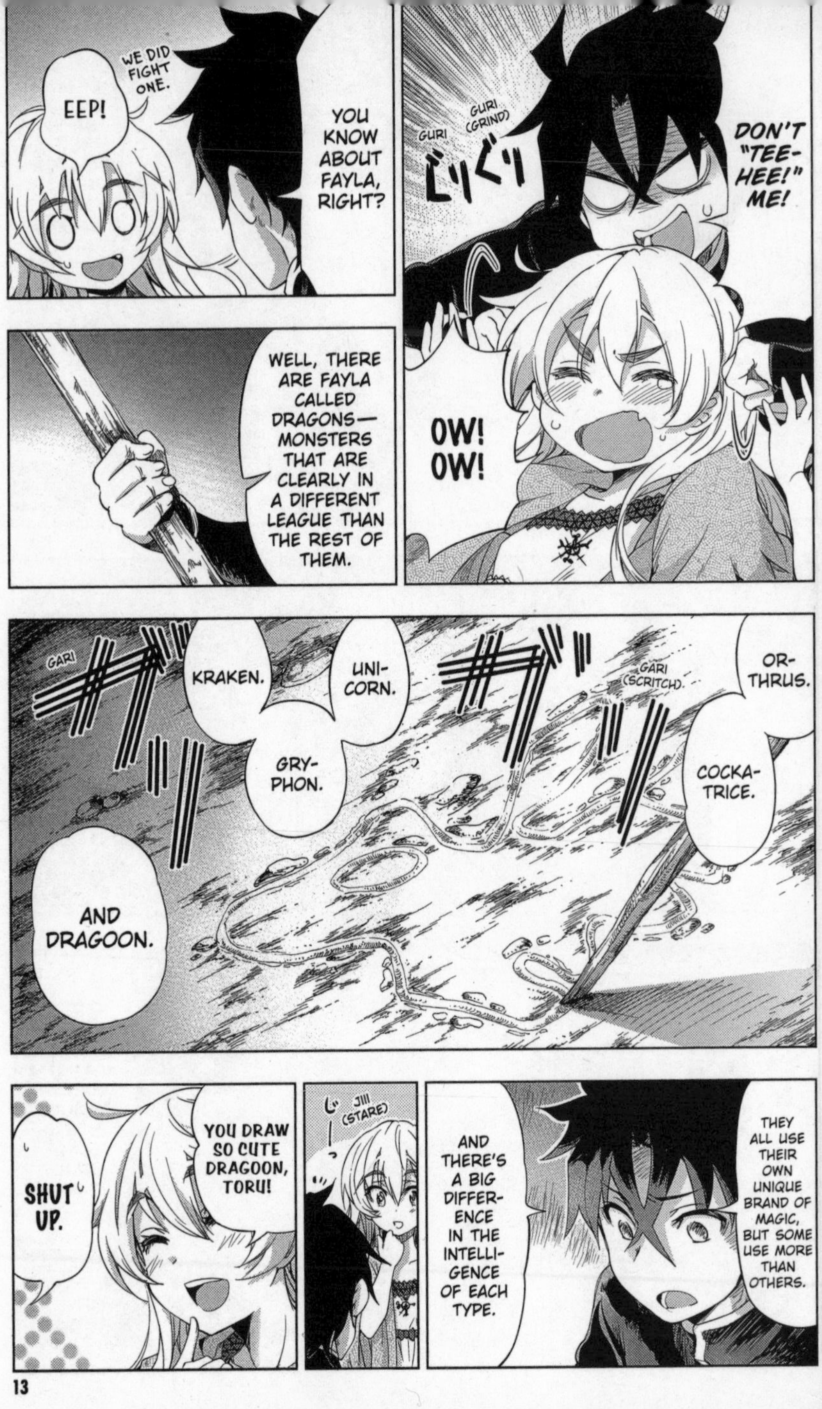
DON'T "TEE-HEE!" ME!
GURI (GRIND)
GURI
ぐりぐり
OW! OW!
YOU KNOW ABOUT FAYLA, RIGHT?
WE DID FIGHT ONE.
EEP!
WELL, THERE ARE FAYLA CALLED DRAGONS—MONSTERS THAT ARE CLEARLY IN A DIFFERENT LEAGUE THAN THE REST OF THEM.
OR-THRUS.
GARI (SCRITCH)
COCKA-TRICE.
UNI-CORN.
KRAKEN.
GRY-PHON.
GARI
AND DRAGOON.
THEY ALL USE THEIR OWN UNIQUE BRAND OF MAGIC, BUT SOME USE MORE THAN OTHERS.
AND THERE'S A BIG DIFFER-ENCE IN THE INTELLI-GENCE OF EACH TYPE.
JIII (STARE)
じー
YOU DRAW SO CUTE DRAGOON, TORU!
SHUT UP.

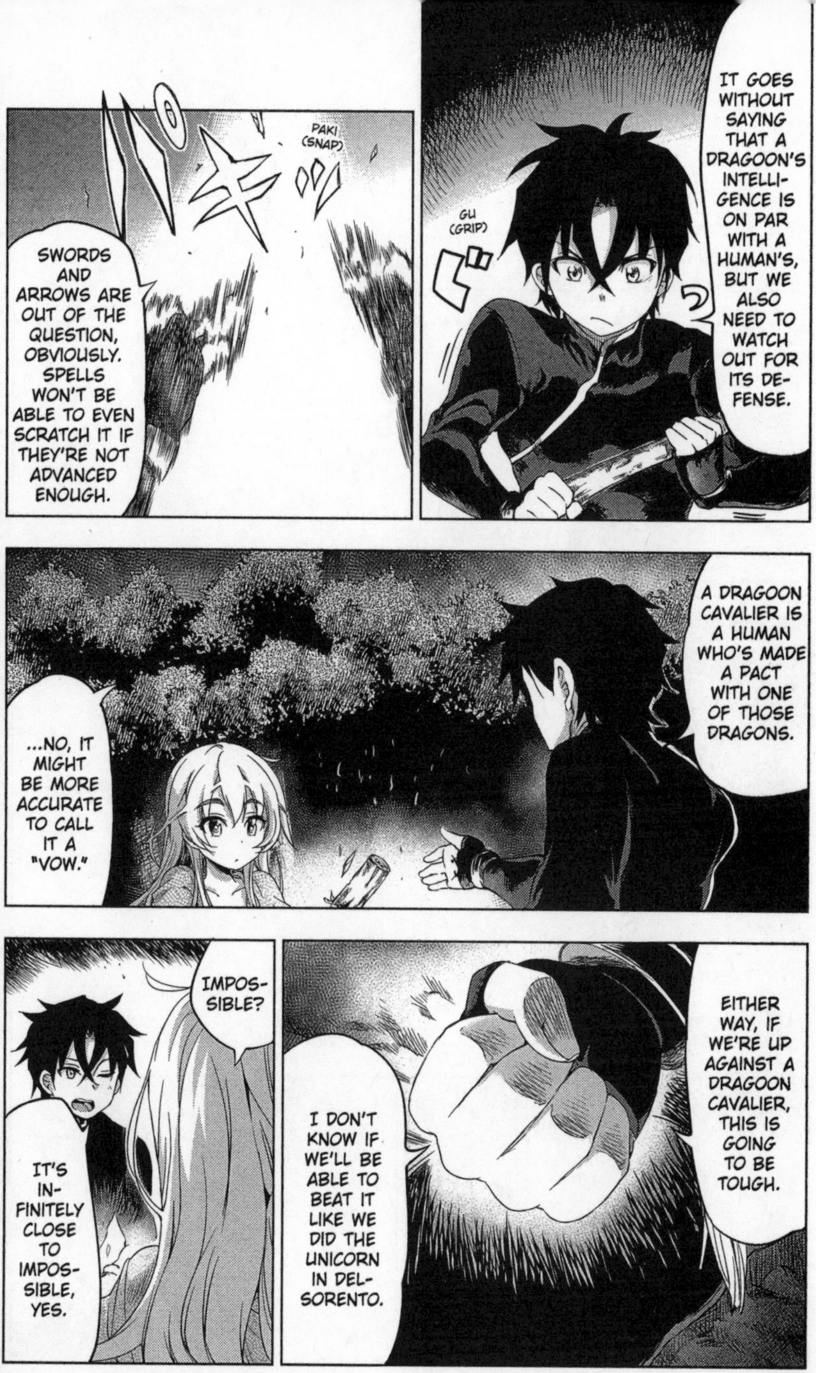
IT GOES WITHOUT SAYING THAT A DRAGOON'S INTELLIGENCE IS ON PAR WITH A HUMAN'S, BUT WE ALSO NEED TO WATCH OUT FOR ITS DEFENSE.
GU (GRIP)
PAKI (SNAP)
SWORDS AND ARROWS ARE OUT OF THE QUESTION, OBVIOUSLY. SPELLS WON'T BE ABLE TO EVEN SCRATCH IT IF THEY'RE NOT ADVANCED ENOUGH.
A DRAGOON CAVALIER IS A HUMAN WHO'S MADE A PACT WITH ONE OF THOSE DRAGONS.
...NO, IT MIGHT BE MORE ACCURATE TO CALL IT A "VOW."
EITHER WAY, IF WE'RE UP AGAINST A DRAGOON CAVALIER, THIS IS GOING TO BE TOUGH.
I DON'T KNOW IF WE'LL BE ABLE TO BEAT IT LIKE WE DID THE UNICORN IN DELSORENTO.
IMPOSSIBLE?
IT'S INFINITELY CLOSE TO IMPOSSIBLE, YES.

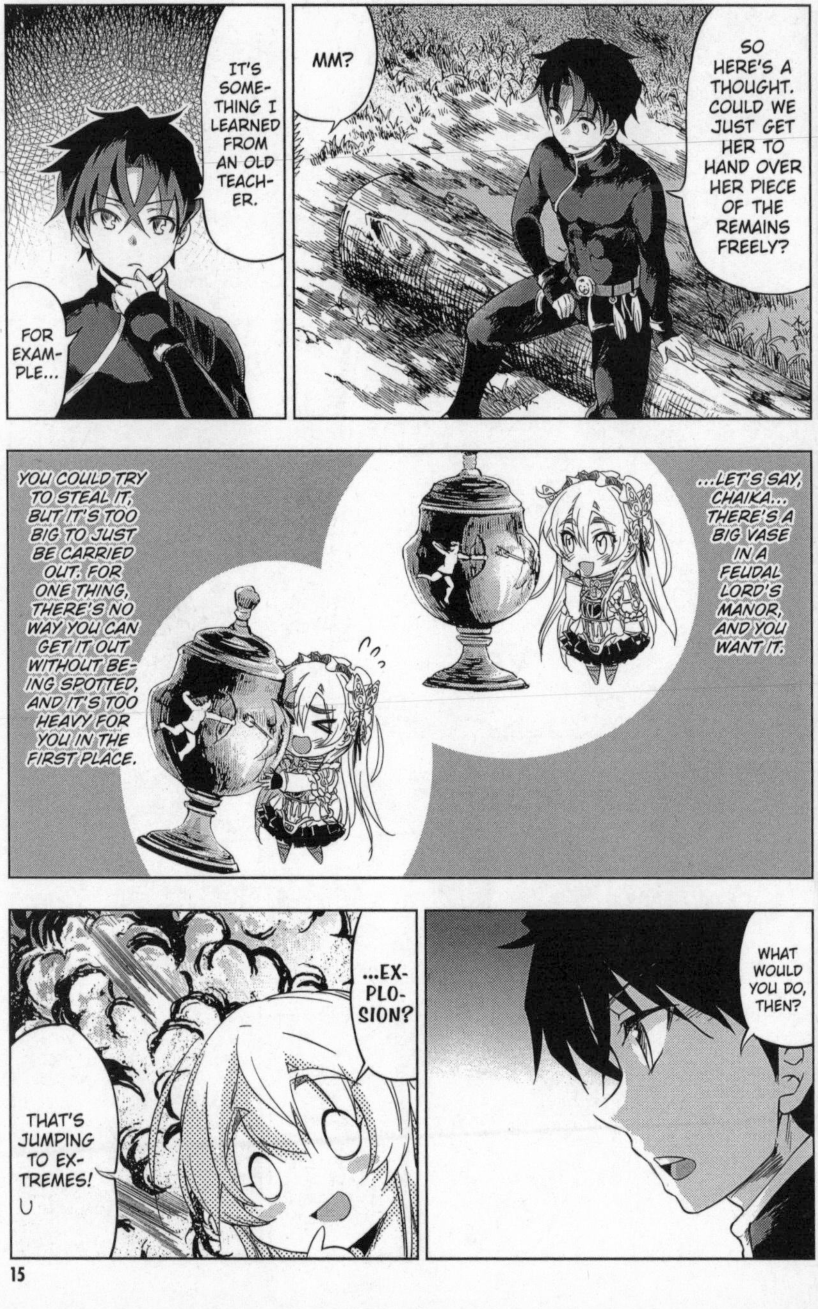
SO HERE'S A THOUGHT. COULD WE JUST GET HER TO HAND OVER HER PIECE OF THE REMAINS FREELY?
MM?
IT'S SOME-THING I LEARNED FROM AN OLD TEACH-ER.
FOR EXAM-PLE...
...LET'S SAY, CHAIKA... THERE'S A BIG VASE IN A FEUDAL LORD'S MANOR, AND YOU WANT IT.
YOU COULD TRY TO STEAL IT, BUT IT'S TOO BIG TO JUST BE CARRIED OUT. FOR ONE THING, THERE'S NO WAY YOU CAN GET IT OUT WITHOUT BE-ING SPOTTED, AND IT'S TOO HEAVY FOR YOU IN THE FIRST PLACE.
WHAT WOULD YOU DO, THEN?
...EX-PLO-SION?
THAT'S JUMPING TO EX-TREMES!

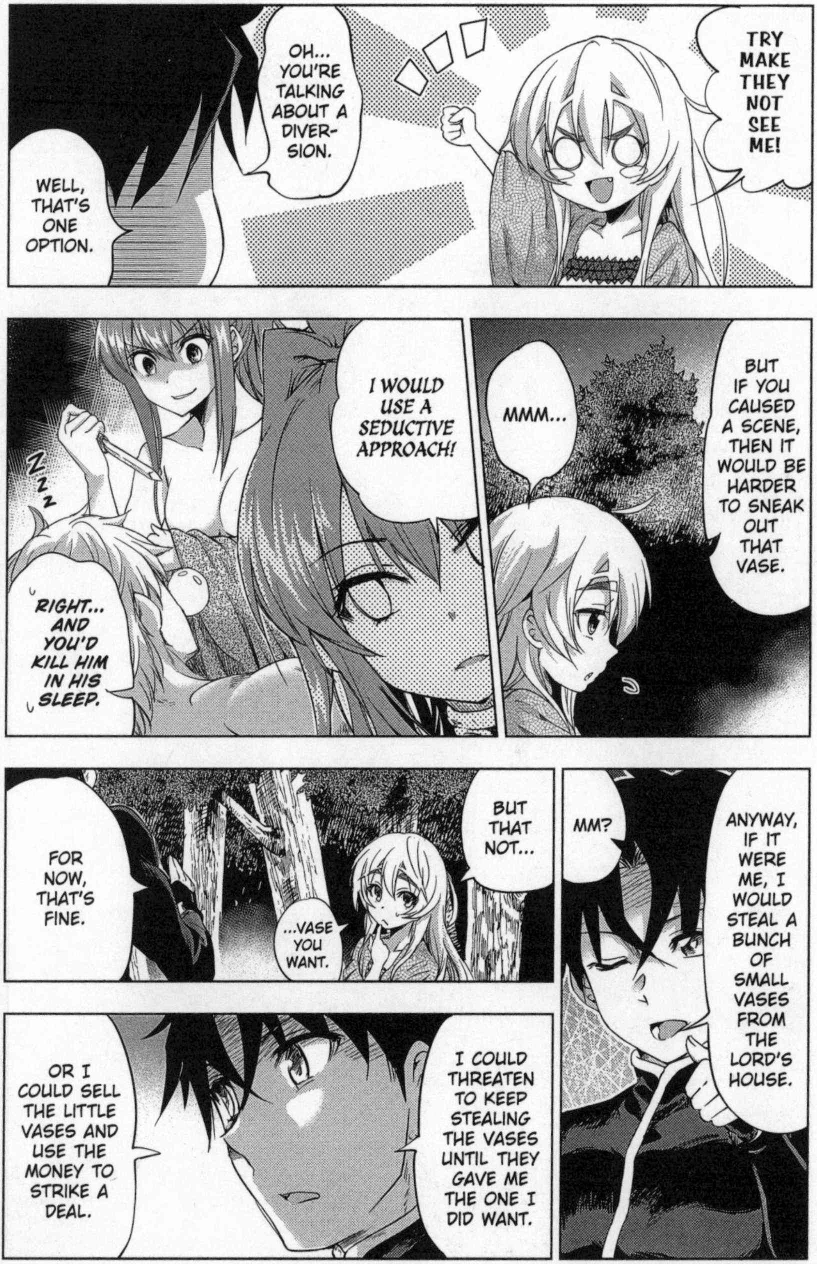
TRY MAKE THEY NOT SEE ME!
OH... YOU'RE TALKING ABOUT A DIVERSION.
WELL, THAT'S ONE OPTION.
BUT IF YOU CAUSED A SCENE, THEN IT WOULD BE HARDER TO SNEAK OUT THAT VASE.
MMM...
I WOULD USE A SEDUCTIVE APPROACH!
Z Z Z
RIGHT... AND YOU'D KILL HIM IN HIS SLEEP.
ANYWAY, IF IT WERE ME, I WOULD STEAL A BUNCH OF SMALL VASES FROM THE LORD'S HOUSE.
MM?
BUT THAT NOT...
...VASE YOU WANT.
FOR NOW, THAT'S FINE.
I COULD THREATEN TO KEEP STEALING THE VASES UNTIL THEY GAVE ME THE ONE I DID WANT.
OR I COULD SELL THE LITTLE VASES AND USE THE MONEY TO STRIKE A DEAL.

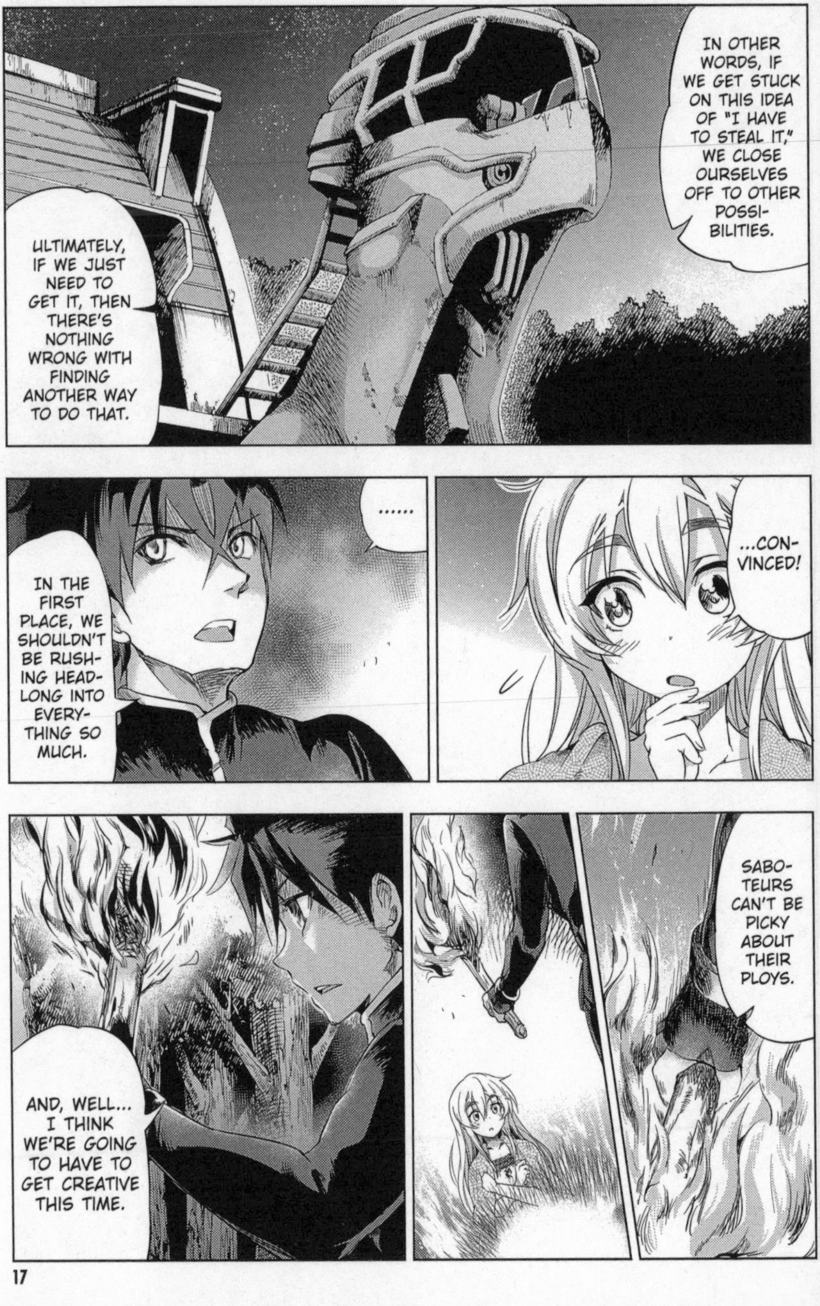
IN OTHER WORDS, IF WE GET STUCK ON THIS IDEA OF "I HAVE TO STEAL IT," WE CLOSE OURSELVES OFF TO OTHER POSSI-BILITIES.
ULTIMATELY, IF WE JUST NEED TO GET IT, THEN THERE'S NOTHING WRONG WITH FINDING ANOTHER WAY TO DO THAT.
...CON-VINCED!
......
IN THE FIRST PLACE, WE SHOULDN'T BE RUSH-ING HEAD-LONG INTO EVERY-THING SO MUCH.
SABO-TEURS CAN'T BE PICKY ABOUT THEIR PLOYS.
AND, WELL... I THINK WE'RE GOING TO HAVE TO GET CREATIVE THIS TIME.

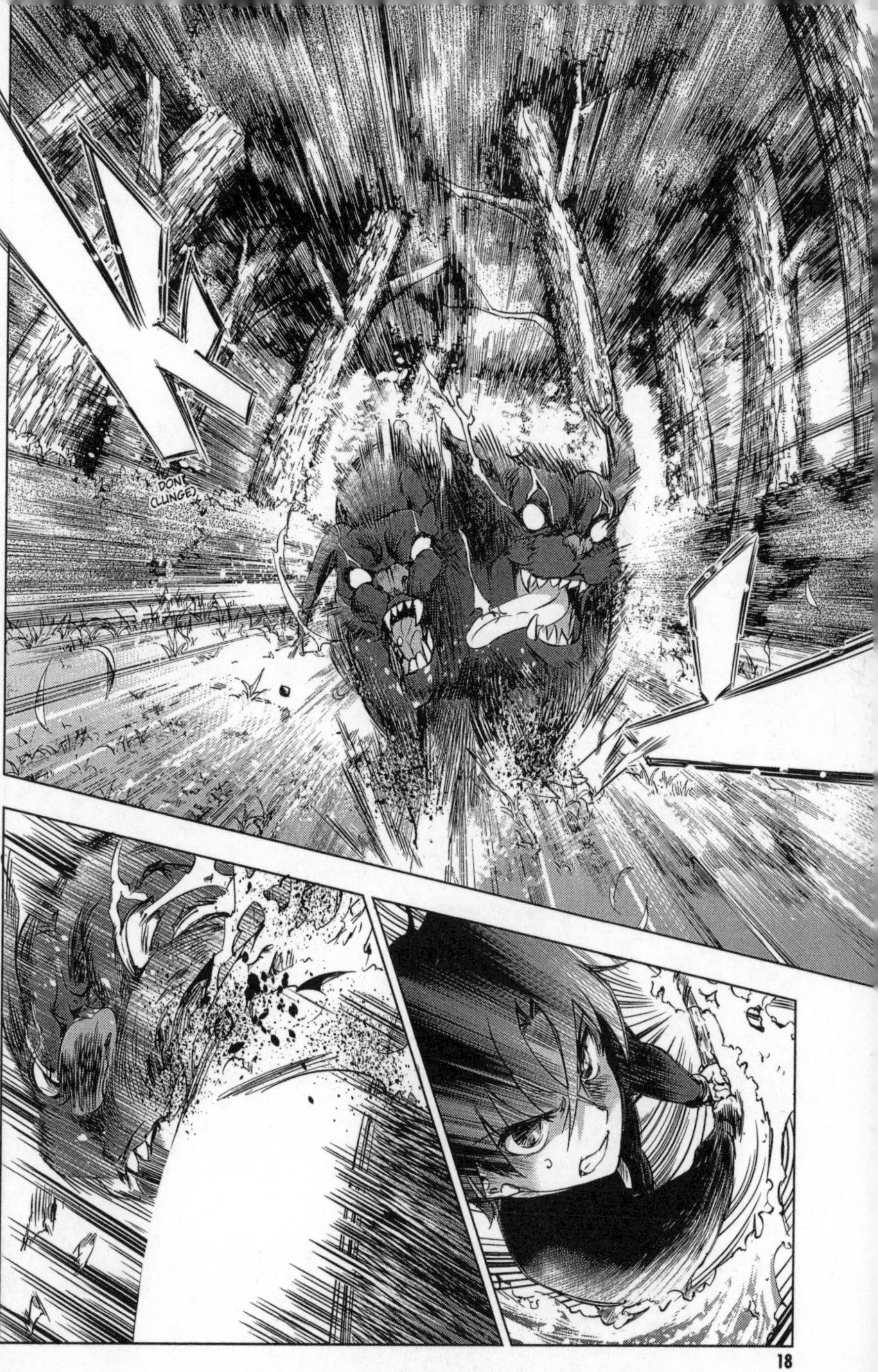
DON
(LUNGE)

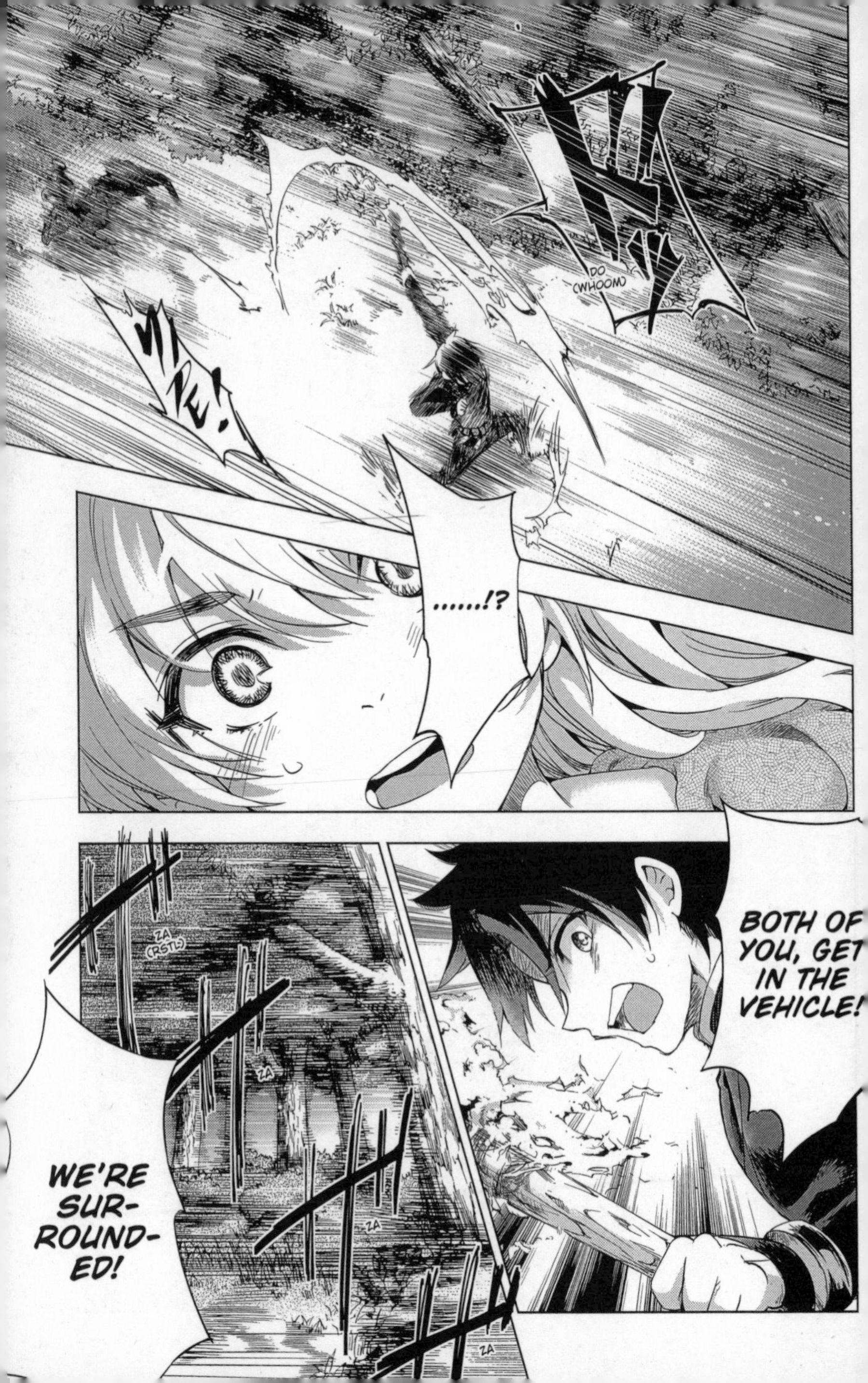
DO (WHOOM)
MINE!
......!?
BOTH OF YOU, GET IN THE VEHICLE!
ZA (RSTL)
ZA
ZA
ZA
WE'RE SUR-ROUND-ED!

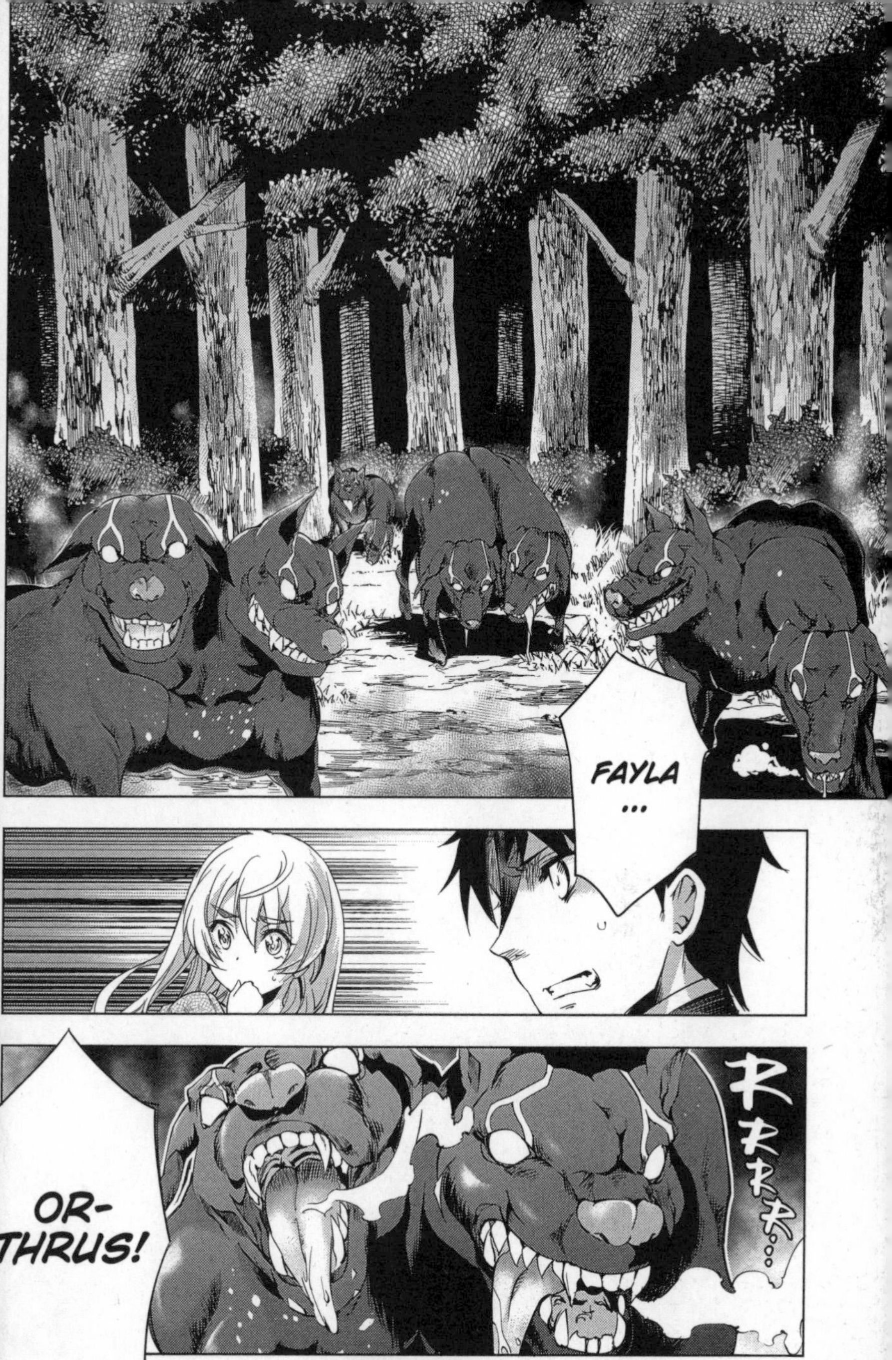
FAYLA ...
RRRR...
OR-THRUS!

episode 18: END

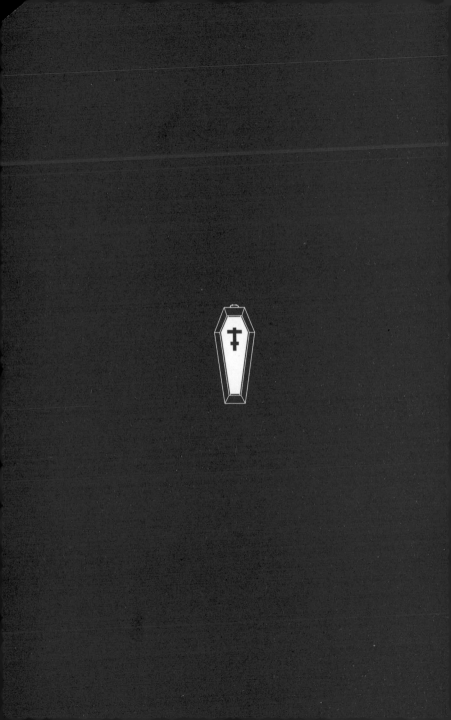

CHAIKA: THE COFFIN PRINCESS

episode 19: Two-headed Dogs

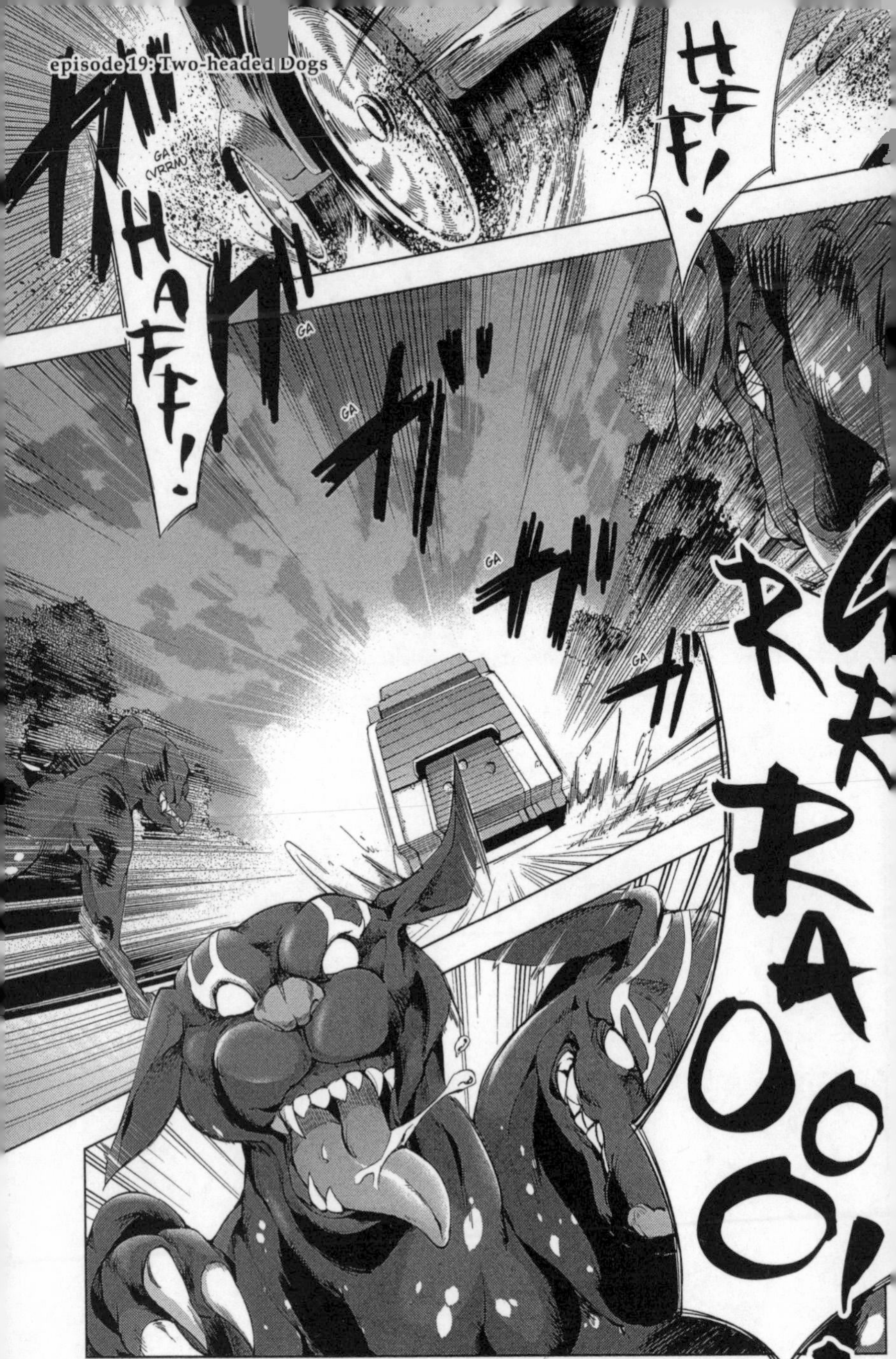
HFF!
GA (VRRM)
HAFF!
GA
GA
GA
GA
GRRRAOOO!

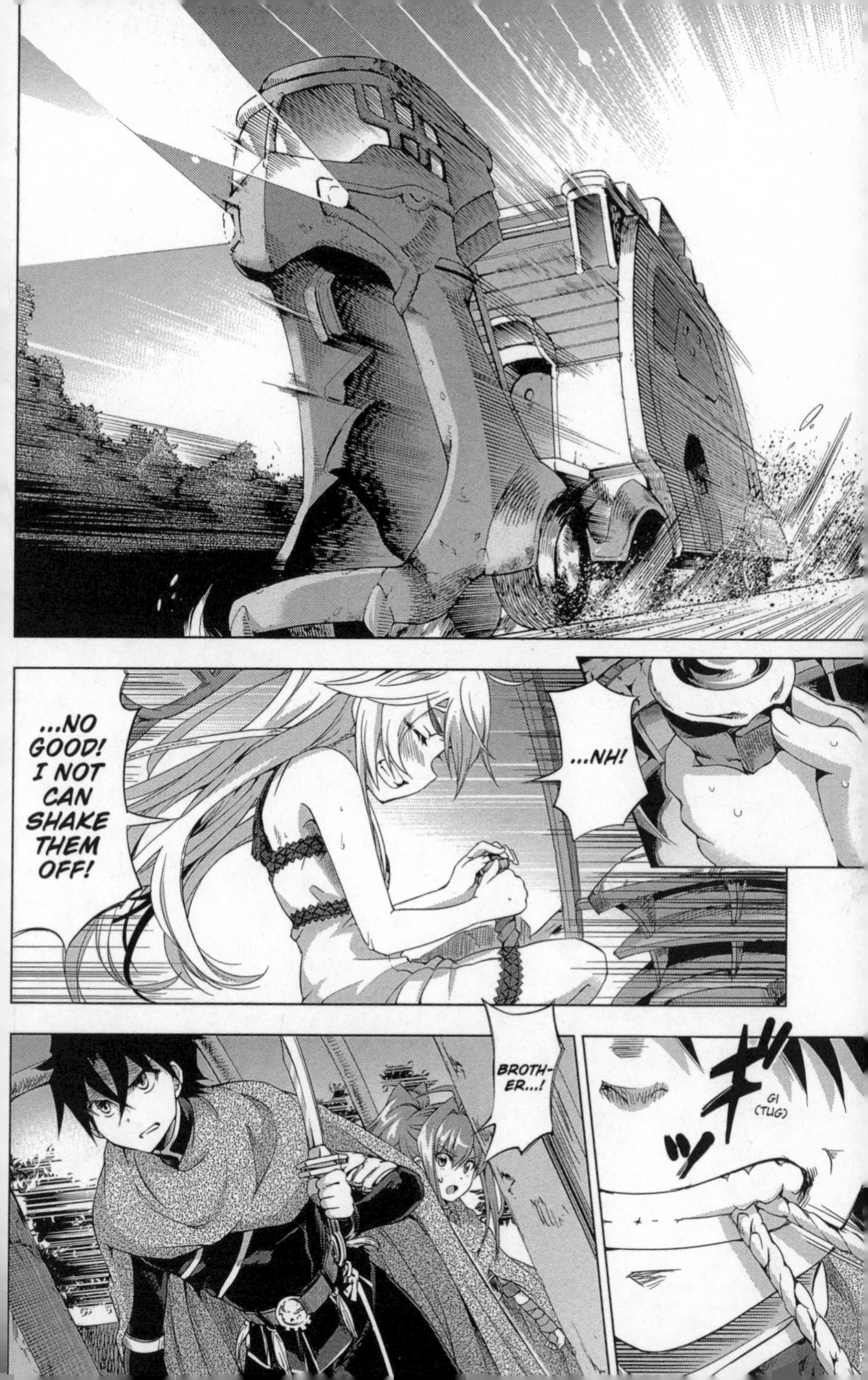
...NH!
...NO GOOD! I NOT CAN SHAKE THEM OFF!
GI (TUG)
BROTHER...!

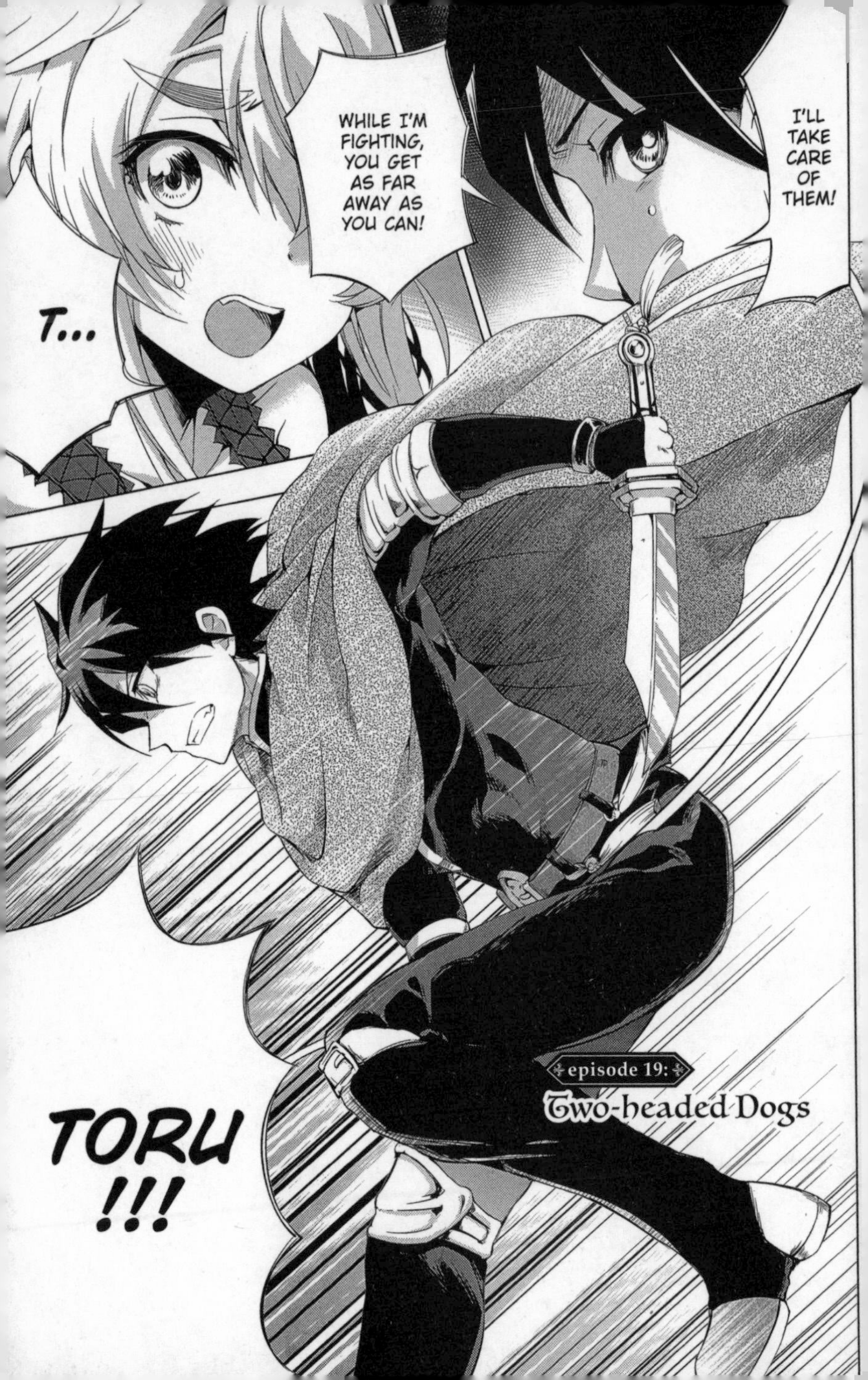
I'LL TAKE CARE OF THEM!
WHILE I'M FIGHTING, YOU GET AS FAR AWAY AS YOU CAN!
T...
episode 19:
Two-headed Dogs
TORU!!!

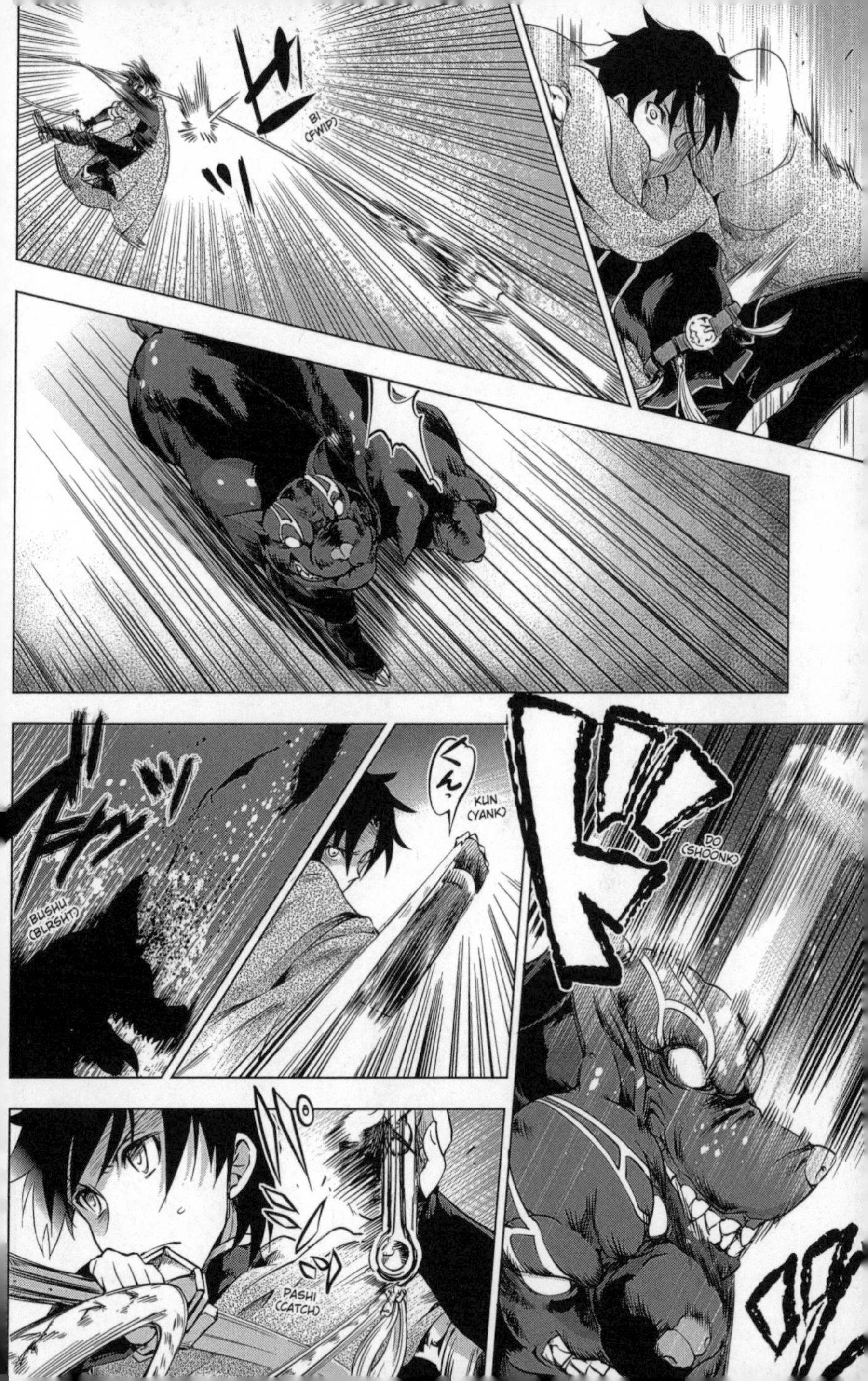
BI
(FWIP)
DO
(SHOONK)
KUN
(YANK)
BUSHU
(BLRSHT)
PASHI
(CATCH)

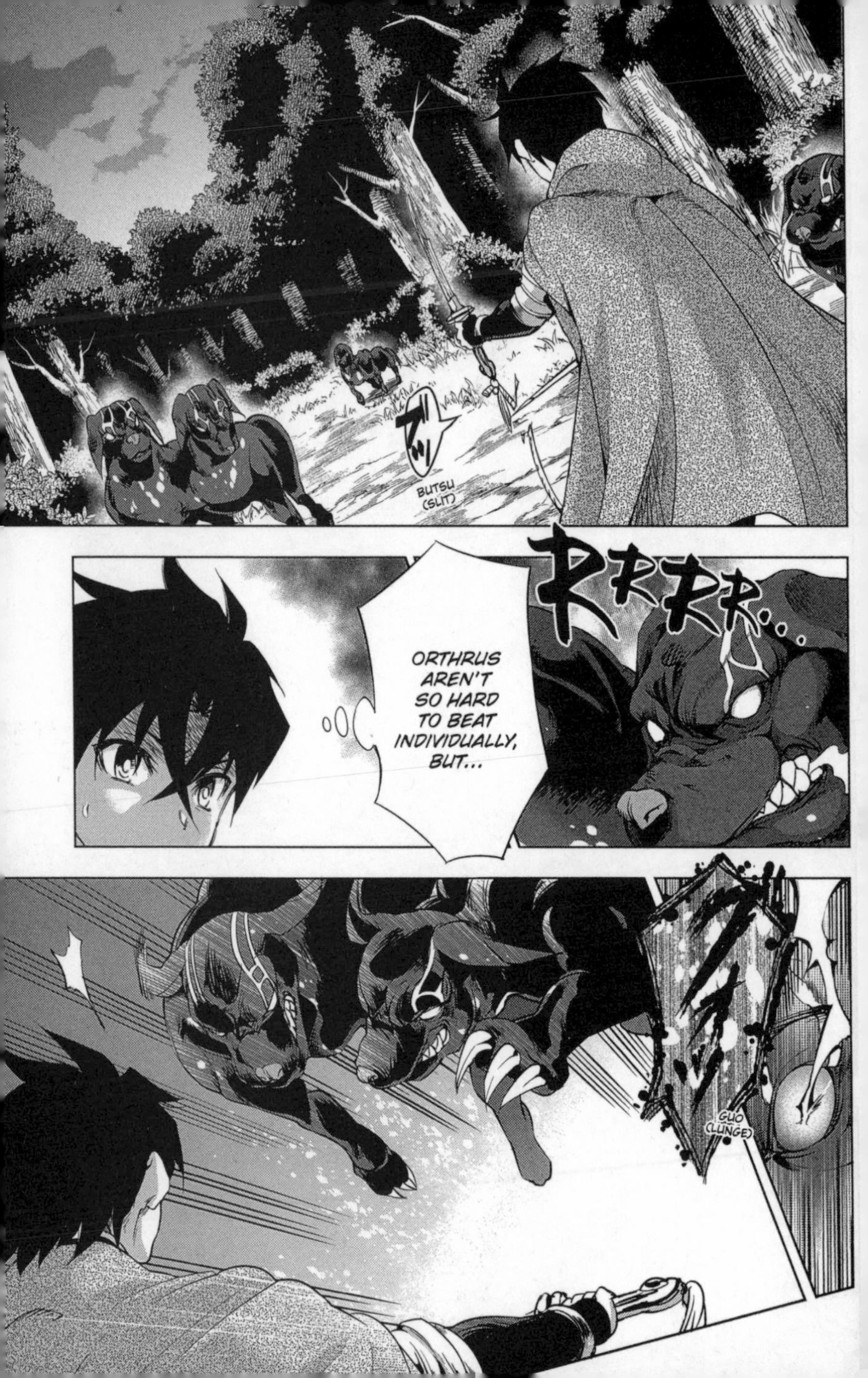

BUTSU (SLIT)
RRRR...
ORTHRUS AREN'T SO HARD TO BEAT INDIVIDUALLY, BUT...
GUO (LUNGE)

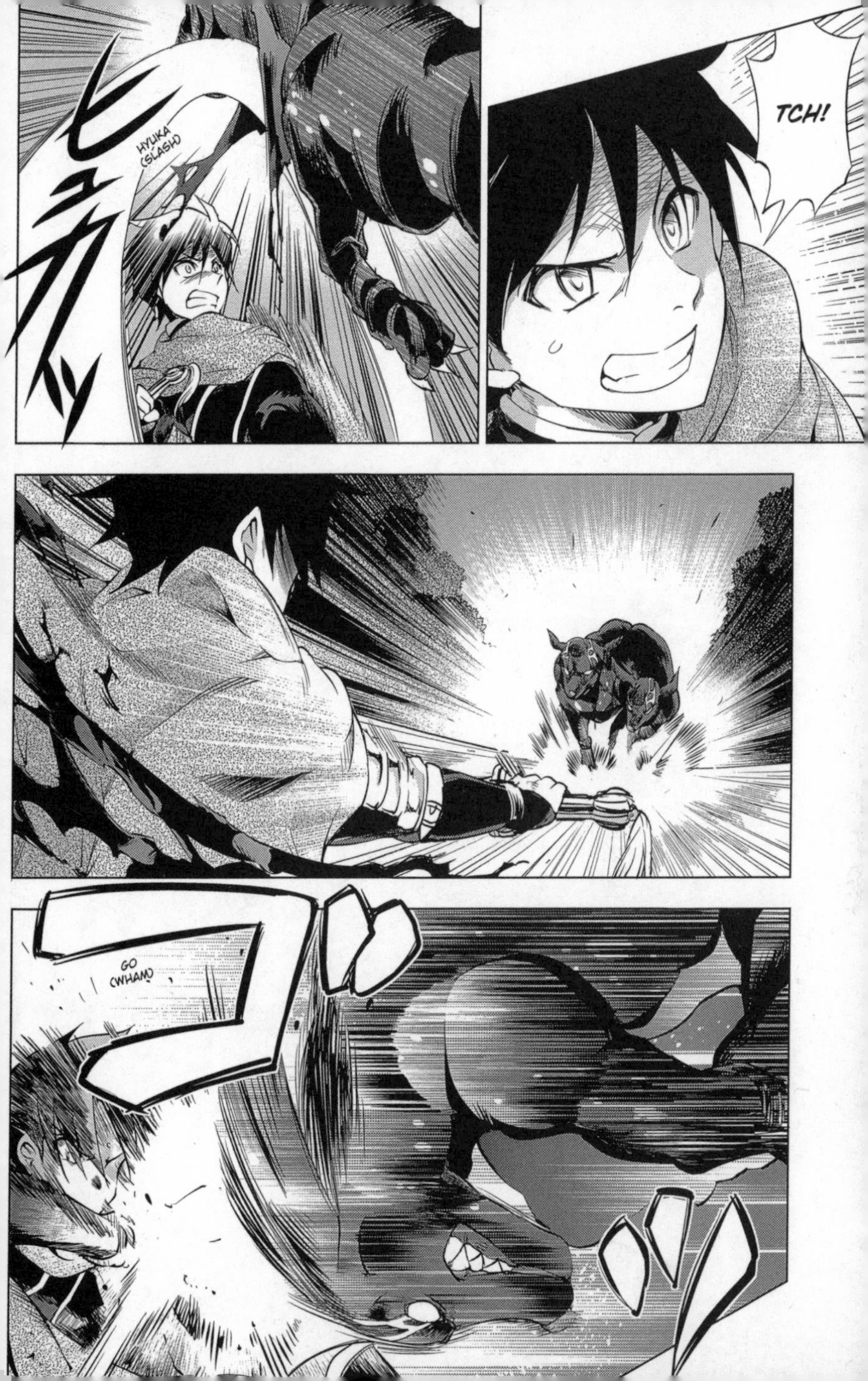
TCH!
HYUKA (SLASH)
GO (WHAM)

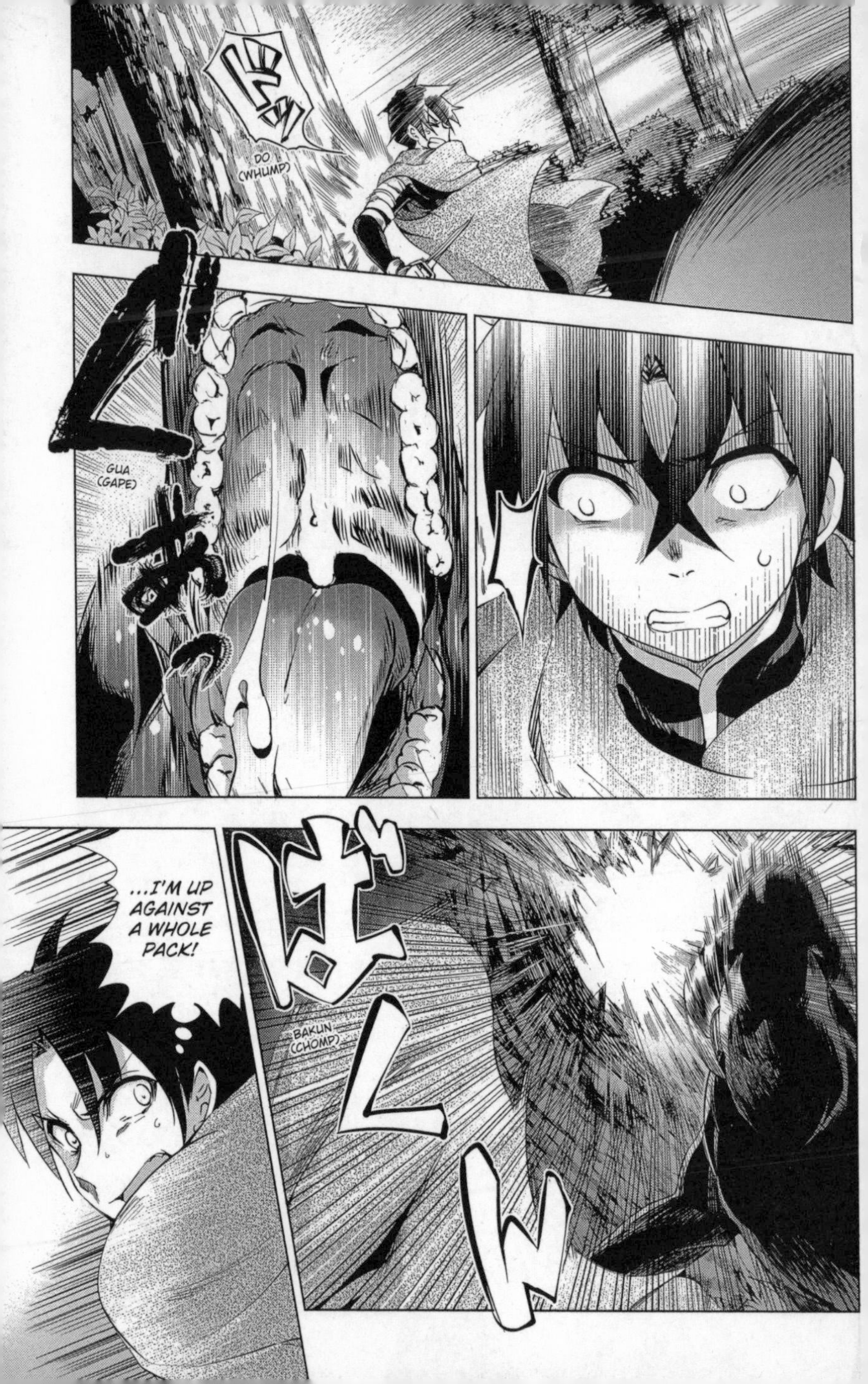
DO (WHUMP)
GUA (GAPE)
BAKUN (CHOMP)
...I'M UP AGAINST A WHOLE PACK!

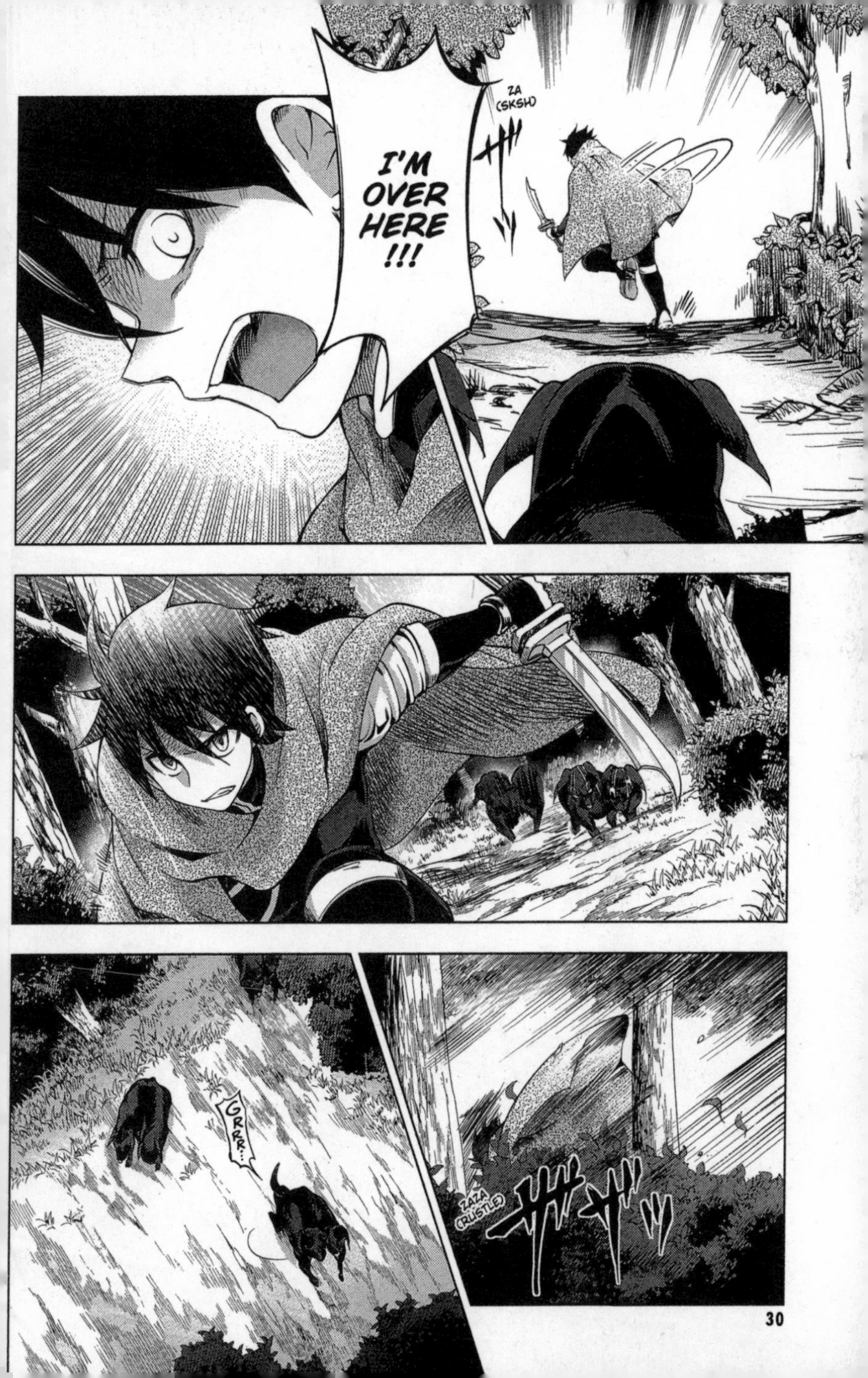
ZA (SKSH)
I'M OVER HERE!!!
ZAZA (RUSTLE)
GRRR...

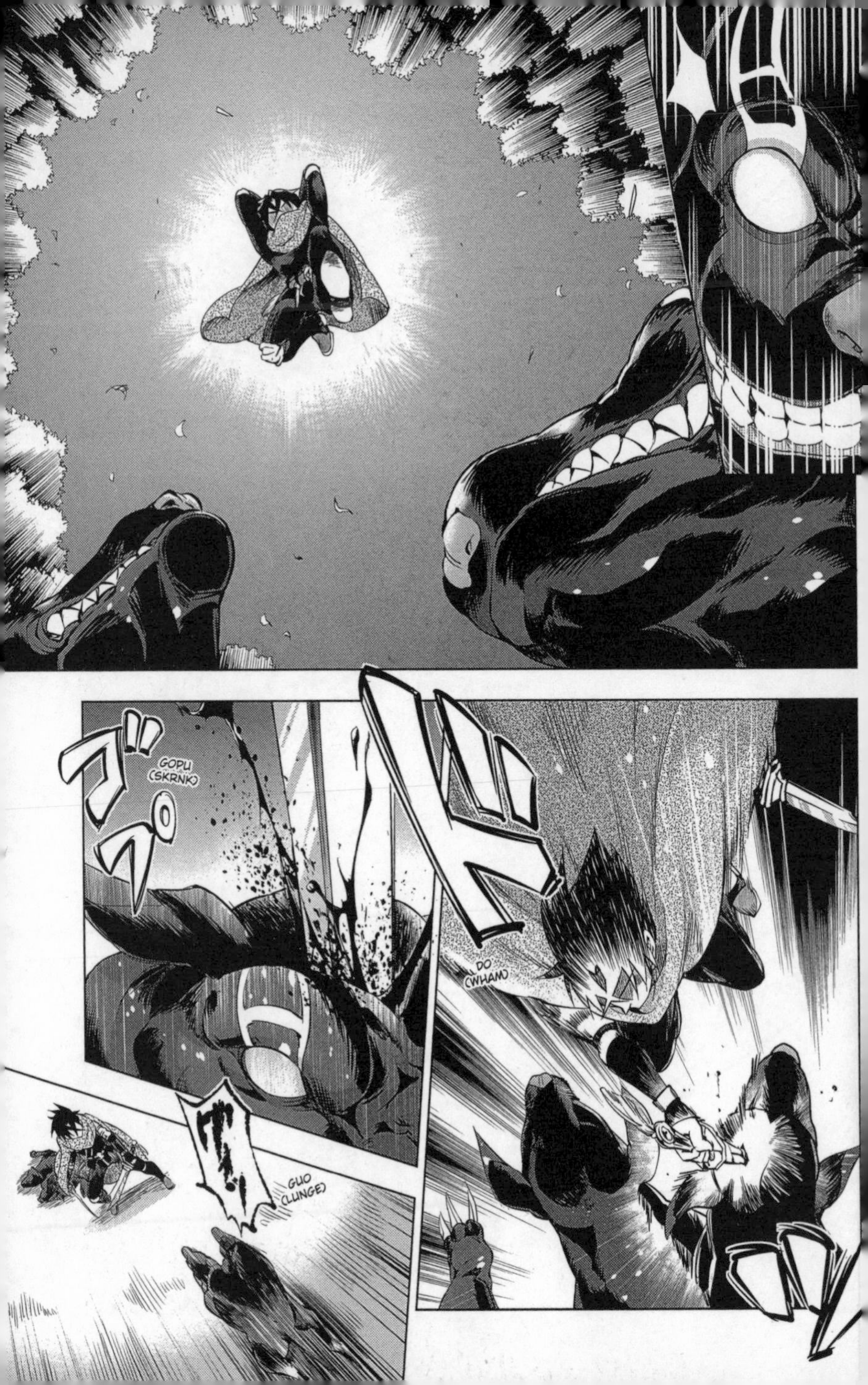
DO (WHAM)
GOPU (SKRNK)
GUO (LUNGE)

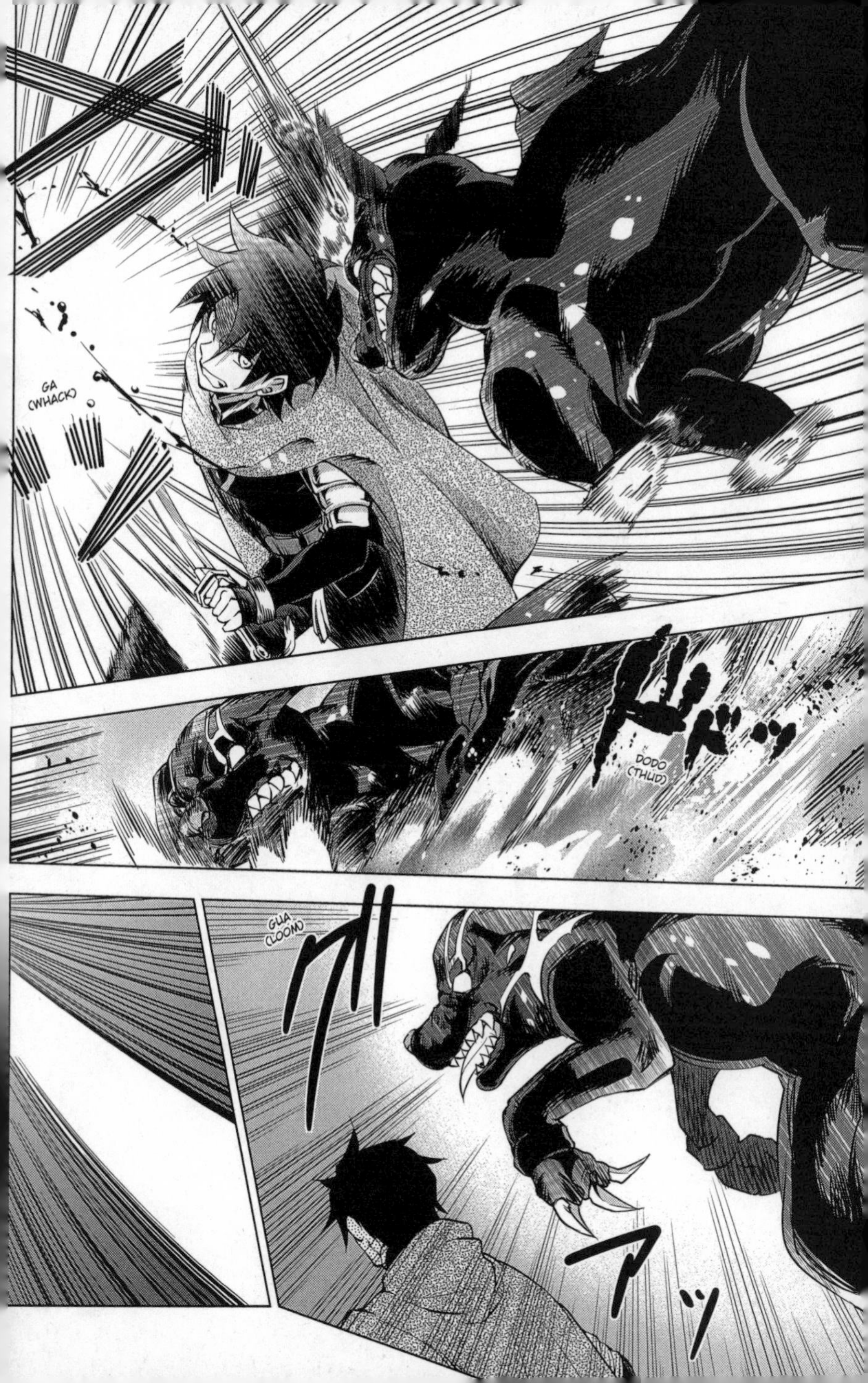
GA
(WHACK)
DODO
(THUD)
GUA
(LOOM)

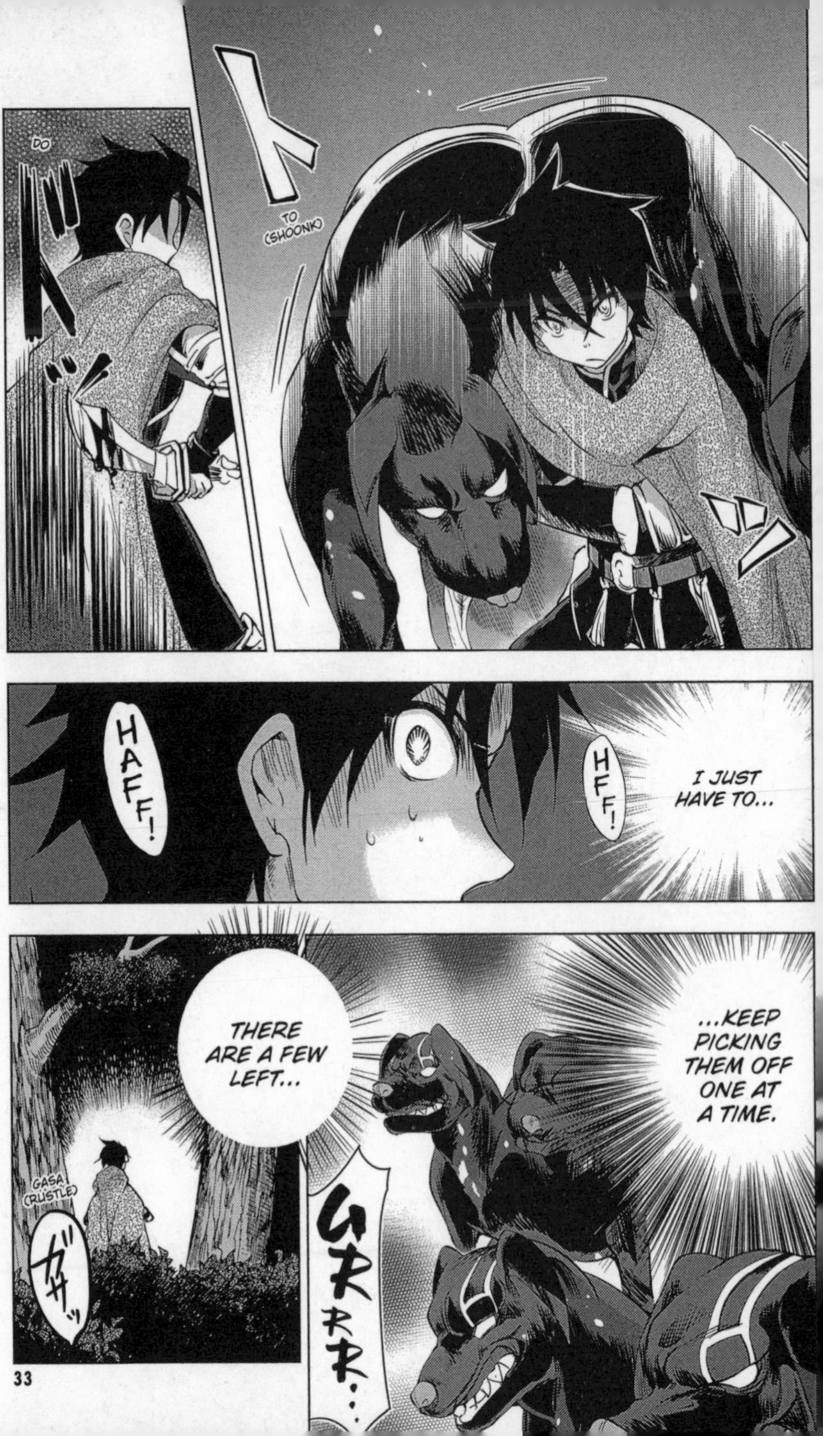
TO (SHOONK)
DO
I JUST HAVE TO...
HFF!
HAFF!
...KEEP PICKING THEM OFF ONE AT A TIME.
THERE ARE A FEW LEFT...
URRRR...
GASA (RUSTLE)

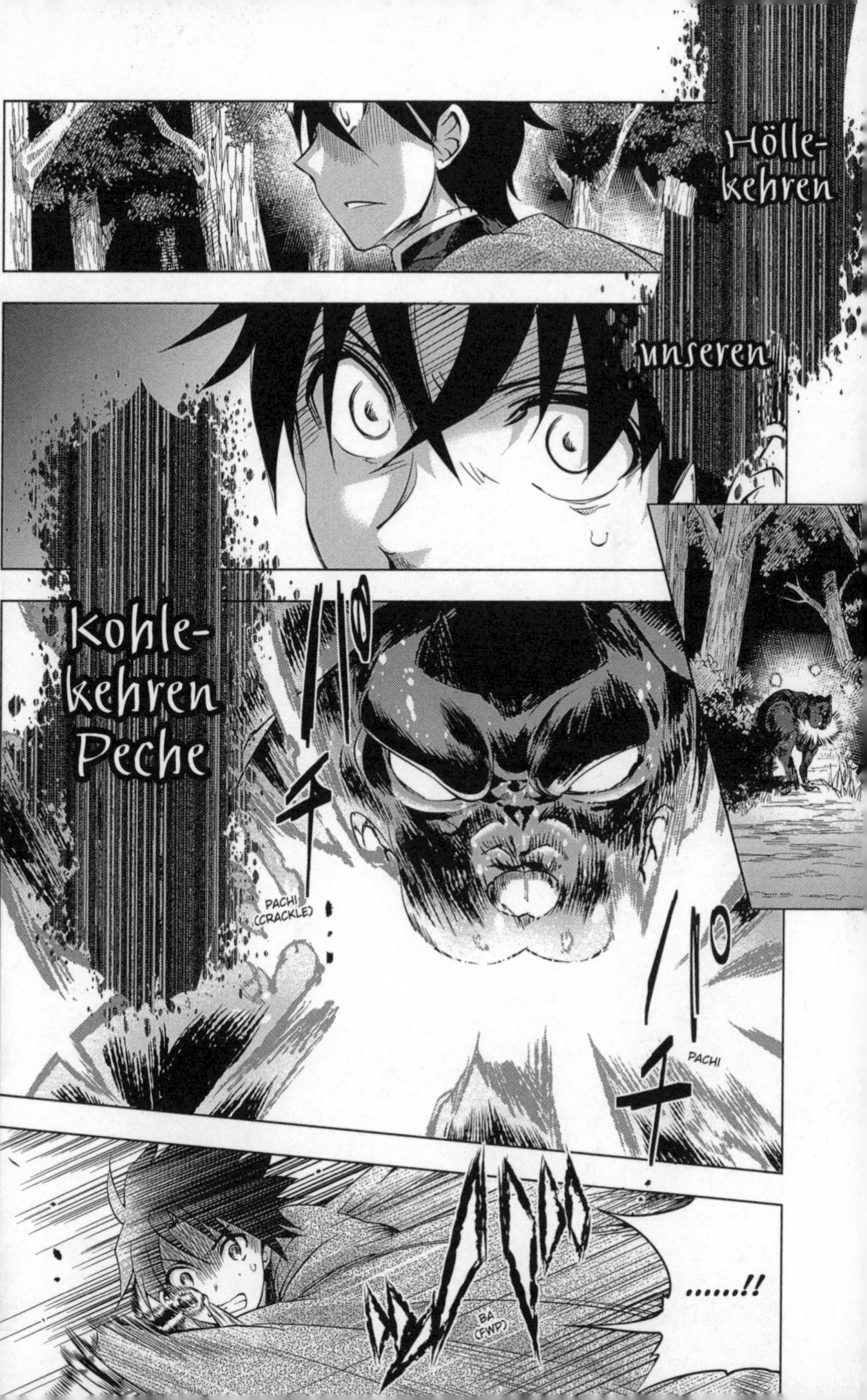
Hölle-
kehren
unseren
Kohle-
kehren
Peche
PACHI
(CRACKLE)
PACHI
BA
(FWP)
......!!

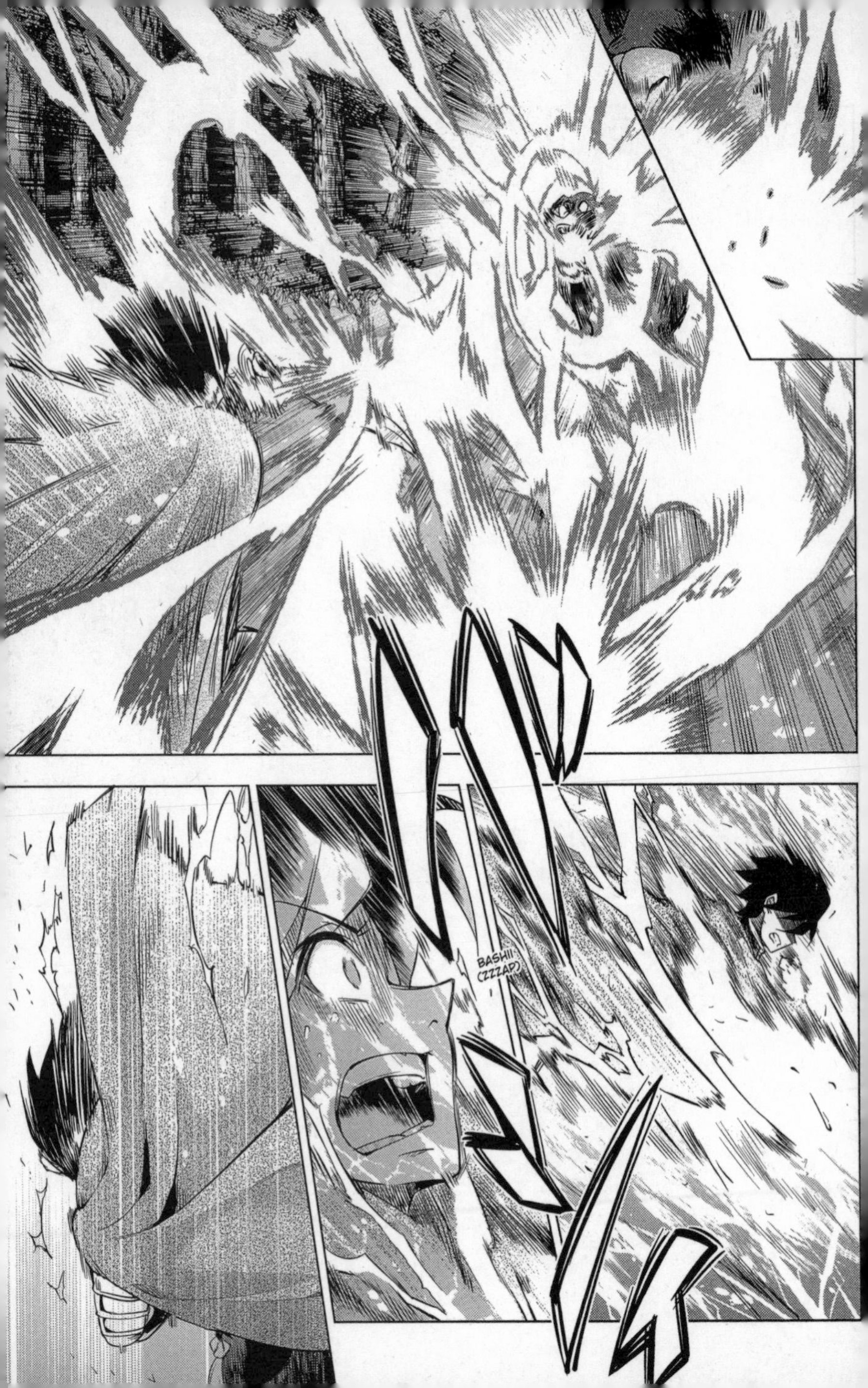
BASHII
(ZZZAP)

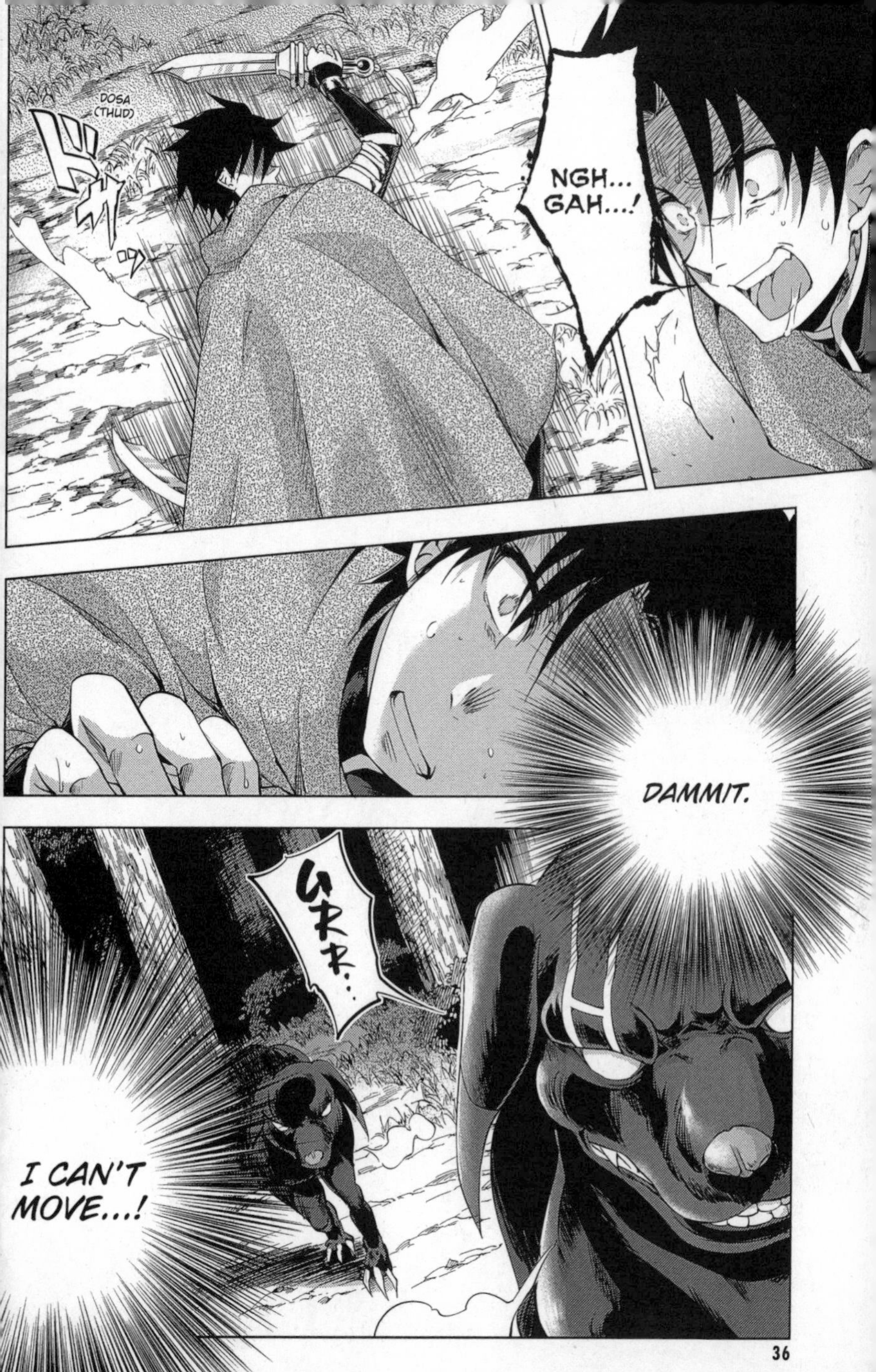
NGH... GAH...!
ドサッ
DOSA (THUD)
DAMMIT.
URRR...
I CAN'T MOVE...!

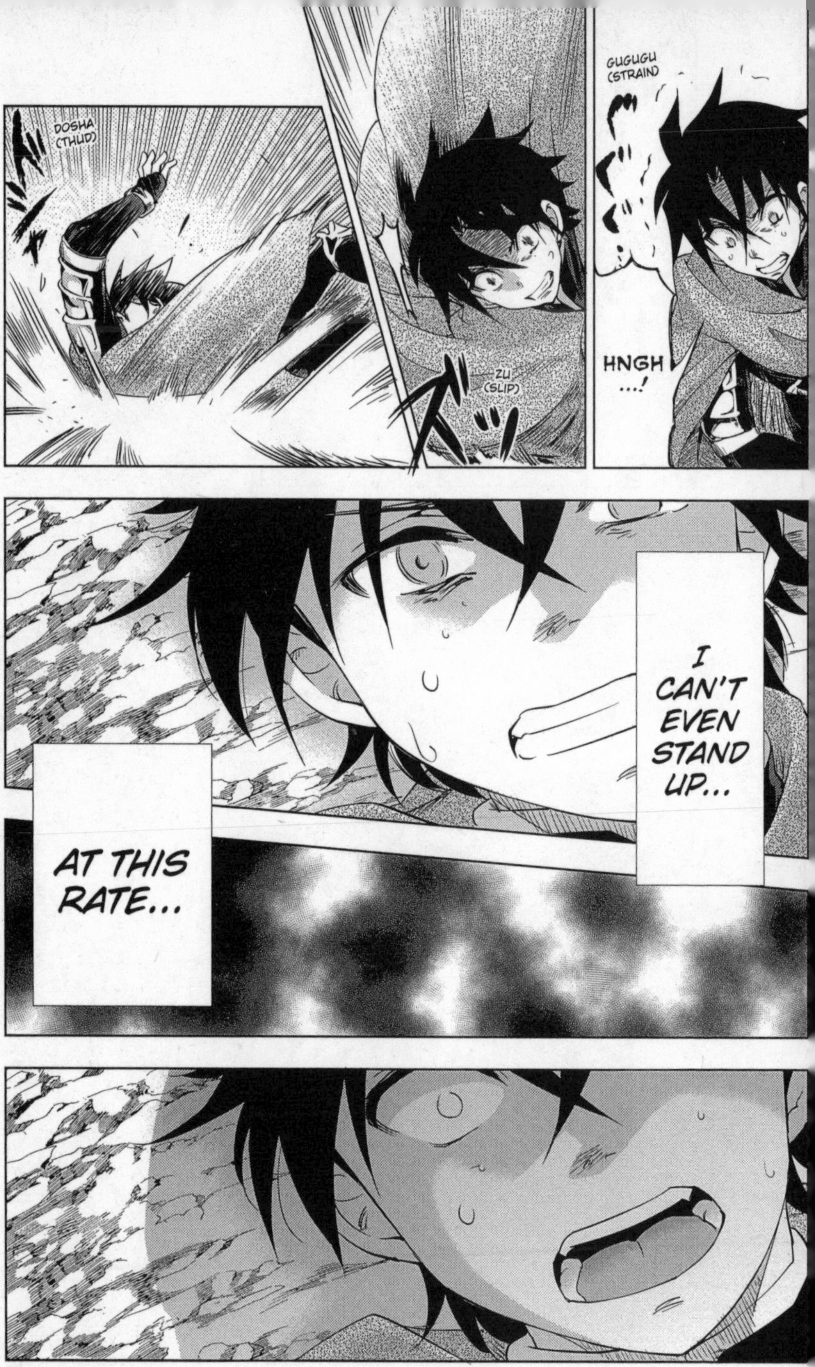
GUGUGU (STRAIN)
HNGH ...!
ZU (SLIP)
DOSHA (THUD)
I CAN'T EVEN STAND UP...
AT THIS RATE...

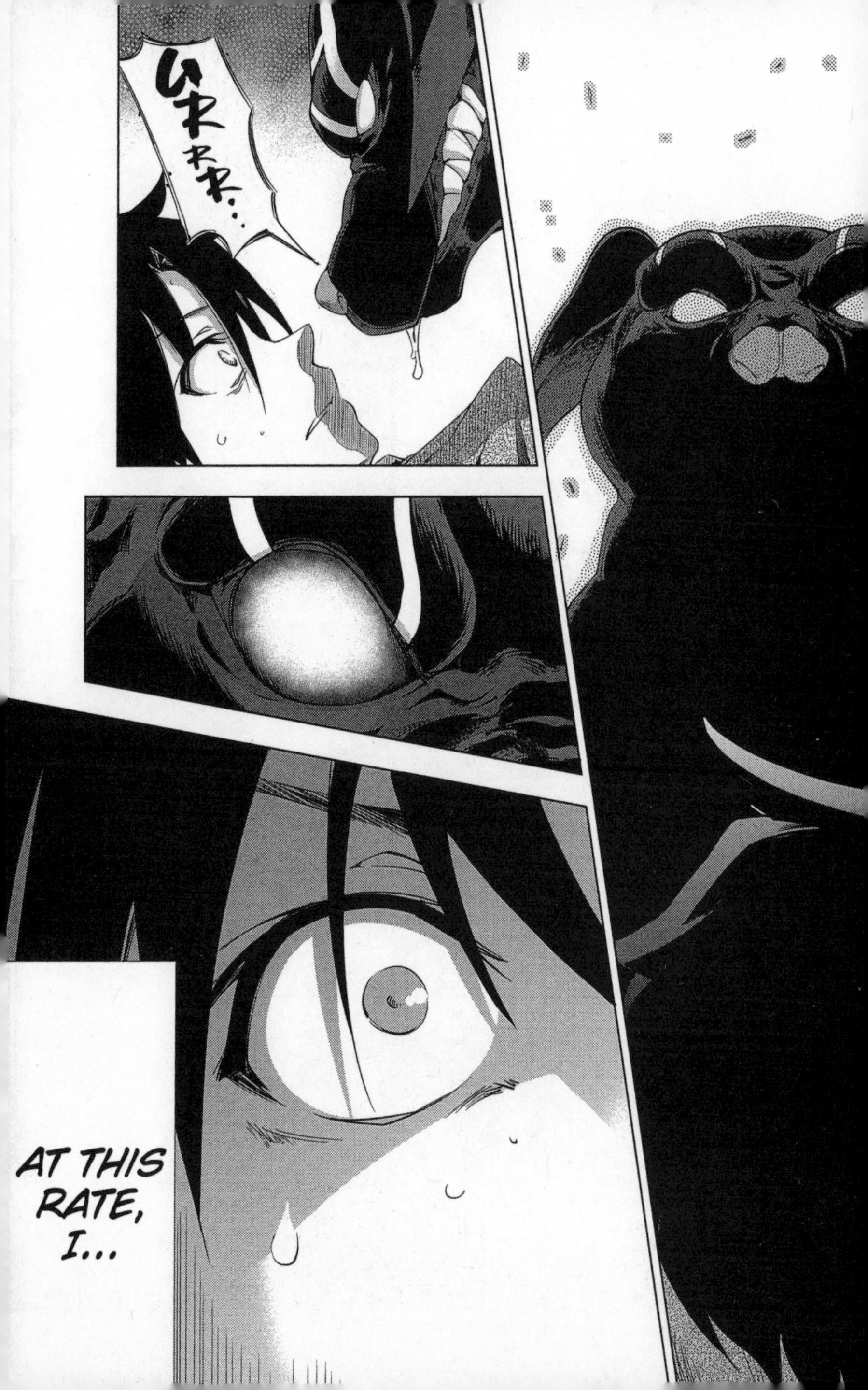
URRRR...
AT THIS RATE, I...

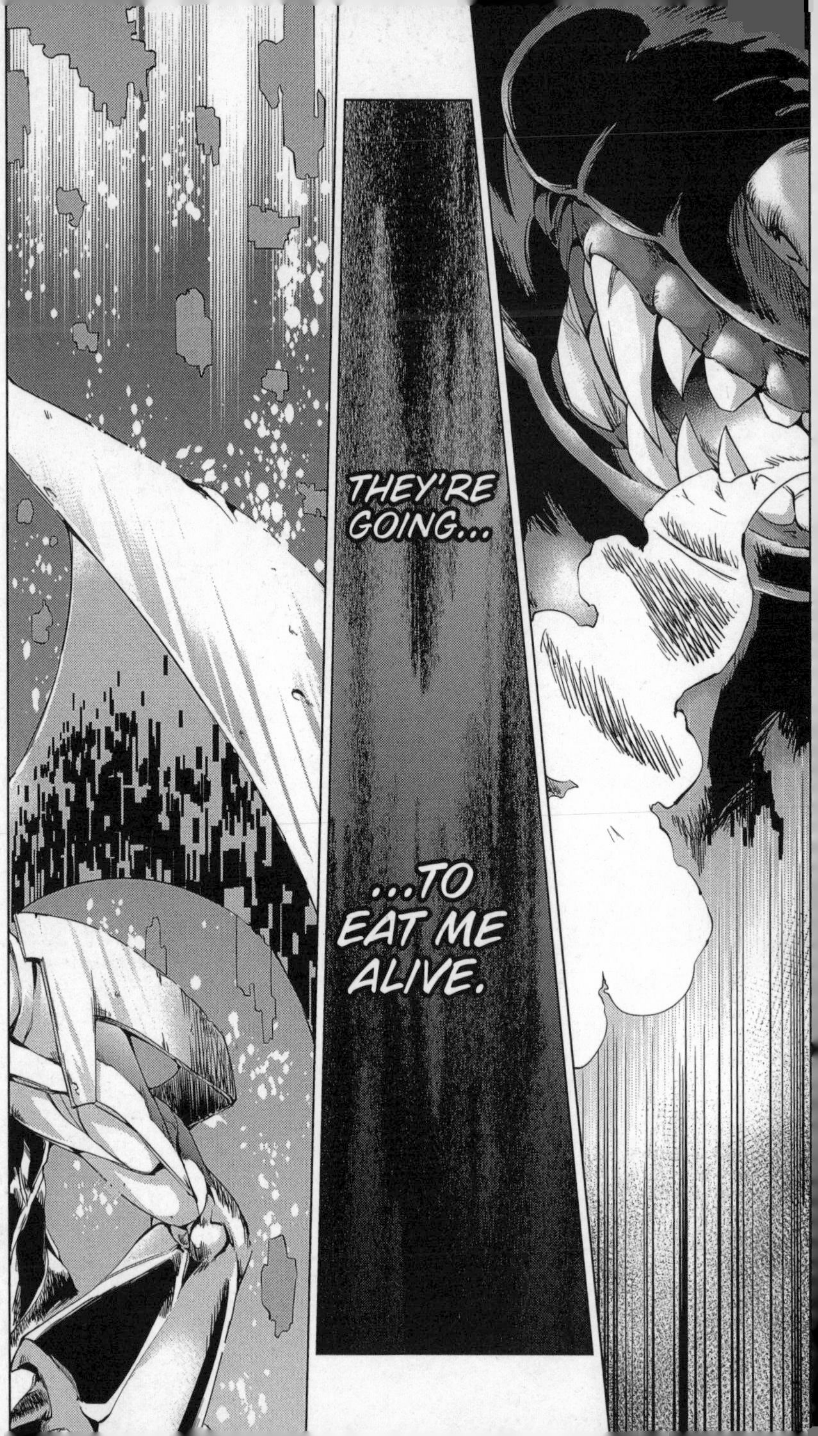
THEY'RE GOING...
...TO EAT ME ALIVE.

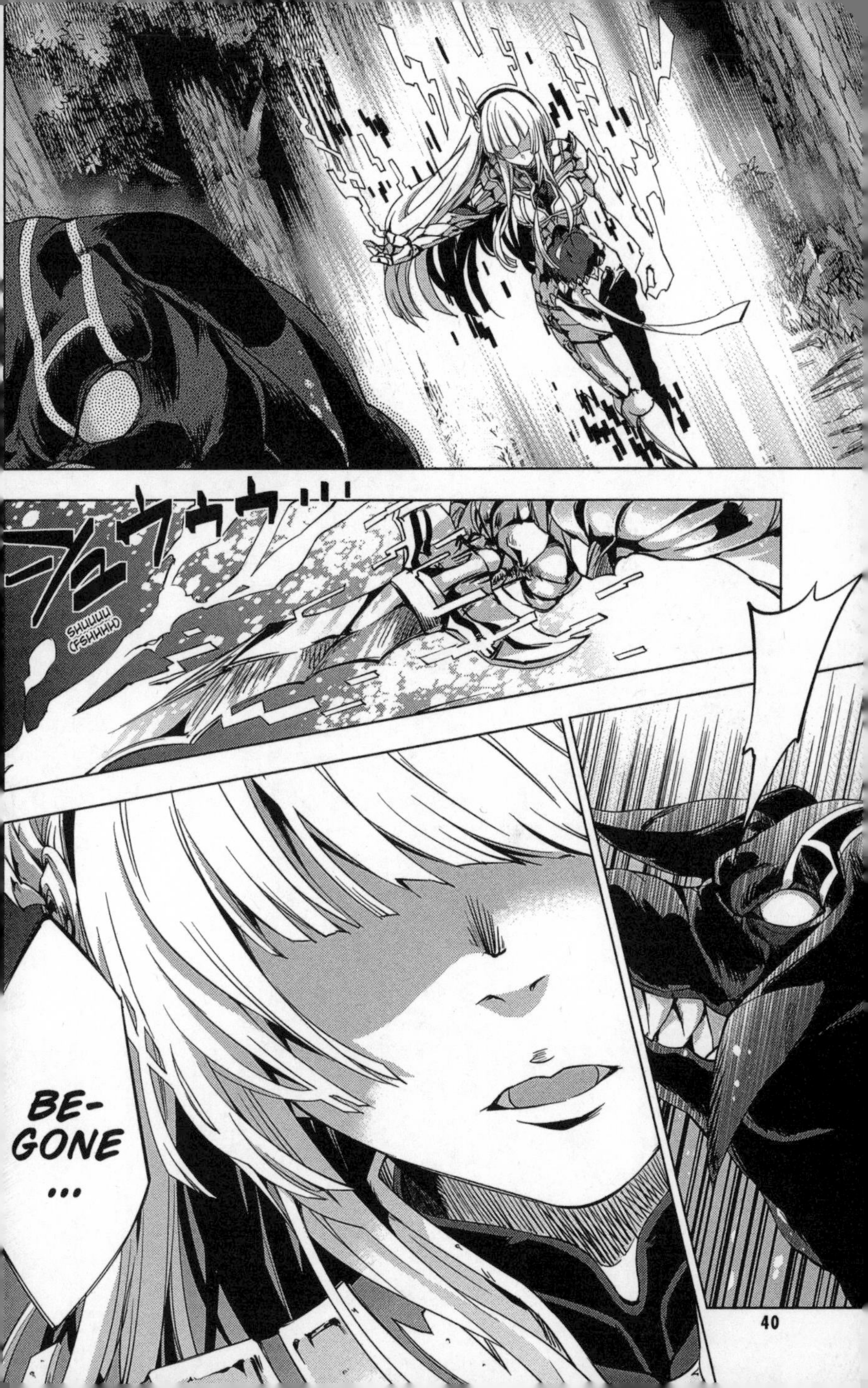
ジュウウウッ
SHUUUUU (FSHHHH)
BE-GONE...

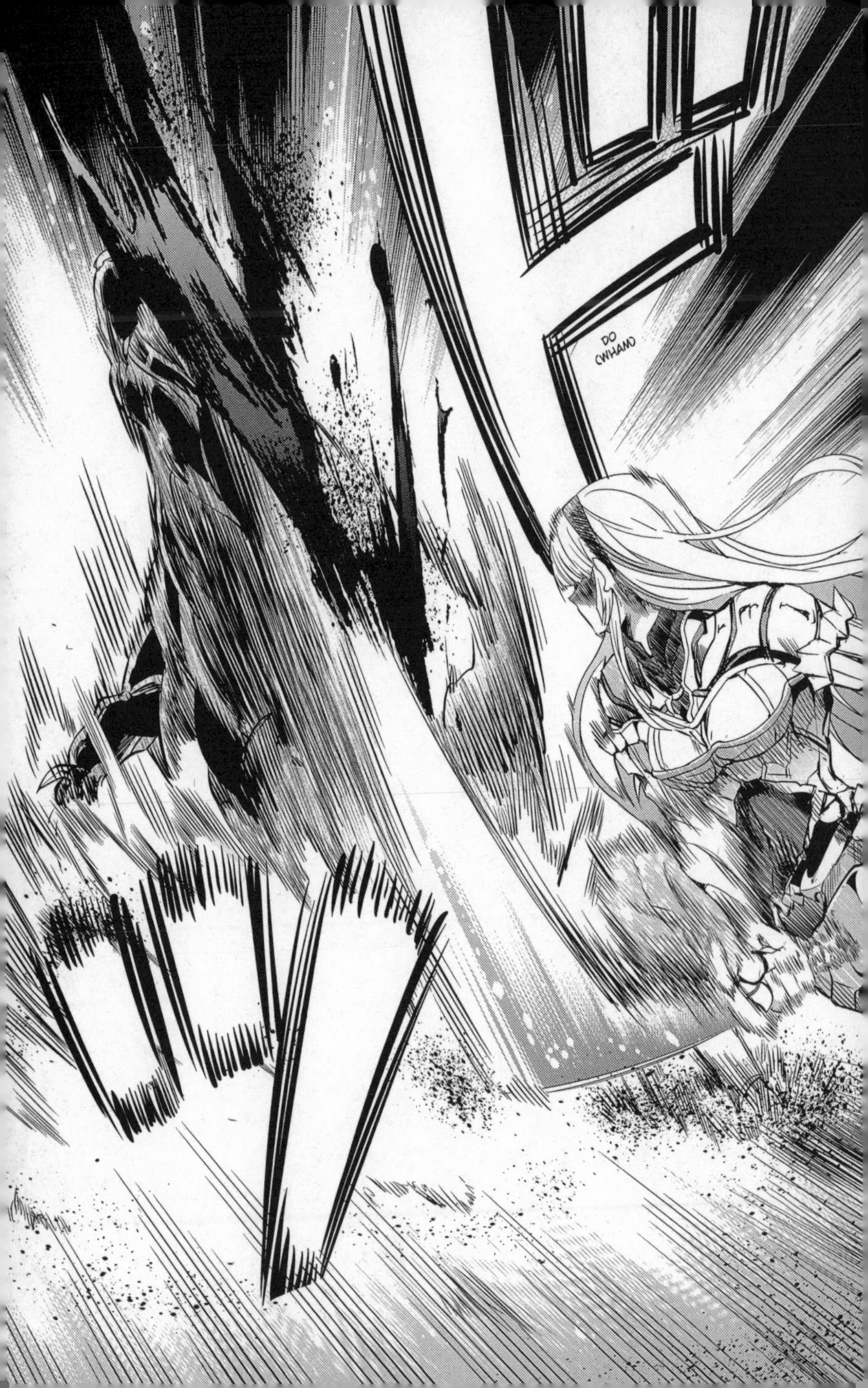
DO
(WHAM)

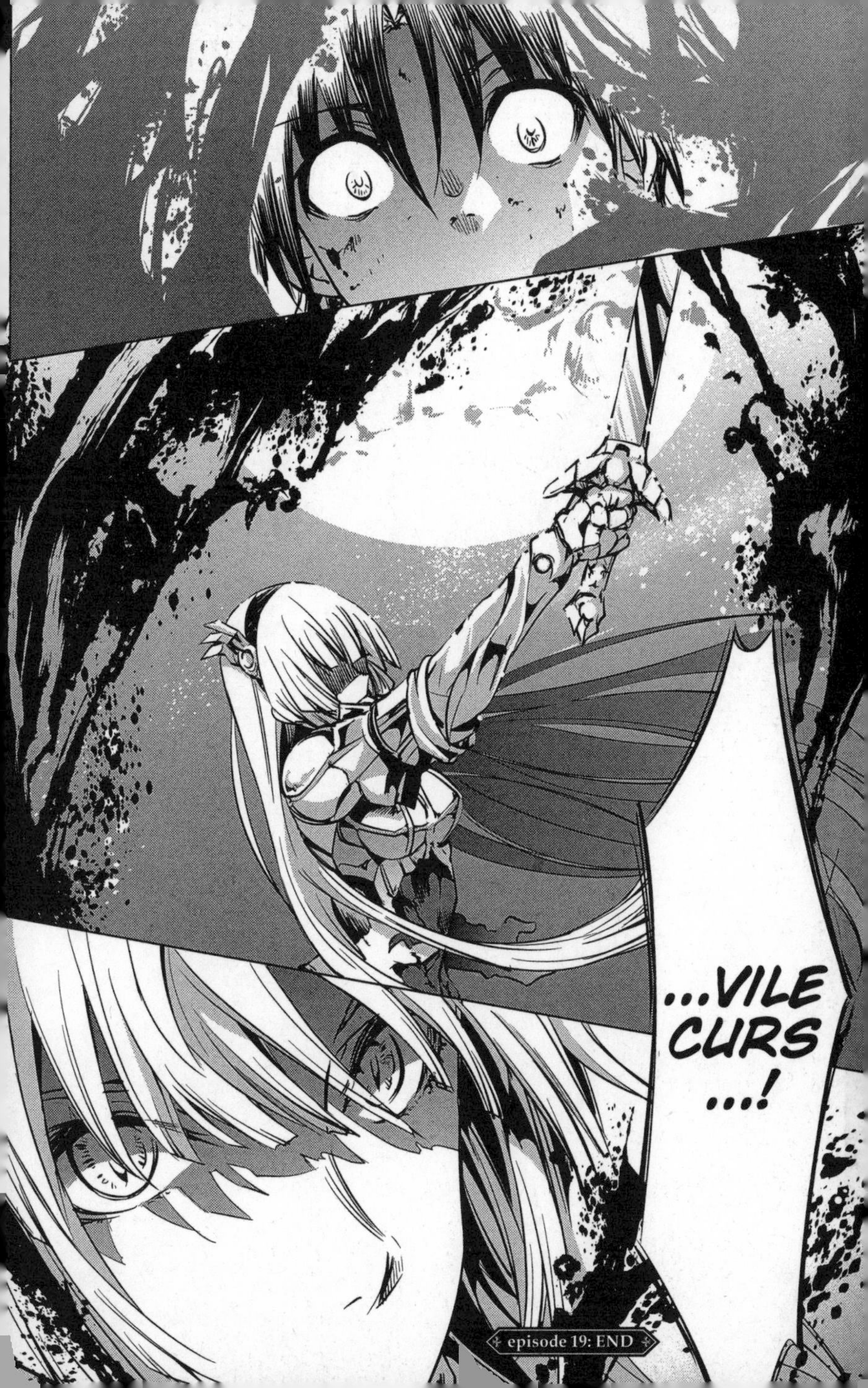
...VILE CURS ...!
episode 19: END

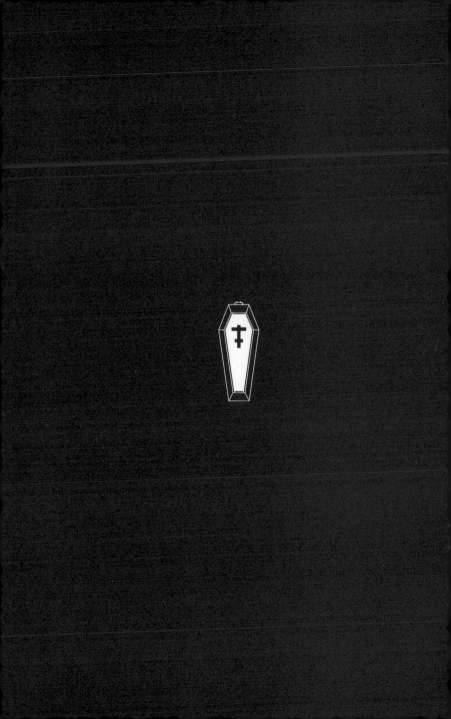

CHAIKA: THE COFFIN PRINCESS

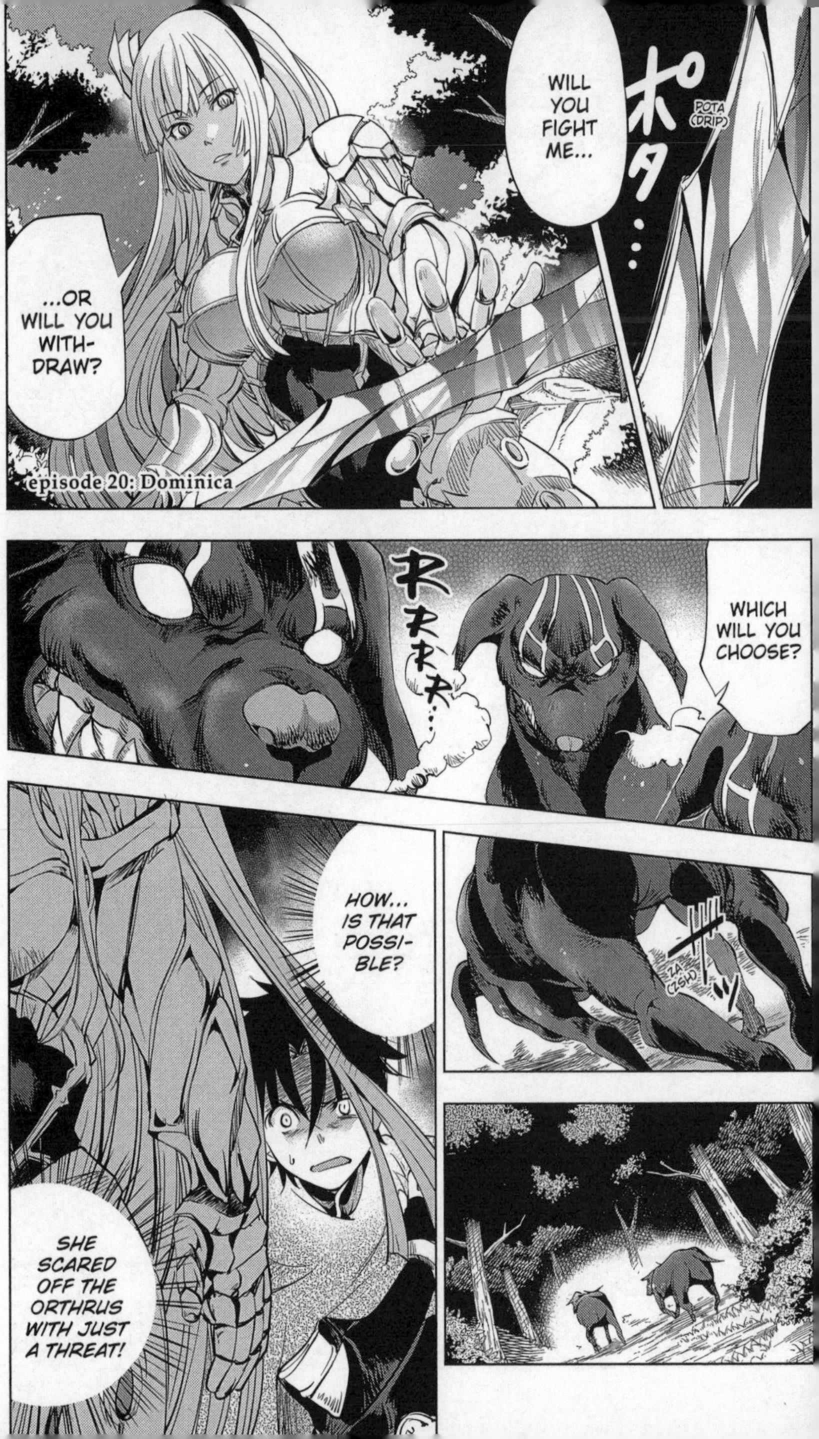
WILL YOU FIGHT ME...
ポタ...
POTA (DRIP)
...OR WILL YOU WITH-DRAW?
episode 20: Dominica
WHICH WILL YOU CHOOSE?
RRRR...
ZA (ZSH)
HOW... IS THAT POSSI-BLE?
SHE SCARED OFF THE ORTHRUS WITH JUST A THREAT!

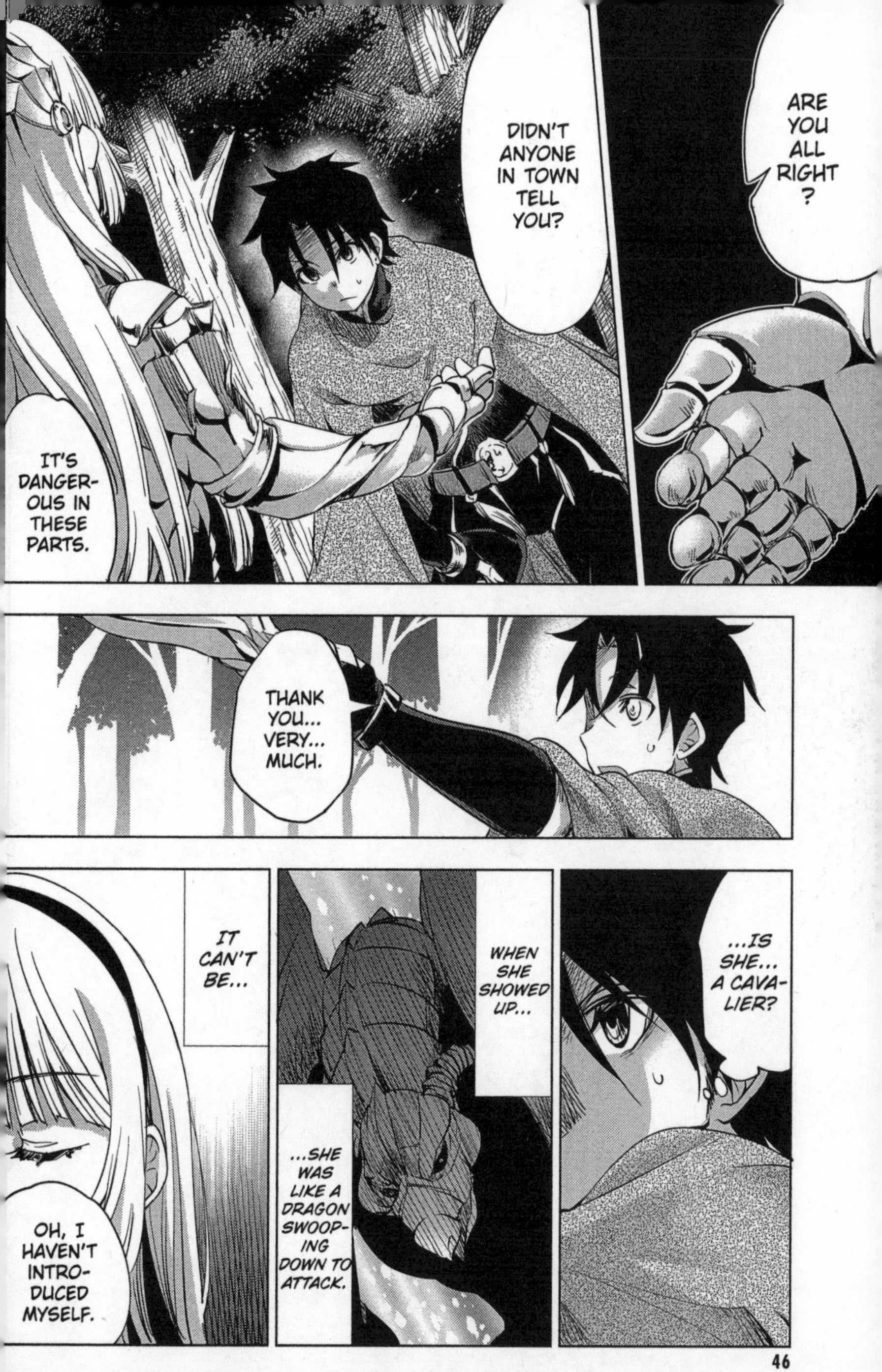
ARE YOU ALL RIGHT?
DIDN'T ANYONE IN TOWN TELL YOU?
IT'S DANGEROUS IN THESE PARTS.
THANK YOU... VERY... MUCH.
...IS SHE... A CAVALIER?
WHEN SHE SHOWED UP...
...SHE WAS LIKE A DRAGON SWOOPING DOWN TO ATTACK.
IT CAN'T BE...
OH, I HAVEN'T INTRODUCED MYSELF.

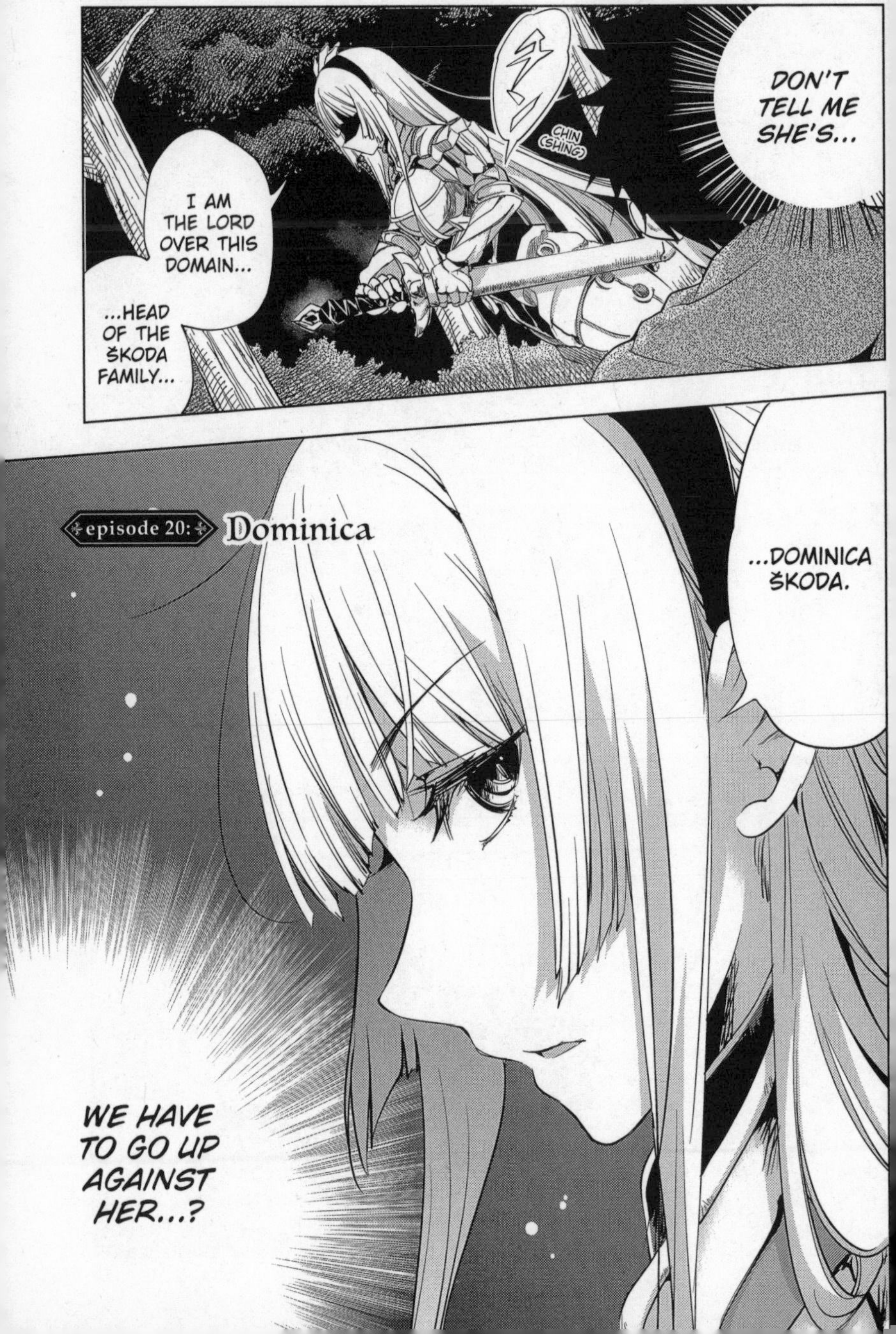
DON'T TELL ME SHE'S...
CHIN (SHING)
I AM THE LORD OVER THIS DOMAIN...
...HEAD OF THE ŠKODA FAMILY...
...DOMINICA ŠKODA.
episode 20: Dominica
WE HAVE TO GO UP AGAINST HER...?

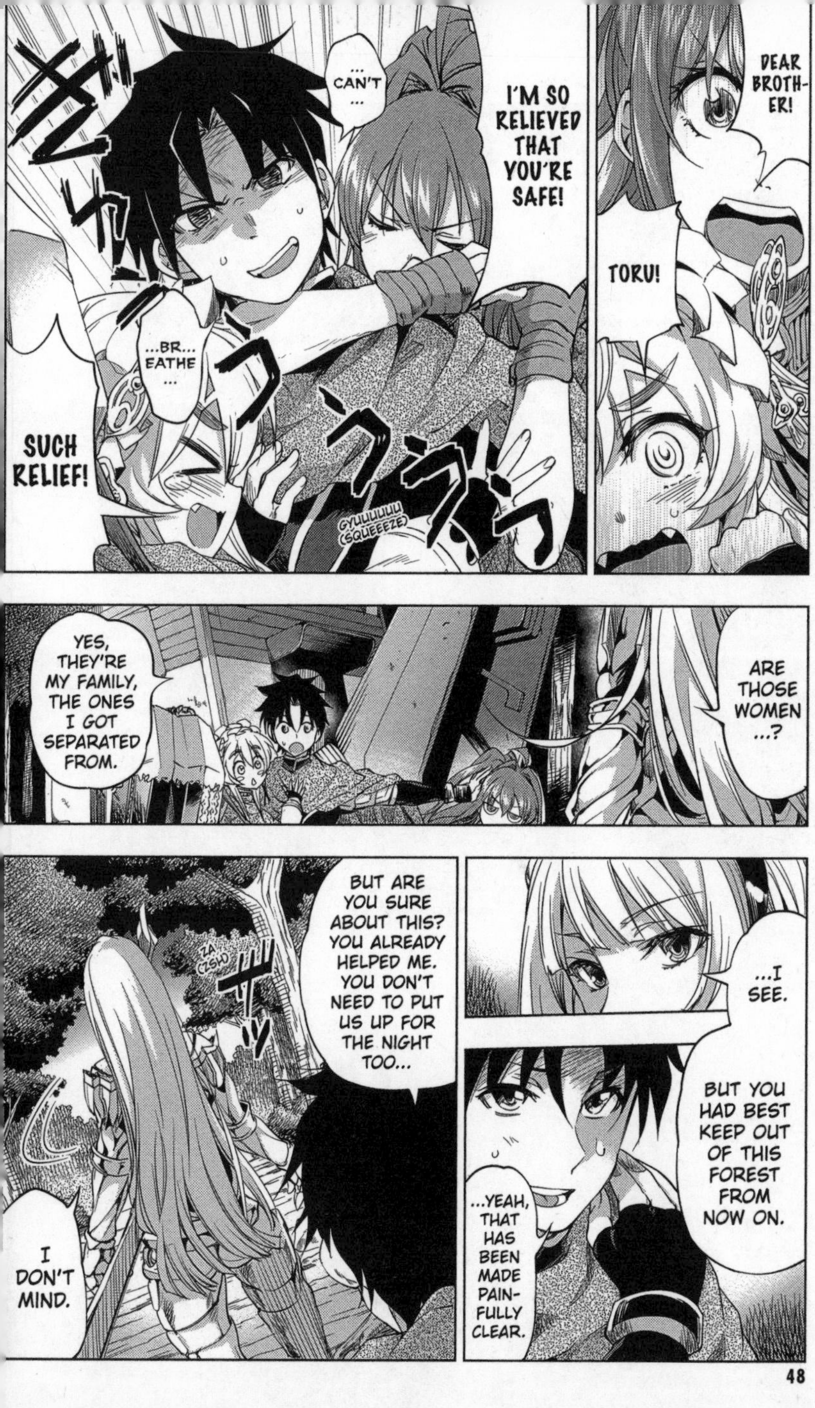
DEAR BROTHER-ER!
TORU!
I'M SO RELIEVED THAT YOU'RE SAFE!
...CAN'T...
...BR...EATHE...
SUCH RELIEF!
GYUUUUUU (SQUEEEZE)
ARE THOSE WOMEN...?
YES, THEY'RE MY FAMILY, THE ONES I GOT SEPARATED FROM.
...I SEE.
BUT YOU HAD BEST KEEP OUT OF THIS FOREST FROM NOW ON.
...YEAH, THAT HAS BEEN MADE PAINFULLY CLEAR.
BUT ARE YOU SURE ABOUT THIS? YOU ALREADY HELPED ME. YOU DON'T NEED TO PUT US UP FOR THE NIGHT TOO...
ZA (ZISH)
I DON'T MIND.

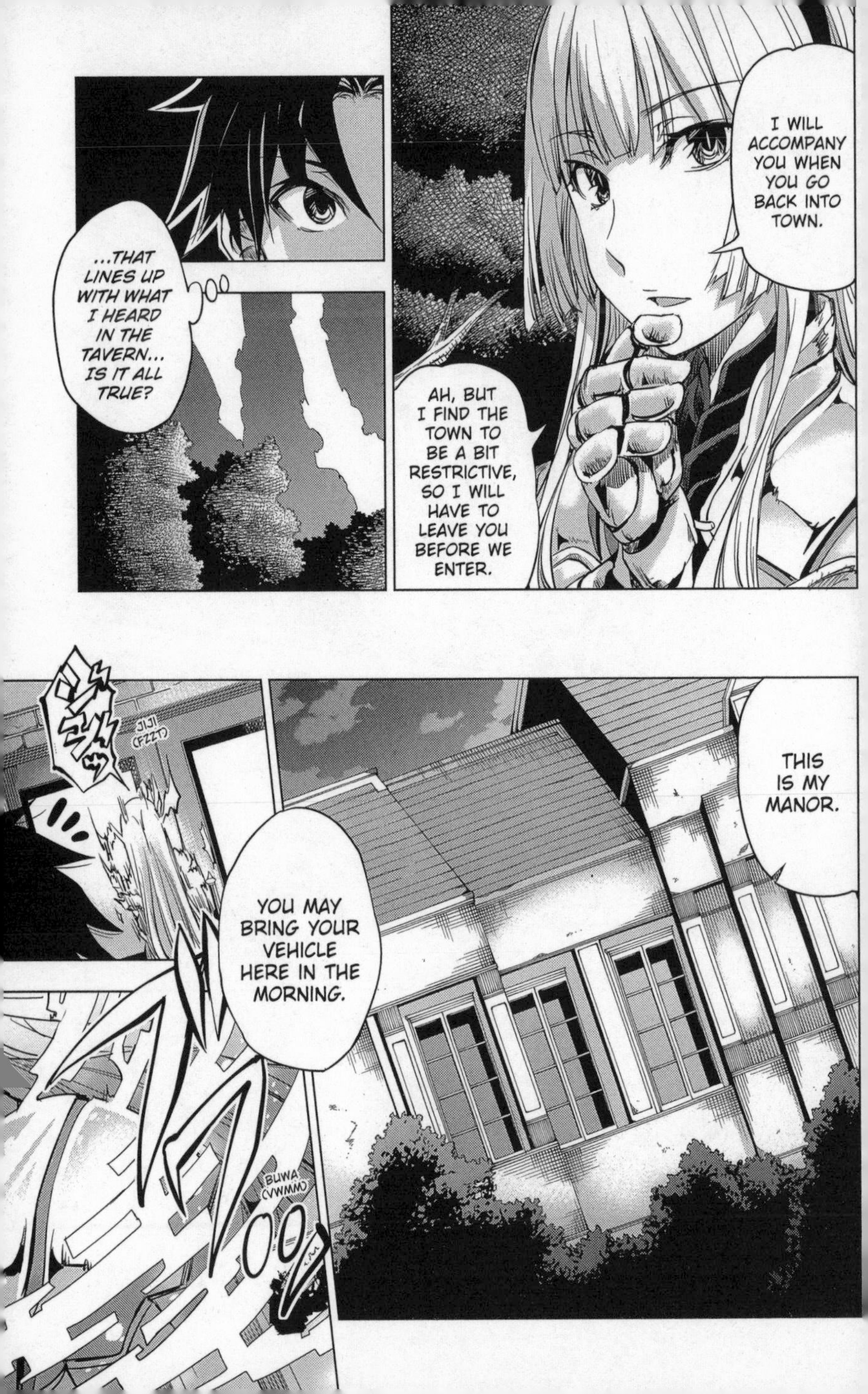
I WILL ACCOMPANY YOU WHEN YOU GO BACK INTO TOWN.
AH, BUT I FIND THE TOWN TO BE A BIT RESTRICTIVE, SO I WILL HAVE TO LEAVE YOU BEFORE WE ENTER.
...THAT LINES UP WITH WHAT I HEARD IN THE TAVERN... IS IT ALL TRUE?
THIS IS MY MANOR.
YOU MAY BRING YOUR VEHICLE HERE IN THE MORNING.
JIJI (FZZT)
BUWA (VWMM)

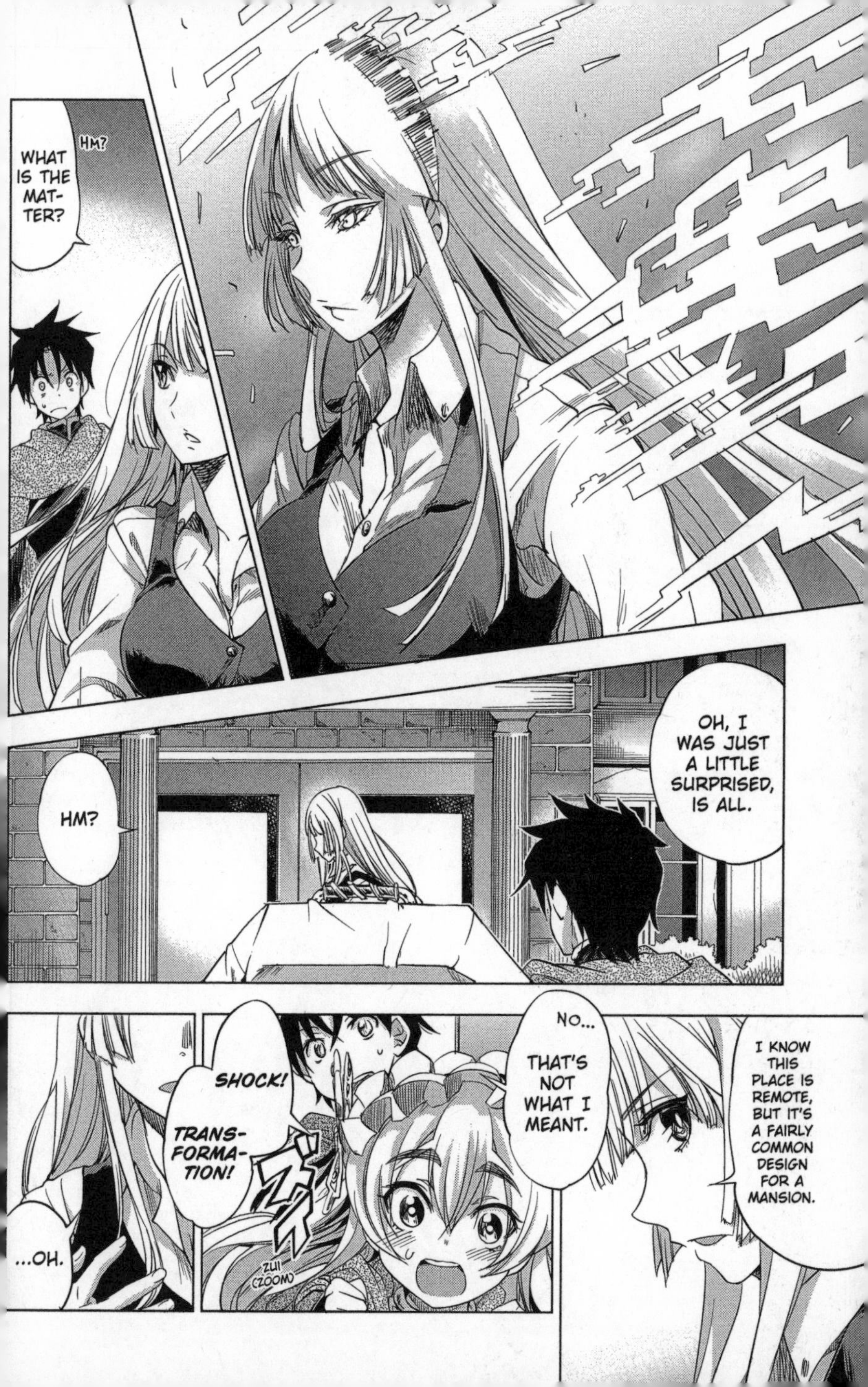
HM?
WHAT IS THE MATTER?
OH, I WAS JUST A LITTLE SURPRISED, IS ALL.
HM?
I KNOW THIS PLACE IS REMOTE, BUT IT'S A FAIRLY COMMON DESIGN FOR A MANSION.
NO...
THAT'S NOT WHAT I MEANT.
SHOCK!
TRANSFORMATION!
ZUI (ZOOM)
...OH.

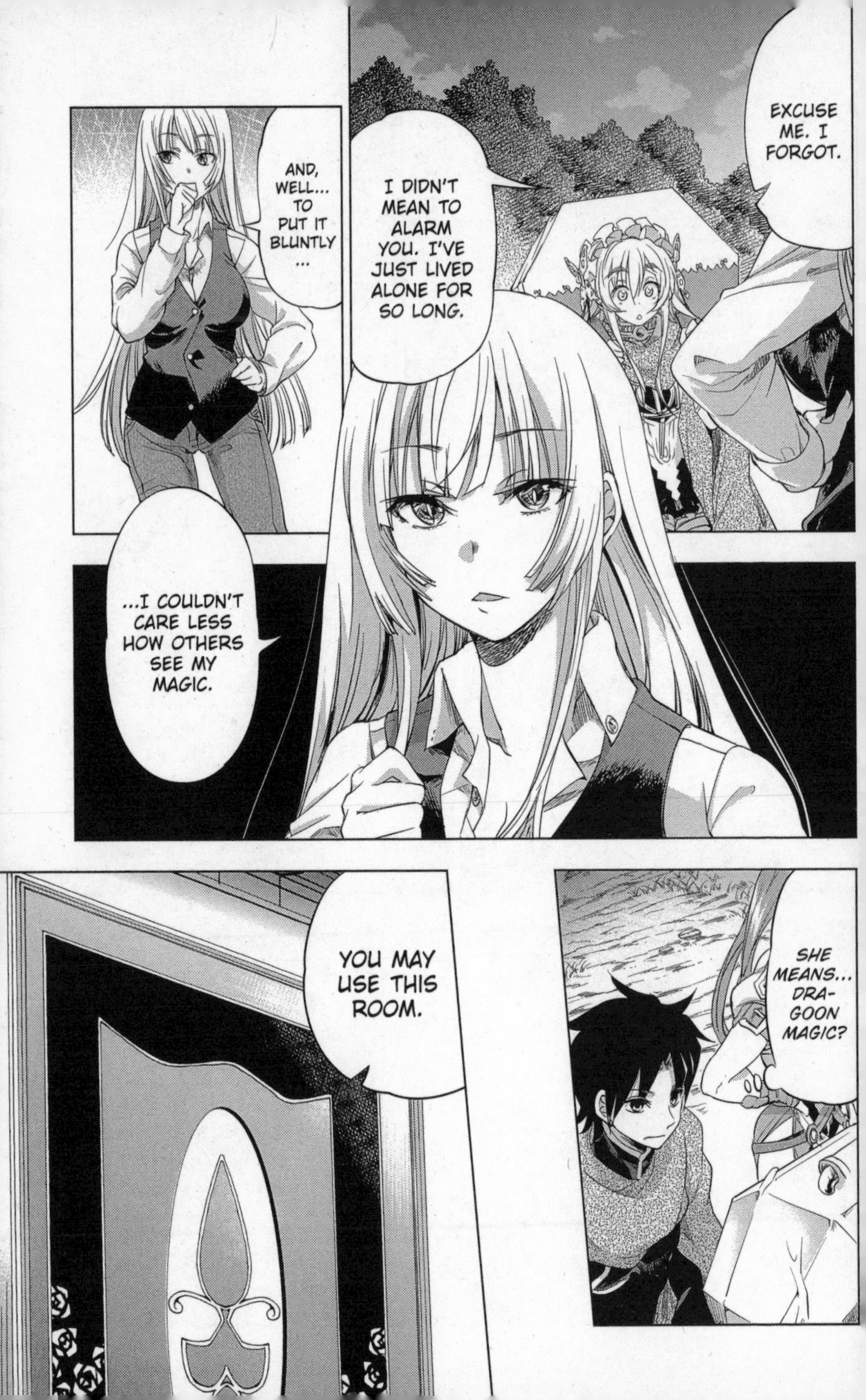
EXCUSE ME. I FORGOT.
I DIDN'T MEAN TO ALARM YOU. I'VE JUST LIVED ALONE FOR SO LONG.
AND, WELL... TO PUT IT BLUNTLY...
...I COULDN'T CARE LESS HOW OTHERS SEE MY MAGIC.
SHE MEANS... DRA-GOON MAGIC?
YOU MAY USE THIS ROOM.

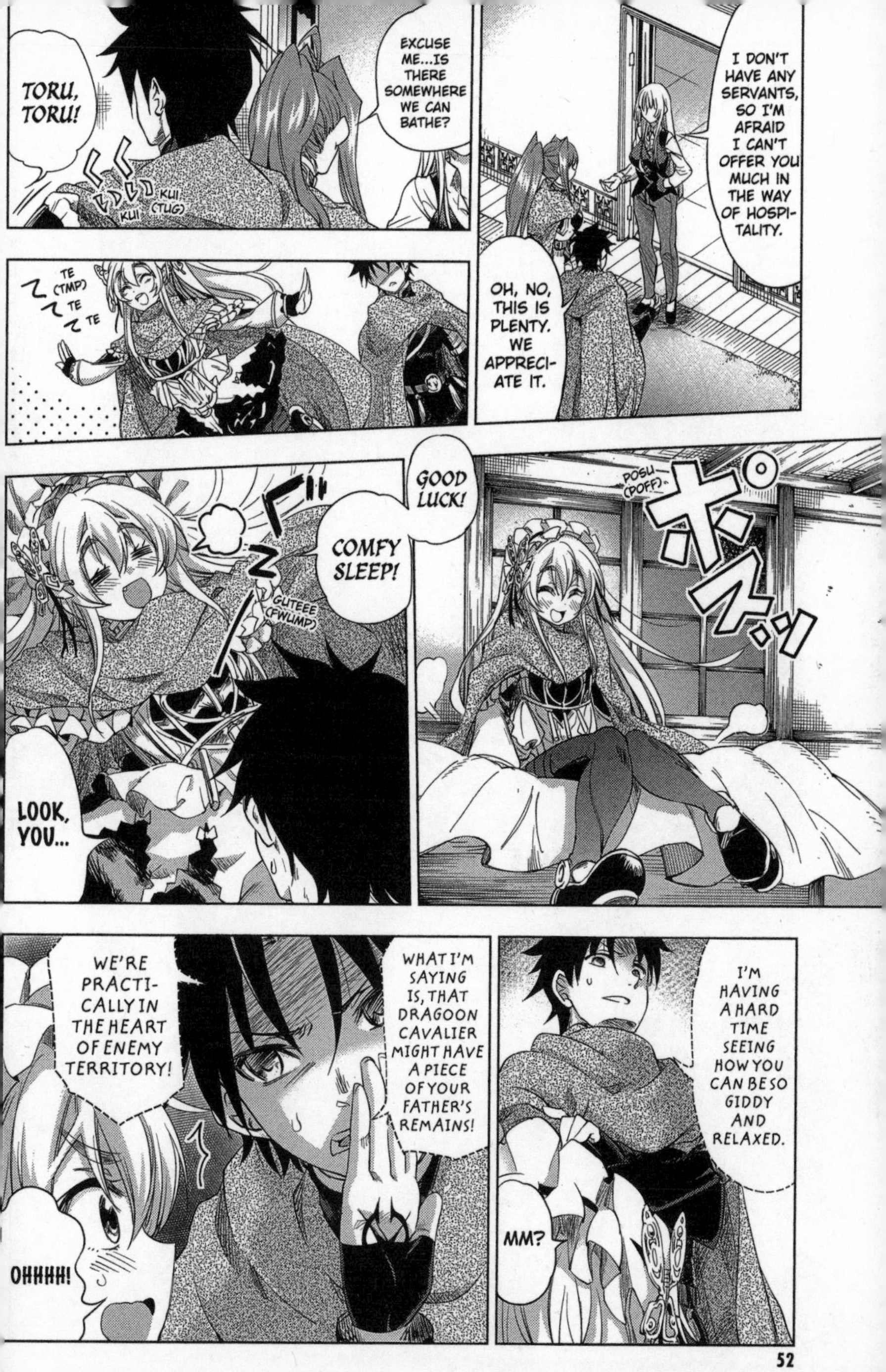
I DON'T HAVE ANY SERVANTS, SO I'M AFRAID I CAN'T OFFER YOU MUCH IN THE WAY OF HOSPI- TALITY.
OH, NO, THIS IS PLENTY. WE APPRECI- ATE IT.
EXCUSE ME...IS THERE SOMEWHERE WE CAN BATHE?
TORU, TORU!
KUI KUI (TUG)
TE (TMP) TE TE
POSU (POFF)
GOOD LUCK!
COMFY SLEEP!
GUTEEE (FWUMP)
LOOK, YOU...
I'M HAVING A HARD TIME SEEING HOW YOU CAN BE SO GIDDY AND RELAXED.
MM?
WHAT I'M SAYING IS, THAT DRAGOON CAVALIER MIGHT HAVE A PIECE OF YOUR FATHER'S REMAINS!
WE'RE PRACTI- CALLY IN THE HEART OF ENEMY TERRITORY!
OHHHH!

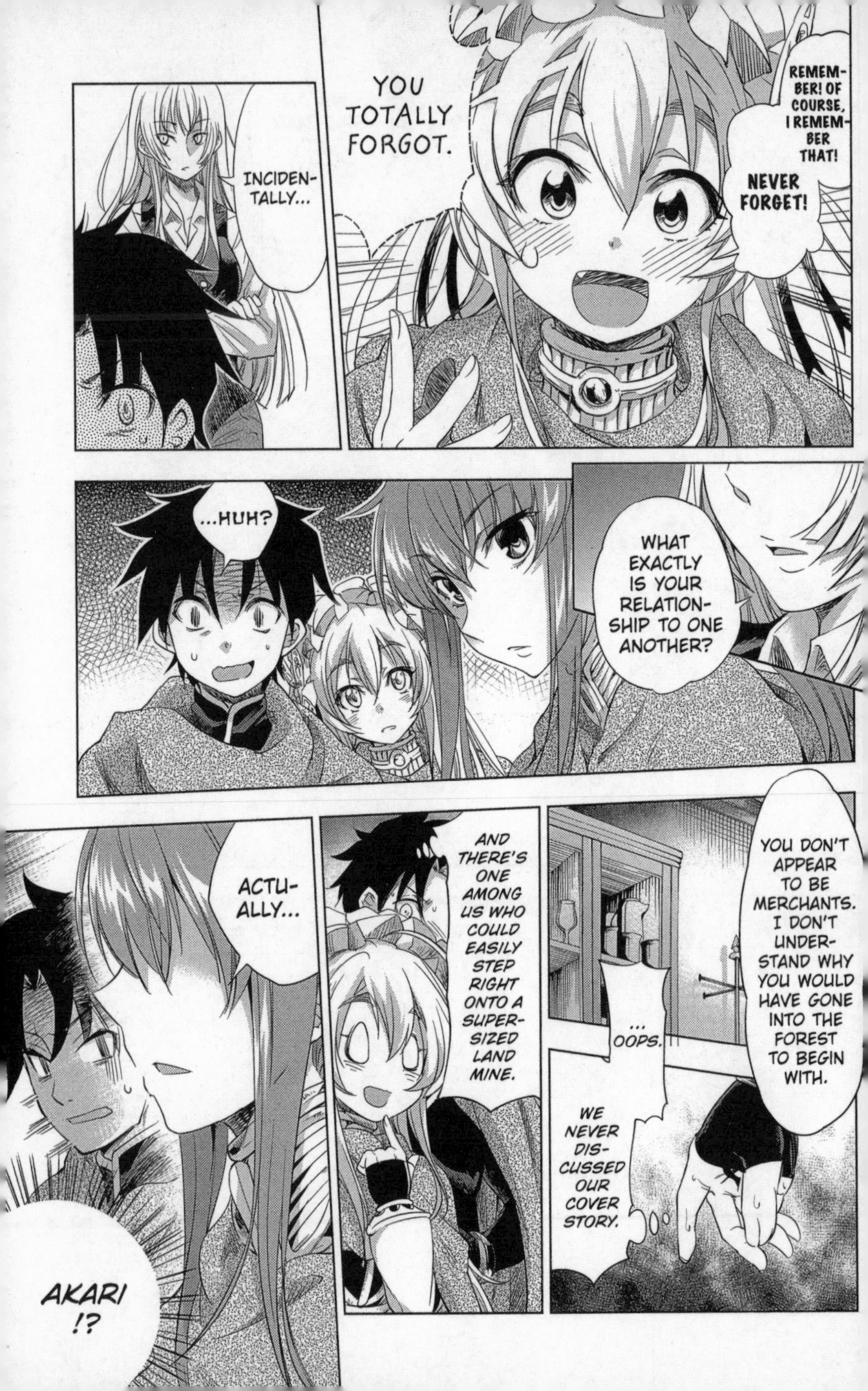
REMEMBER! OF COURSE, I REMEMBER THAT!
NEVER FORGET!
YOU TOTALLY FORGOT.
INCIDENTALLY...
WHAT EXACTLY IS YOUR RELATIONSHIP TO ONE ANOTHER?
...HUH?
YOU DON'T APPEAR TO BE MERCHANTS. I DON'T UNDERSTAND WHY YOU WOULD HAVE GONE INTO THE FOREST TO BEGIN WITH.
...OOPS.
WE NEVER DISCUSSED OUR COVER STORY.
AND THERE'S ONE AMONG US WHO COULD EASILY STEP RIGHT ONTO A SUPER-SIZED LAND MINE.
ACTUALLY...
AKARI!?

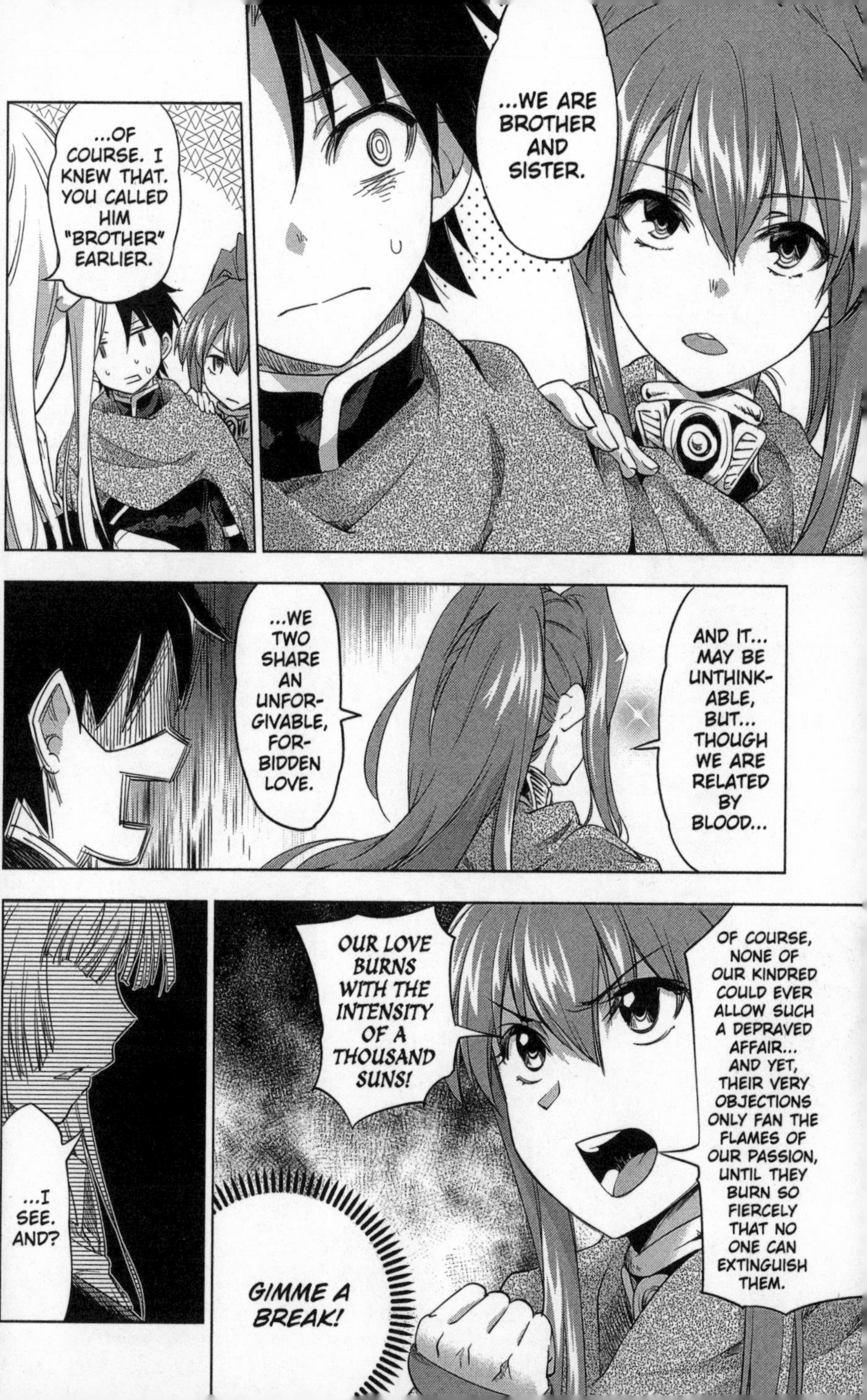
...WE ARE BROTHER AND SISTER.
...OF COURSE. I KNEW THAT. YOU CALLED HIM "BROTHER" EARLIER.
AND IT... MAY BE UNTHINKABLE, BUT... THOUGH WE ARE RELATED BY BLOOD...
...WE TWO SHARE AN UNFORGIVABLE, FORBIDDEN LOVE.
OF COURSE, NONE OF OUR KINDRED COULD EVER ALLOW SUCH A DEPRAVED AFFAIR... AND YET, THEIR VERY OBJECTIONS ONLY FAN THE FLAMES OF OUR PASSION, UNTIL THEY BURN SO FIERCELY THAT NO ONE CAN EXTINGUISH THEM.
OUR LOVE BURNS WITH THE INTENSITY OF A THOUSAND SUNS!
GIMME A BREAK!
...I SEE. AND?

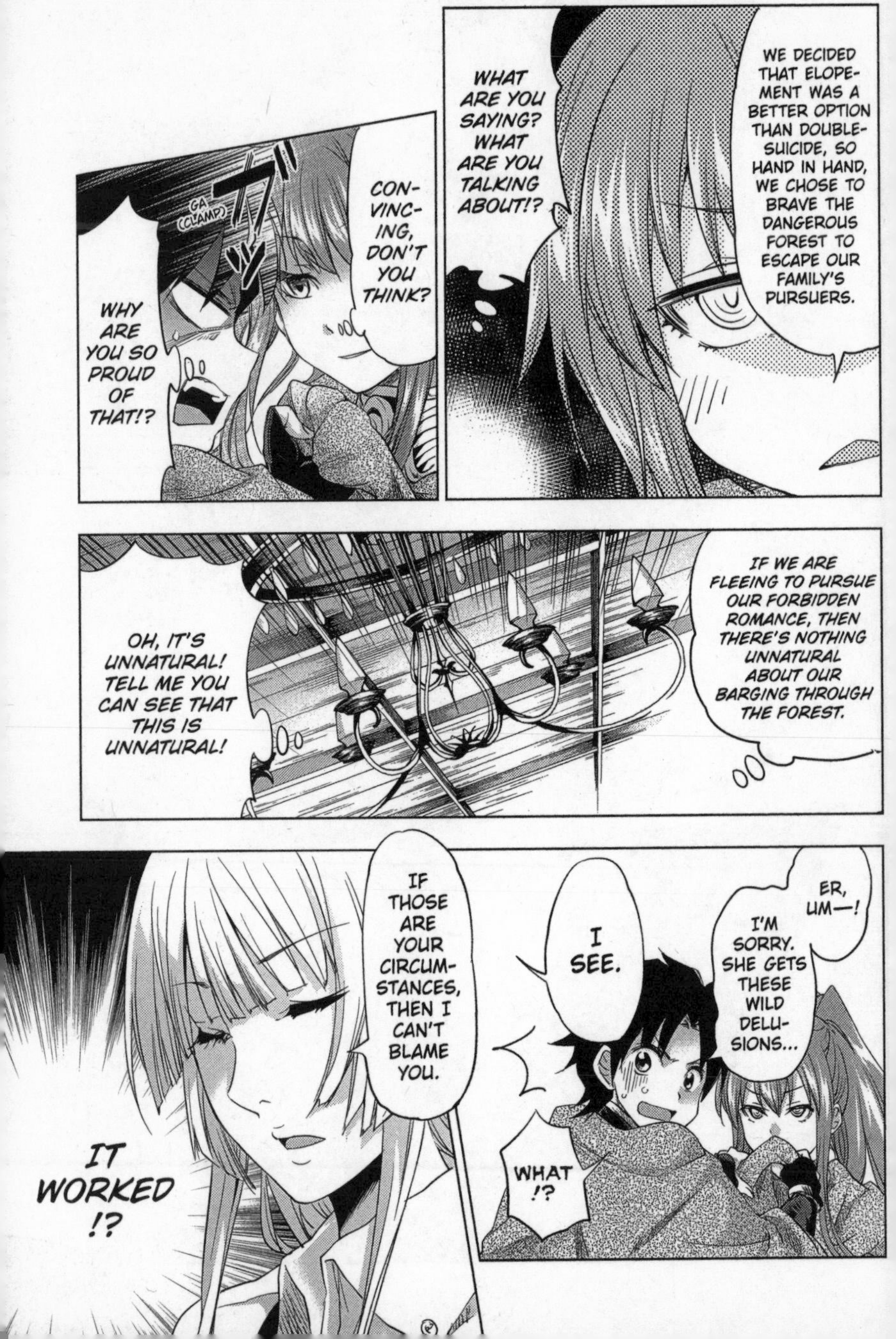
WE DECIDED THAT ELOPEMENT WAS A BETTER OPTION THAN DOUBLE-SUICIDE, SO HAND IN HAND, WE CHOSE TO BRAVE THE DANGEROUS FOREST TO ESCAPE OUR FAMILY'S PURSUERS.
WHAT ARE YOU SAYING? WHAT ARE YOU TALKING ABOUT!?
CONVINCING, DON'T YOU THINK?
GA (CLAMP)
WHY ARE YOU SO PROUD OF THAT!?
IF WE ARE FLEEING TO PURSUE OUR FORBIDDEN ROMANCE, THEN THERE'S NOTHING UNNATURAL ABOUT OUR BARGING THROUGH THE FOREST.
OH, IT'S UNNATURAL! TELL ME YOU CAN SEE THAT THIS IS UNNATURAL!
ER, UM—!
I'M SORRY. SHE GETS THESE WILD DELUSIONS...
I SEE.
WHAT!?
IF THOSE ARE YOUR CIRCUMSTANCES, THEN I CAN'T BLAME YOU.
IT WORKED!?

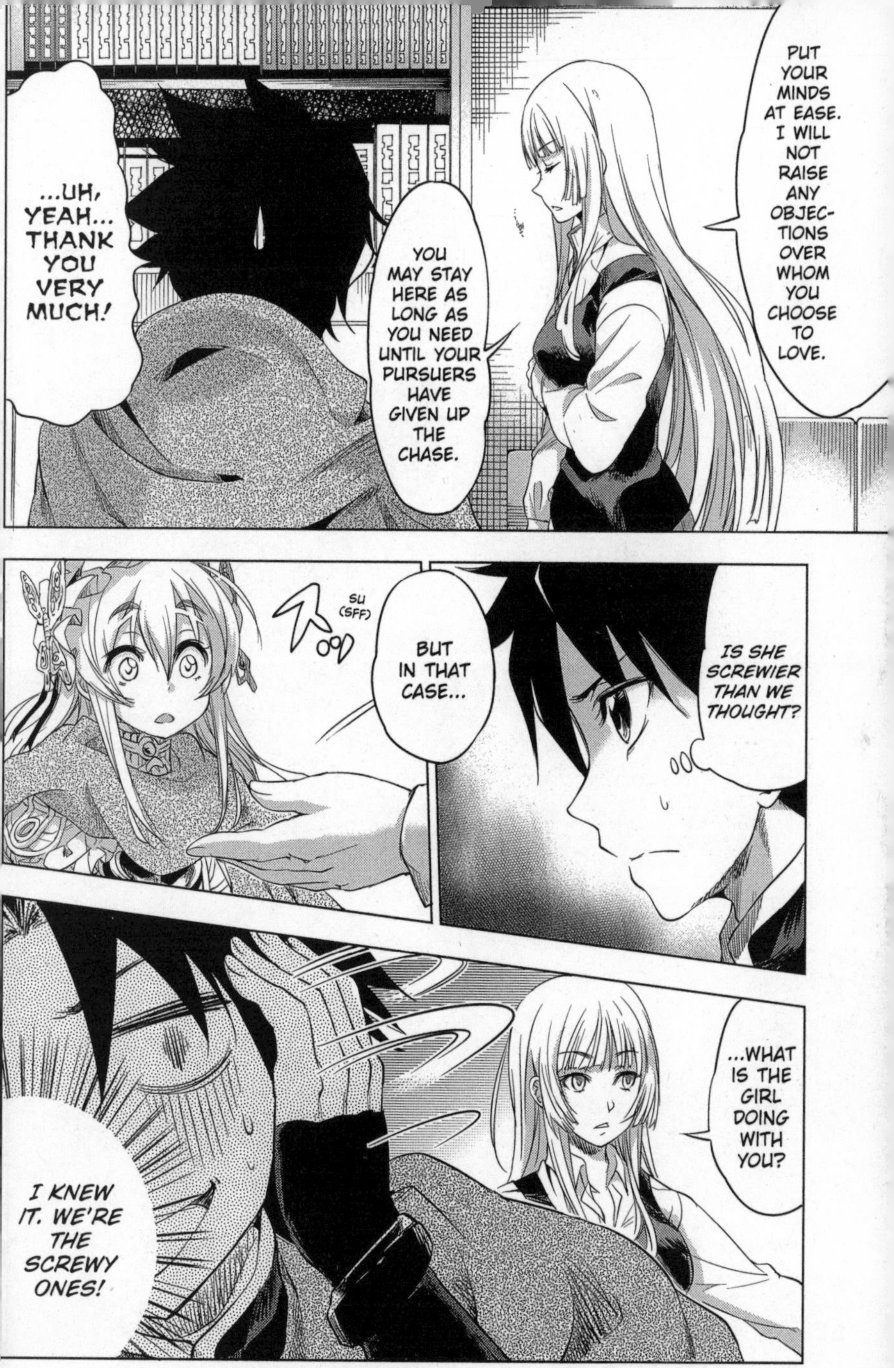
PUT YOUR MINDS AT EASE. I WILL NOT RAISE ANY OBJECTIONS OVER WHOM YOU CHOOSE TO LOVE.
YOU MAY STAY HERE AS LONG AS YOU NEED UNTIL YOUR PURSUERS HAVE GIVEN UP THE CHASE.
...UH, YEAH... THANK YOU VERY MUCH!
IS SHE SCREWIER THAN WE THOUGHT?
BUT IN THAT CASE...
SU (SFF)
...WHAT IS THE GIRL DOING WITH YOU?
I KNEW IT. WE'RE THE SCREWY ONES!

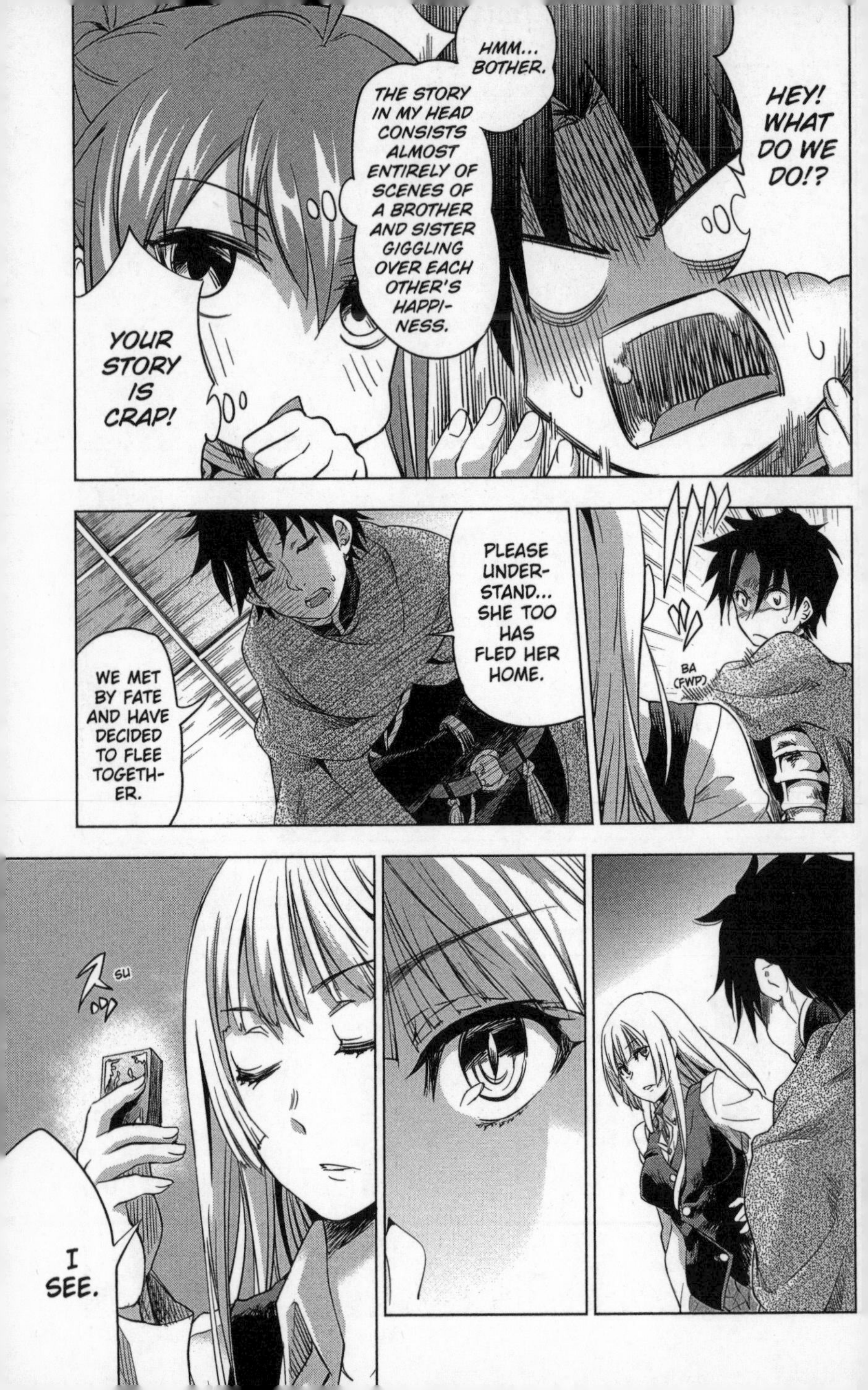
HEY! WHAT DO WE DO!?
HMM... BOTHER.
THE STORY IN MY HEAD CONSISTS ALMOST ENTIRELY OF SCENES OF A BROTHER AND SISTER GIGGLING OVER EACH OTHER'S HAPPI-NESS.
YOUR STORY IS CRAP!
BA (FWP)
PLEASE UNDER-STAND... SHE TOO HAS FLED HER HOME.
WE MET BY FATE AND HAVE DECIDED TO FLEE TOGETH-ER.
SU
I SEE.

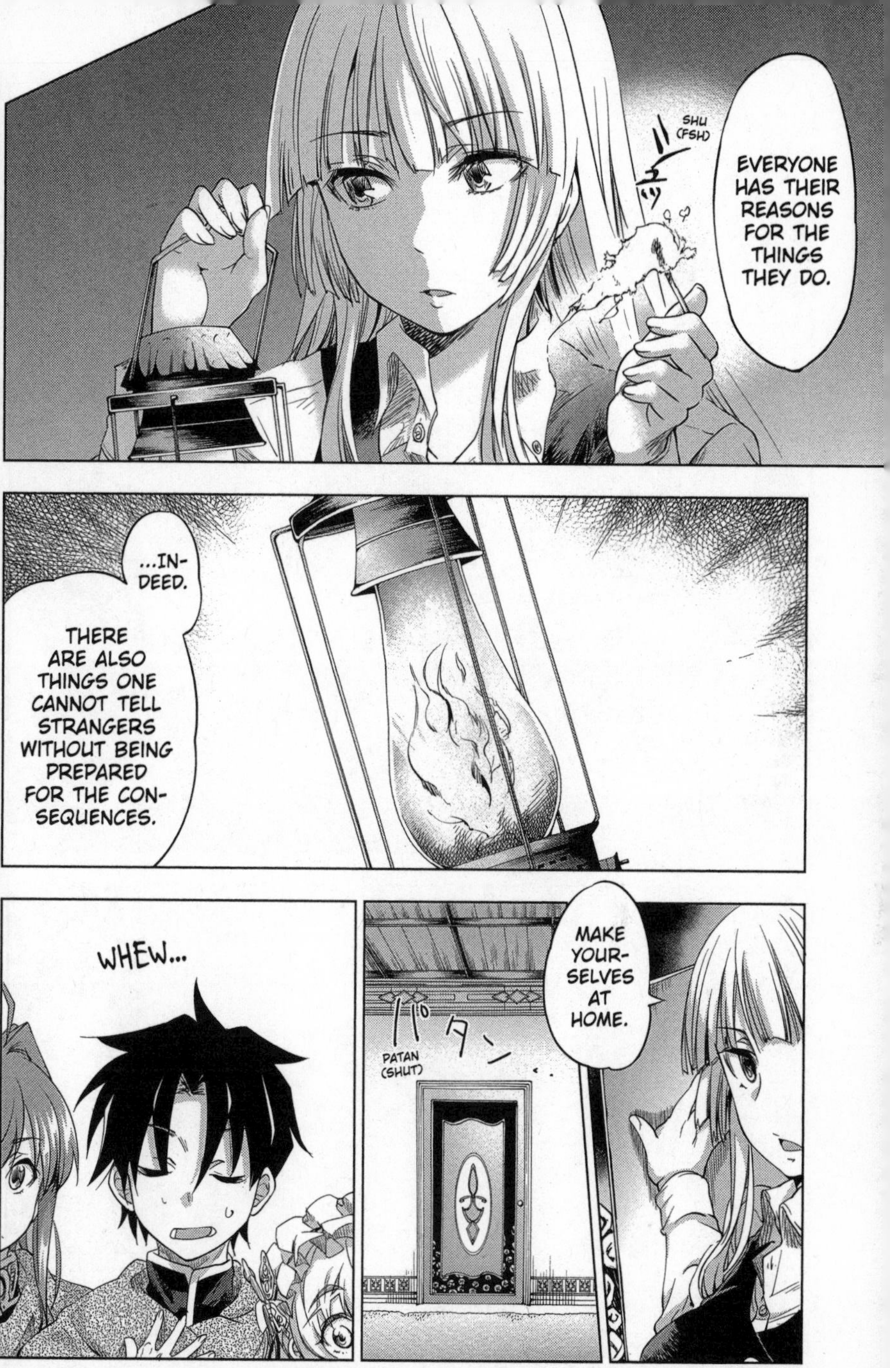
シュッ
SHU (FSH)
EVERYONE HAS THEIR REASONS FOR THE THINGS THEY DO.
...IN-DEED.
THERE ARE ALSO THINGS ONE CANNOT TELL STRANGERS WITHOUT BEING PREPARED FOR THE CON-SEQUENCES.
MAKE YOUR-SELVES AT HOME.
バタン
PATAN (SHUT)
WHEW...

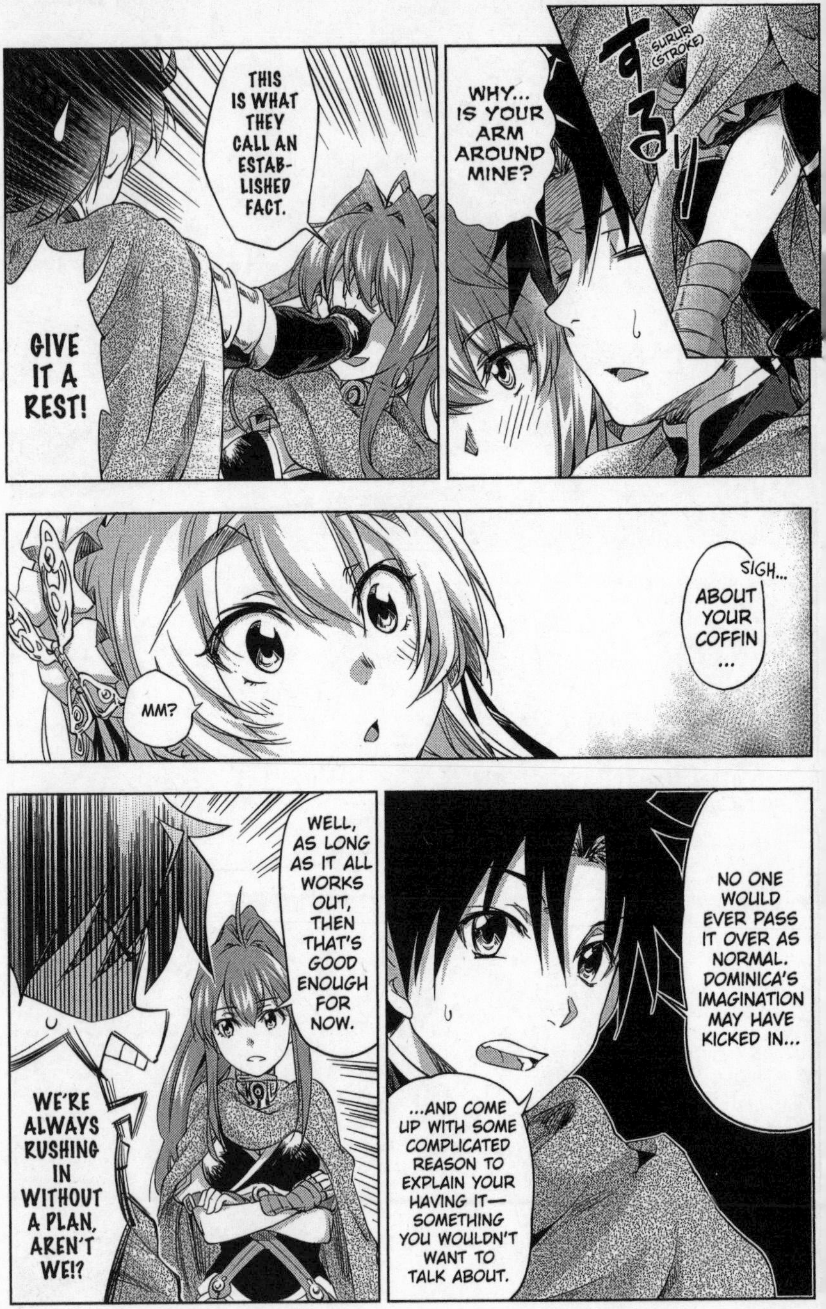

するり
SURURI (STROKE)
WHY... IS YOUR ARM AROUND MINE?
THIS IS WHAT THEY CALL AN ESTAB-LISHED FACT.
GIVE IT A REST!
SIGH...
ABOUT YOUR COFFIN ...
MM?
NO ONE WOULD EVER PASS IT OVER AS NORMAL. DOMINICA'S IMAGINATION MAY HAVE KICKED IN...
...AND COME UP WITH SOME COMPLICATED REASON TO EXPLAIN YOUR HAVING IT—SOMETHING YOU WOULDN'T WANT TO TALK ABOUT.
WELL, AS LONG AS IT ALL WORKS OUT, THEN THAT'S GOOD ENOUGH FOR NOW.
WE'RE ALWAYS RUSHING IN WITHOUT A PLAN, AREN'T WE!?

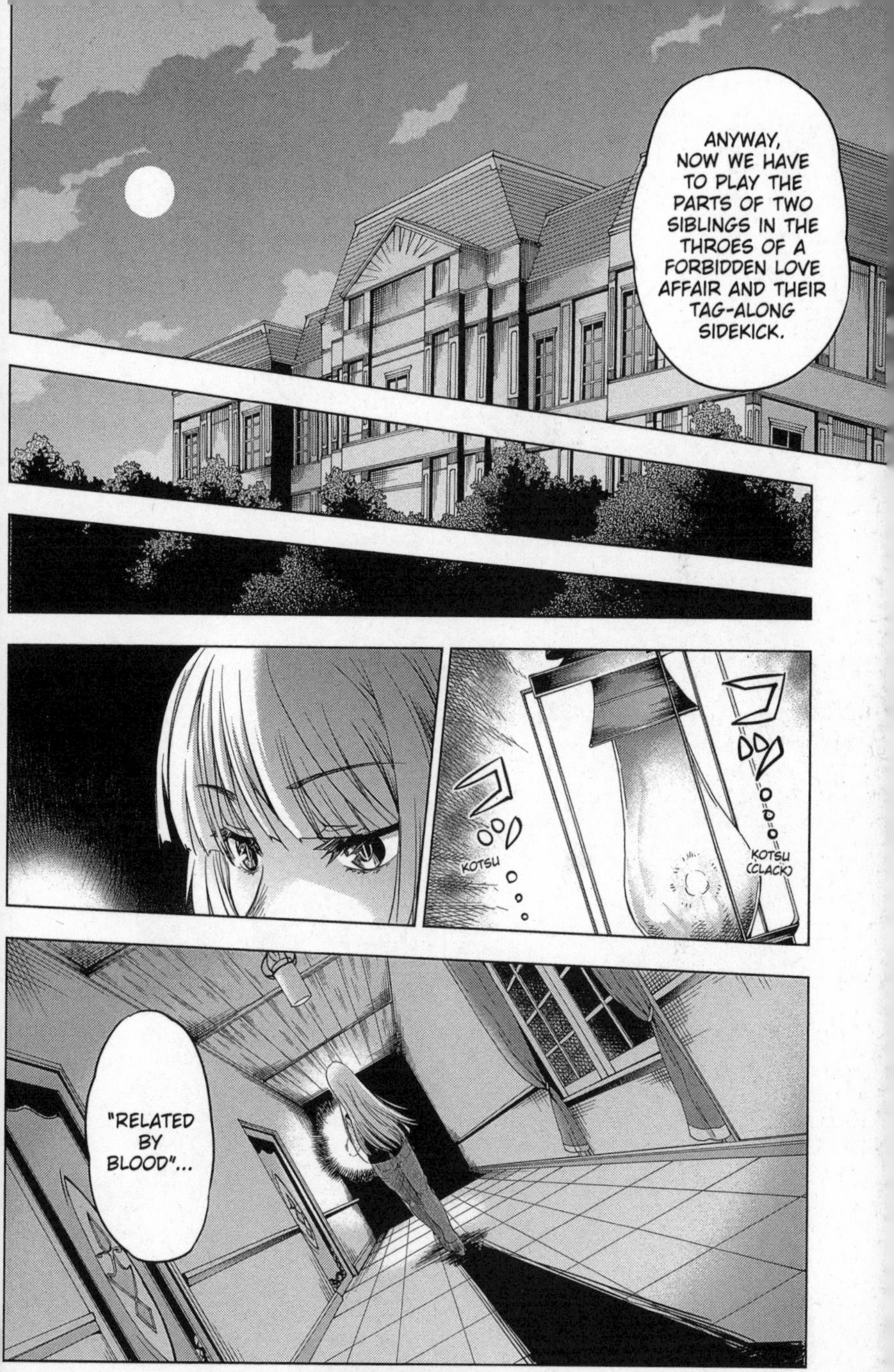
ANYWAY, NOW WE HAVE TO PLAY THE PARTS OF TWO SIBLINGS IN THE THROES OF A FORBIDDEN LOVE AFFAIR AND THEIR TAG-ALONG SIDEKICK.
KOTSU (CLACK)
KOTSU
"RELATED BY BLOOD"...

episode 20: END

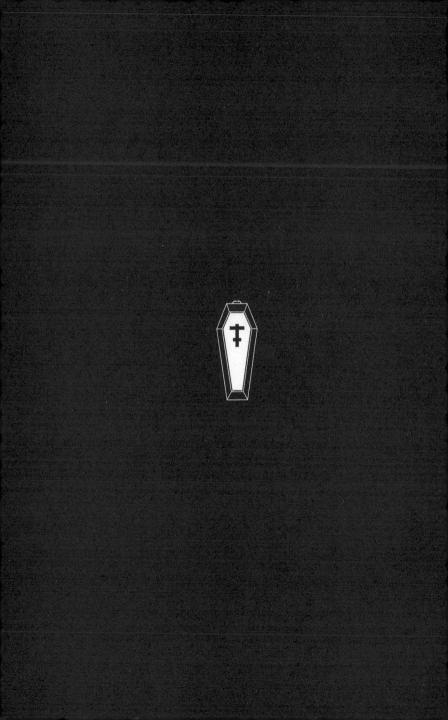

CHAIKA: THE COFFIN PRINCESS

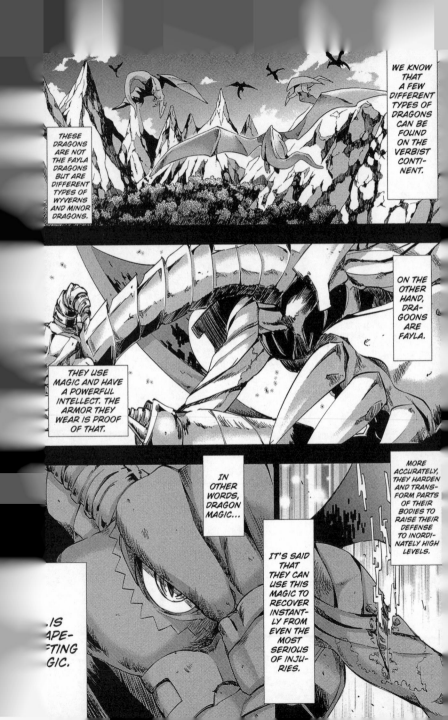

WE KNOW THAT A FEW DIFFERENT TYPES OF DRAGONS CAN BE FOUND ON THE VERBIST CONTINENT.

THESE DRAGONS ARE NOT THE FAYLA DRAGONS BUT ARE DIFFERENT TYPES OF WYVERNS AND MINOR DRAGONS.

ON THE OTHER HAND, DRAGOONS ARE FAYLA.

THEY USE MAGIC AND HAVE A POWERFUL INTELLECT. THE ARMOR THEY WEAR IS PROOF OF THAT.

IN OTHER WORDS, DRAGON MAGIC...

MORE ACCURATELY, THEY HARDEN AND TRANSFORM PARTS OF THEIR BODIES TO RAISE THEIR DEFENSE TO INORDINATELY HIGH LEVELS.

IT'S SAID THAT THEY CAN USE THIS MAGIC TO RECOVER INSTANTLY FROM EVEN THE MOST SERIOUS OF INJURIES.

...IS ...APE- ...FTING ...GIC.

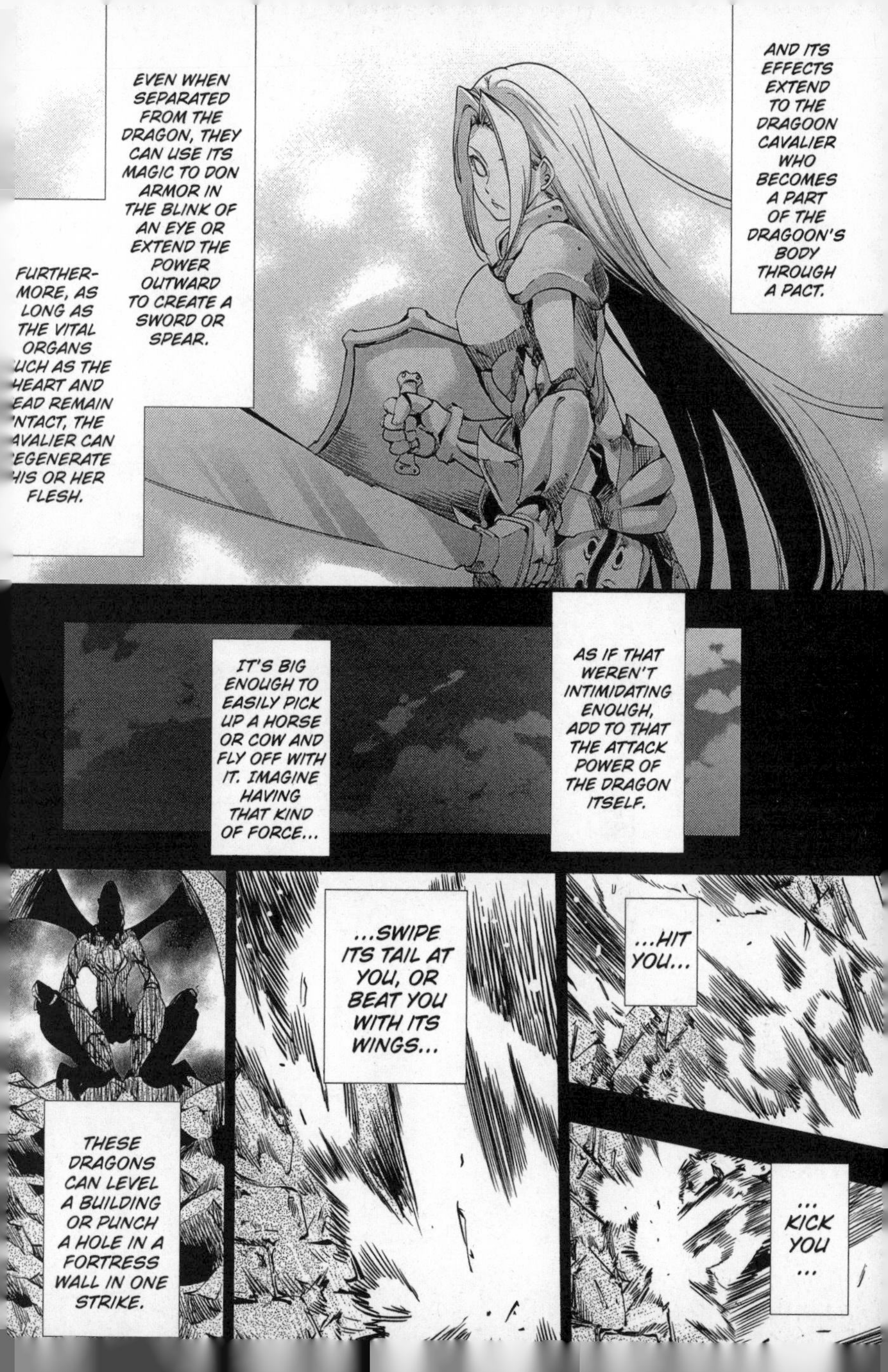
AND ITS EFFECTS EXTEND TO THE DRAGOON CAVALIER WHO BECOMES A PART OF THE DRAGOON'S BODY THROUGH A PACT.
EVEN WHEN SEPARATED FROM THE DRAGON, THEY CAN USE ITS MAGIC TO DON ARMOR IN THE BLINK OF AN EYE OR EXTEND THE POWER OUTWARD TO CREATE A SWORD OR SPEAR.
FURTHER-MORE, AS LONG AS THE VITAL ORGANS UCH AS THE HEART AND EAD REMAIN NTACT, THE AVALIER CAN EGENERATE HIS OR HER FLESH.
IT'S BIG ENOUGH TO EASILY PICK UP A HORSE OR COW AND FLY OFF WITH IT. IMAGINE HAVING THAT KIND OF FORCE...
AS IF THAT WEREN'T INTIMIDATING ENOUGH, ADD TO THAT THE ATTACK POWER OF THE DRAGON ITSELF.
THESE DRAGONS CAN LEVEL A BUILDING OR PUNCH A HOLE IN A FORTRESS WALL IN ONE STRIKE.
...SWIPE ITS TAIL AT YOU, OR BEAT YOU WITH ITS WINGS...
...HIT YOU...
...KICK YOU...

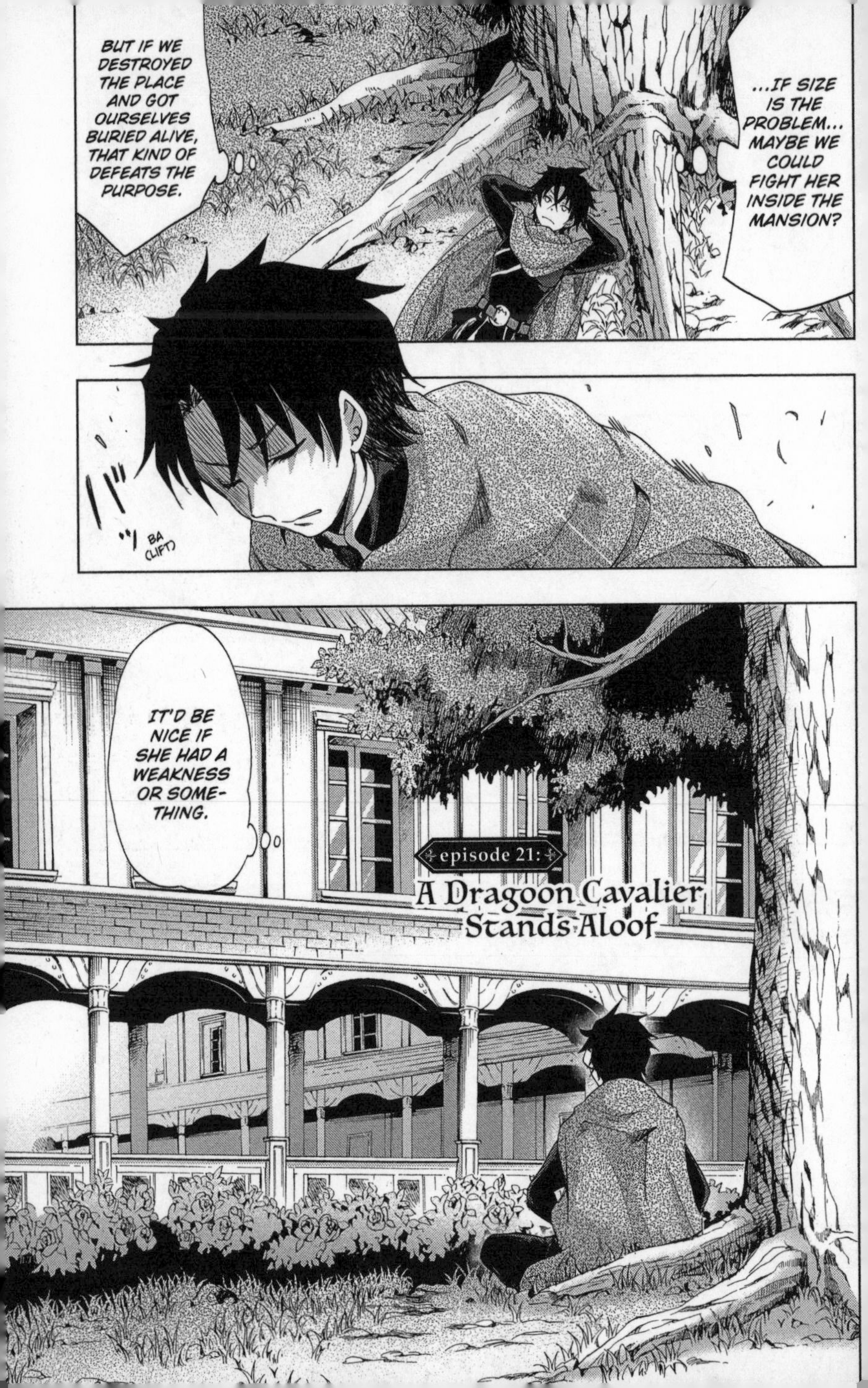
...IF SIZE IS THE PROBLEM... MAYBE WE COULD FIGHT HER INSIDE THE MANSION?
BUT IF WE DESTROYED THE PLACE AND GOT OURSELVES BURIED ALIVE, THAT KIND OF DEFEATS THE PURPOSE.
BA (LIFT)
IT'D BE NICE IF SHE HAD A WEAKNESS OR SOME-THING.
episode 21:
A Dragoon Cavalier Stands Aloof

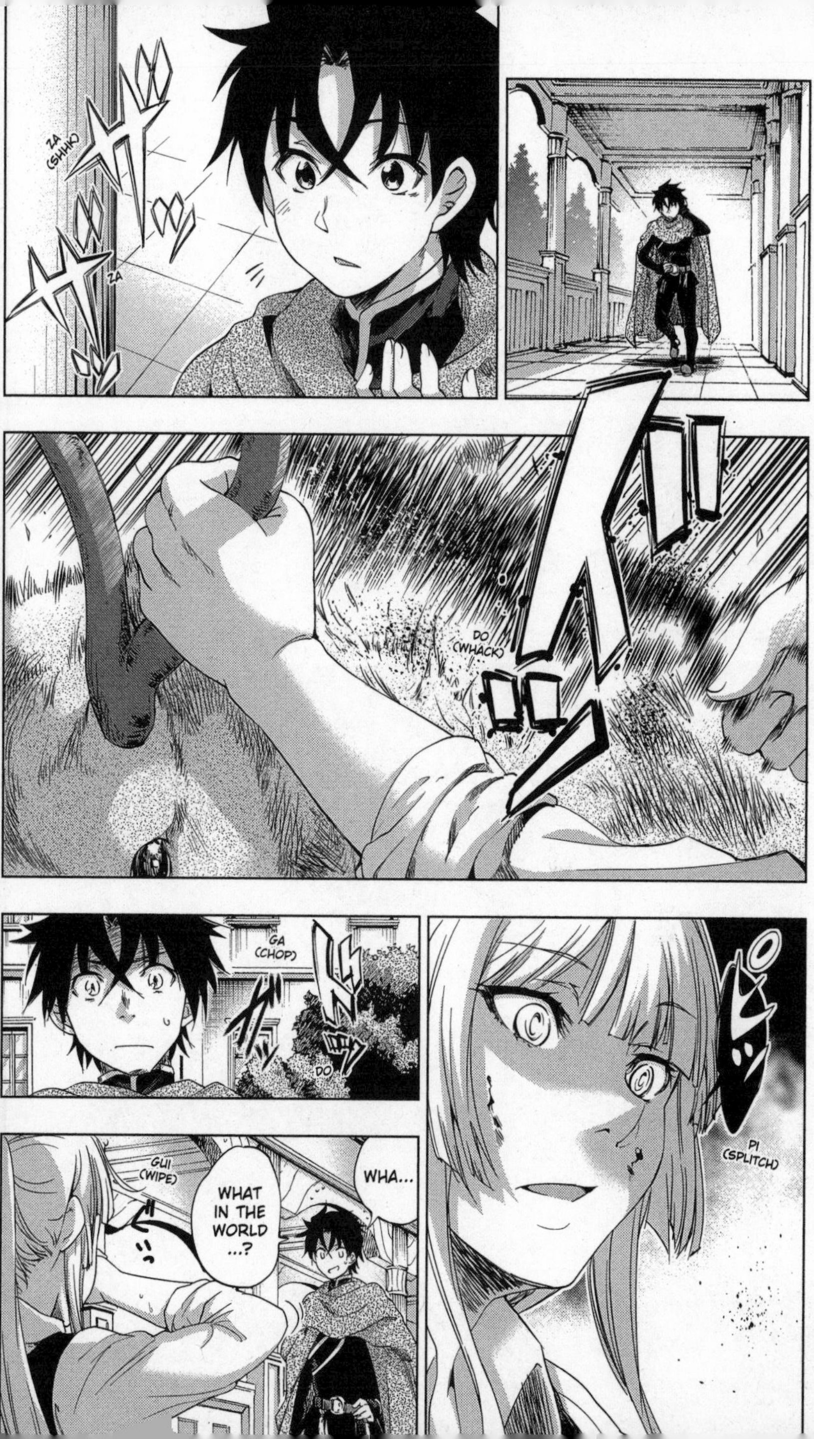
ZA
(SHHK)
ZA
DO
(WHACK)
PI
(SPLITCH)
GA
(CHOP)
DO
WHA...
WHAT IN THE WORLD ...?
GUI
(WIPE)

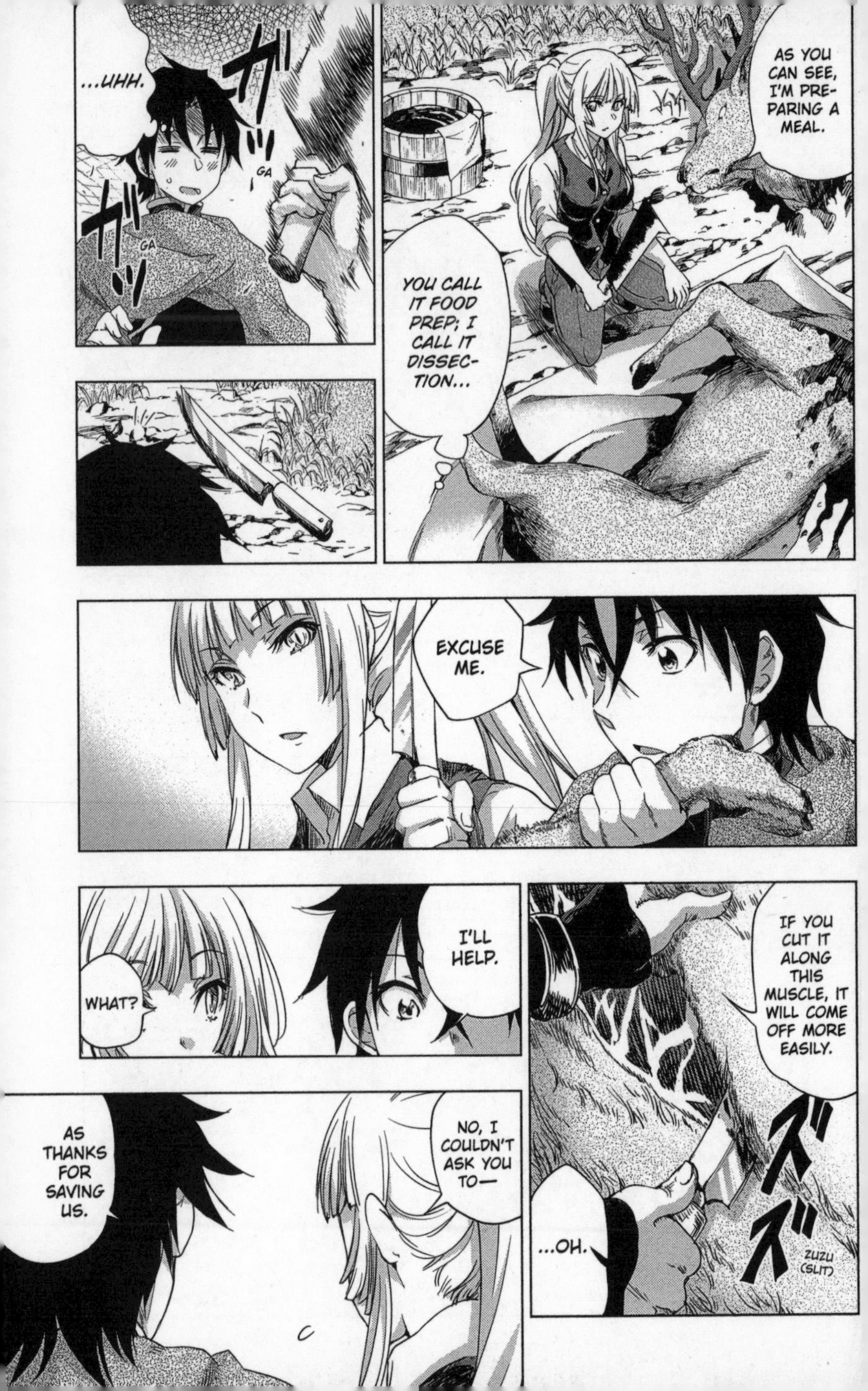
AS YOU CAN SEE, I'M PREPARING A MEAL.
YOU CALL IT FOOD PREP; I CALL IT DISSECTION...
...UHH.
GA
GA
EXCUSE ME.
IF YOU CUT IT ALONG THIS MUSCLE, IT WILL COME OFF MORE EASILY.
ZUZU (SLIT)
...OH.
I'LL HELP.
WHAT?
NO, I COULDN'T ASK YOU TO—
AS THANKS FOR SAVING US.

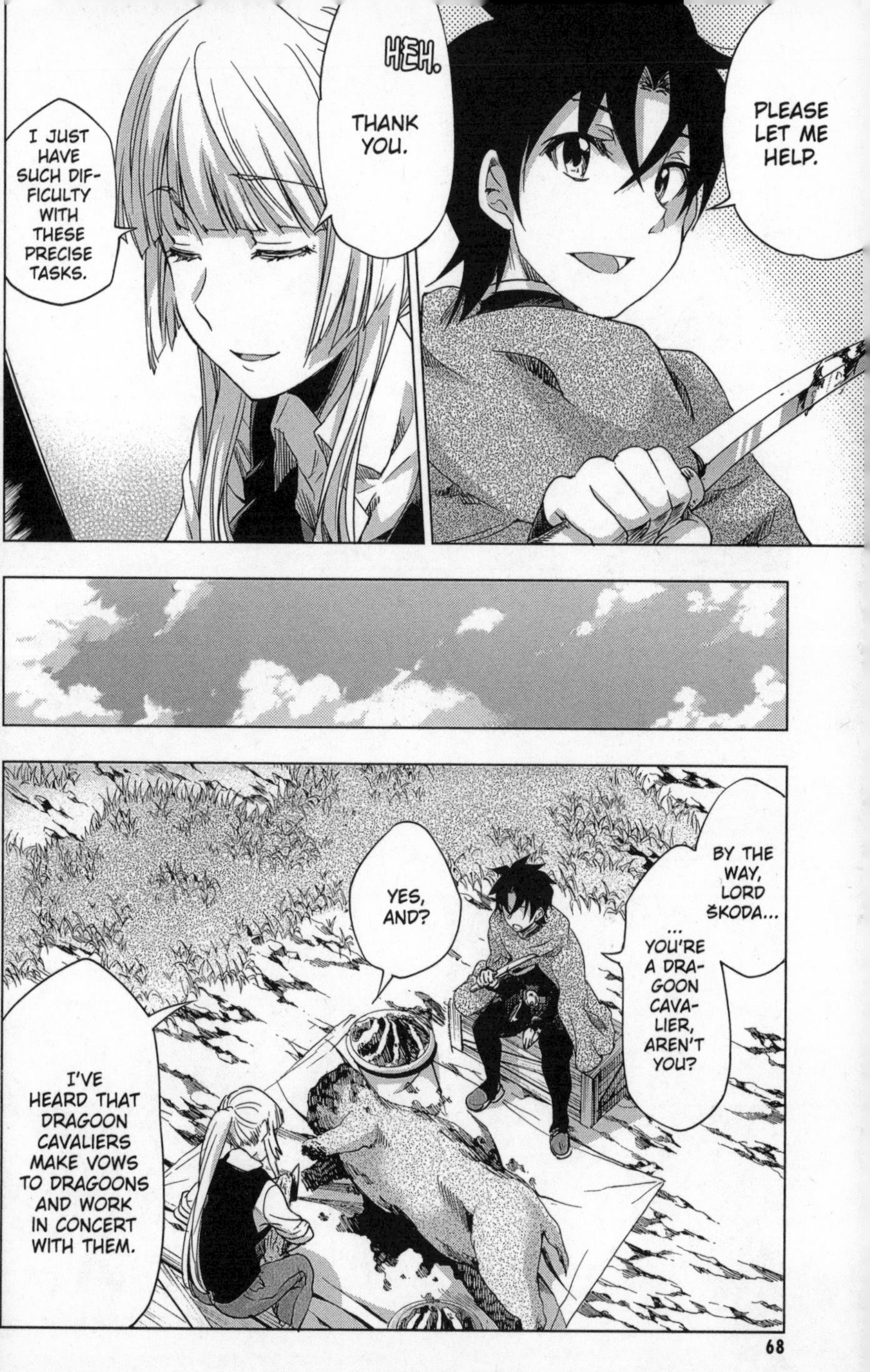
PLEASE LET ME HELP.
HEH.
THANK YOU.
I JUST HAVE SUCH DIFFICULTY WITH THESE PRECISE TASKS.
BY THE WAY, LORD ŠKODA...
...YOU'RE A DRAGOON CAVALIER, AREN'T YOU?
YES, AND?
I'VE HEARD THAT DRAGOON CAVALIERS MAKE VOWS TO DRAGOONS AND WORK IN CONCERT WITH THEM.

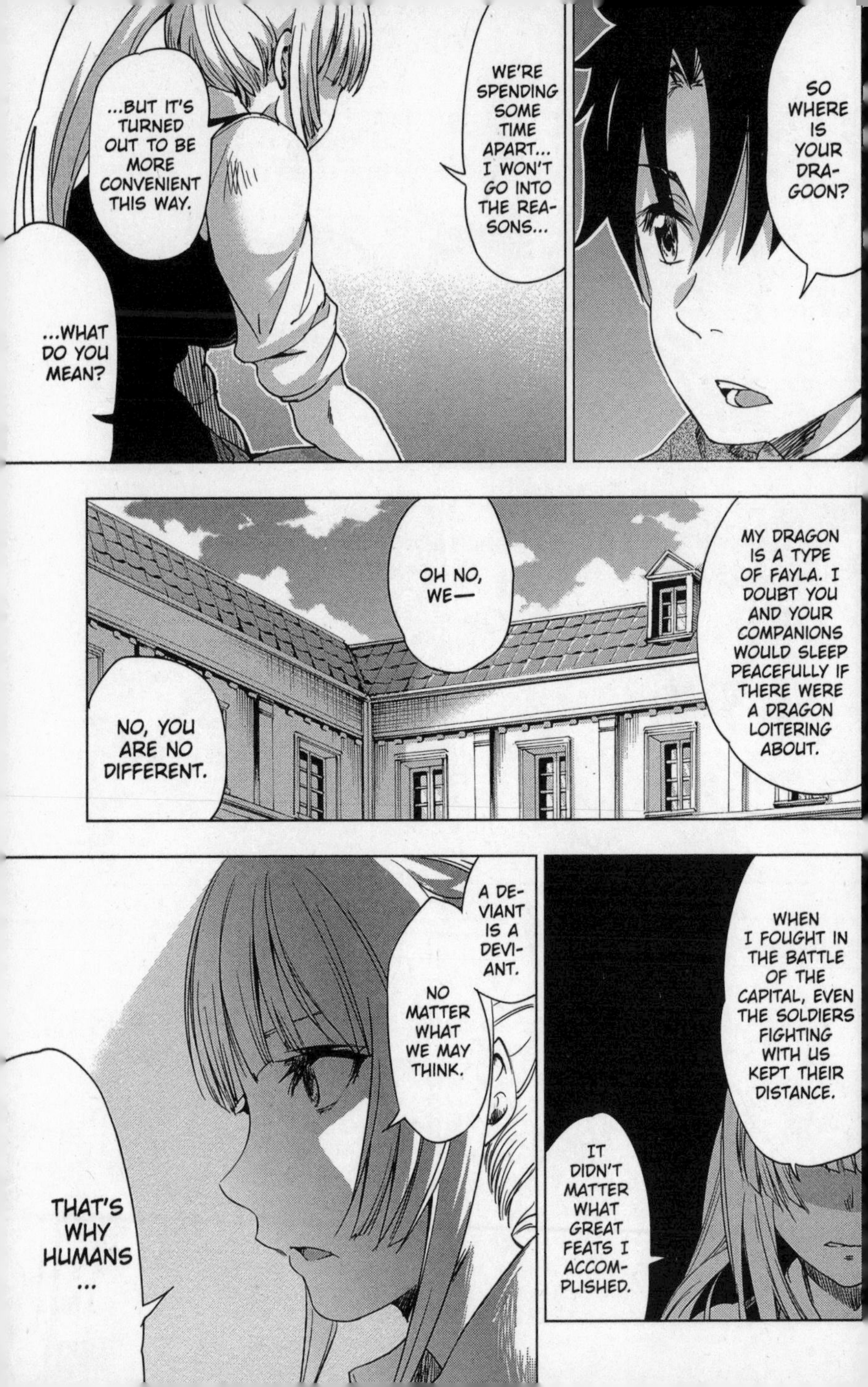
SO WHERE IS YOUR DRAGOON?
WE'RE SPENDING SOME TIME APART... I WON'T GO INTO THE REASONS...
...BUT IT'S TURNED OUT TO BE MORE CONVENIENT THIS WAY.
...WHAT DO YOU MEAN?
MY DRAGON IS A TYPE OF FAYLA. I DOUBT YOU AND YOUR COMPANIONS WOULD SLEEP PEACEFULLY IF THERE WERE A DRAGON LOITERING ABOUT.
OH NO, WE—
NO, YOU ARE NO DIFFERENT.
WHEN I FOUGHT IN THE BATTLE OF THE CAPITAL, EVEN THE SOLDIERS FIGHTING WITH US KEPT THEIR DISTANCE.
IT DIDN'T MATTER WHAT GREAT FEATS I ACCOMPLISHED.
A DEVIANT IS A DEVIANT.
NO MATTER WHAT WE MAY THINK.
THAT'S WHY HUMANS...

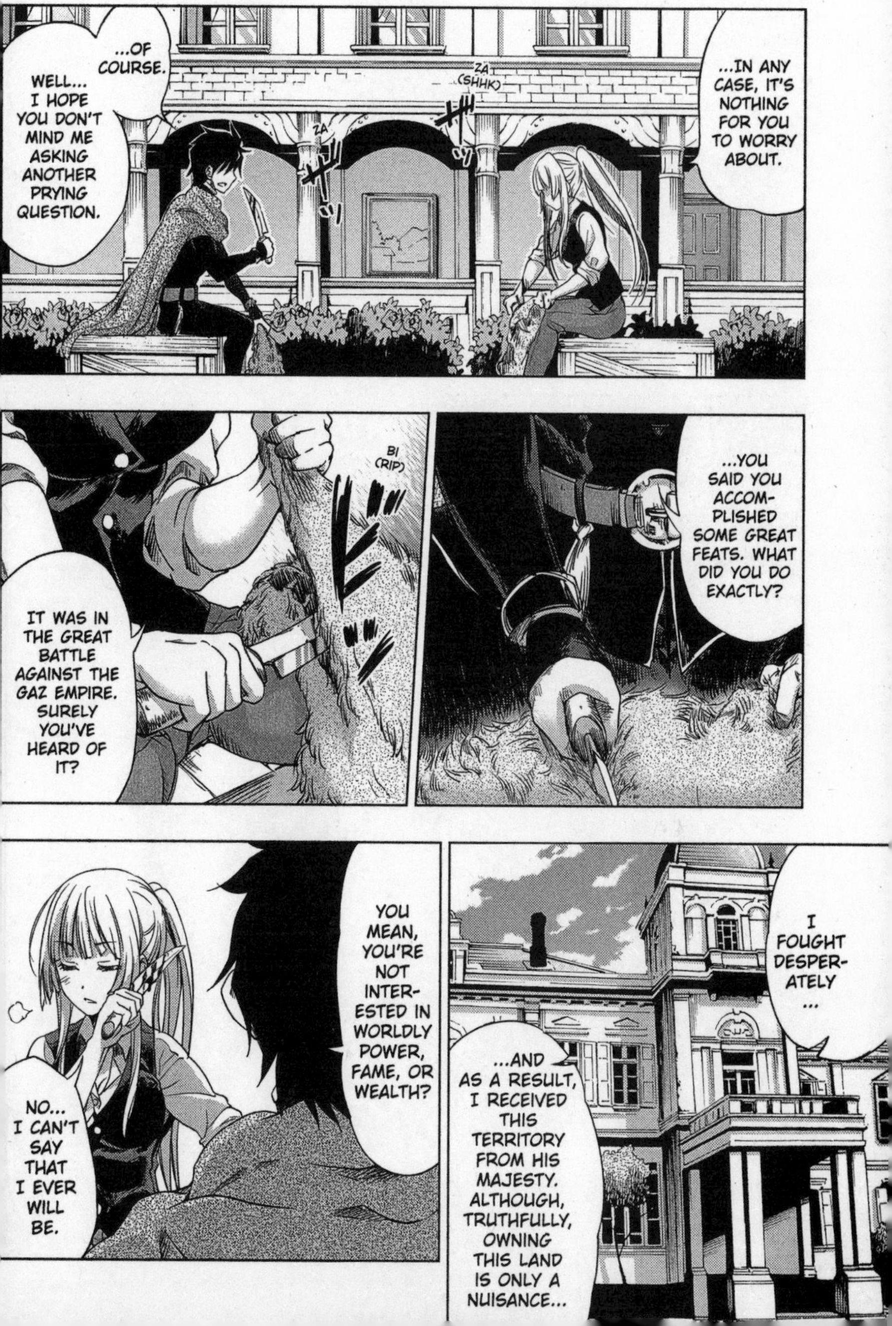
...IN ANY CASE, IT'S NOTHING FOR YOU TO WORRY ABOUT.
ZA (SHHK)
ZA
...OF COURSE.
WELL... I HOPE YOU DON'T MIND ME ASKING ANOTHER PRYING QUESTION.
...YOU SAID YOU ACCOMPLISHED SOME GREAT FEATS. WHAT DID YOU DO EXACTLY?
BI (RIP)
IT WAS IN THE GREAT BATTLE AGAINST THE GAZ EMPIRE. SURELY YOU'VE HEARD OF IT?
I FOUGHT DESPERATELY...
...AND AS A RESULT, I RECEIVED THIS TERRITORY FROM HIS MAJESTY. ALTHOUGH, TRUTHFULLY, OWNING THIS LAND IS ONLY A NUISANCE...
YOU MEAN, YOU'RE NOT INTERESTED IN WORLDLY POWER, FAME, OR WEALTH?
NO... I CAN'T SAY THAT I EVER WILL BE.

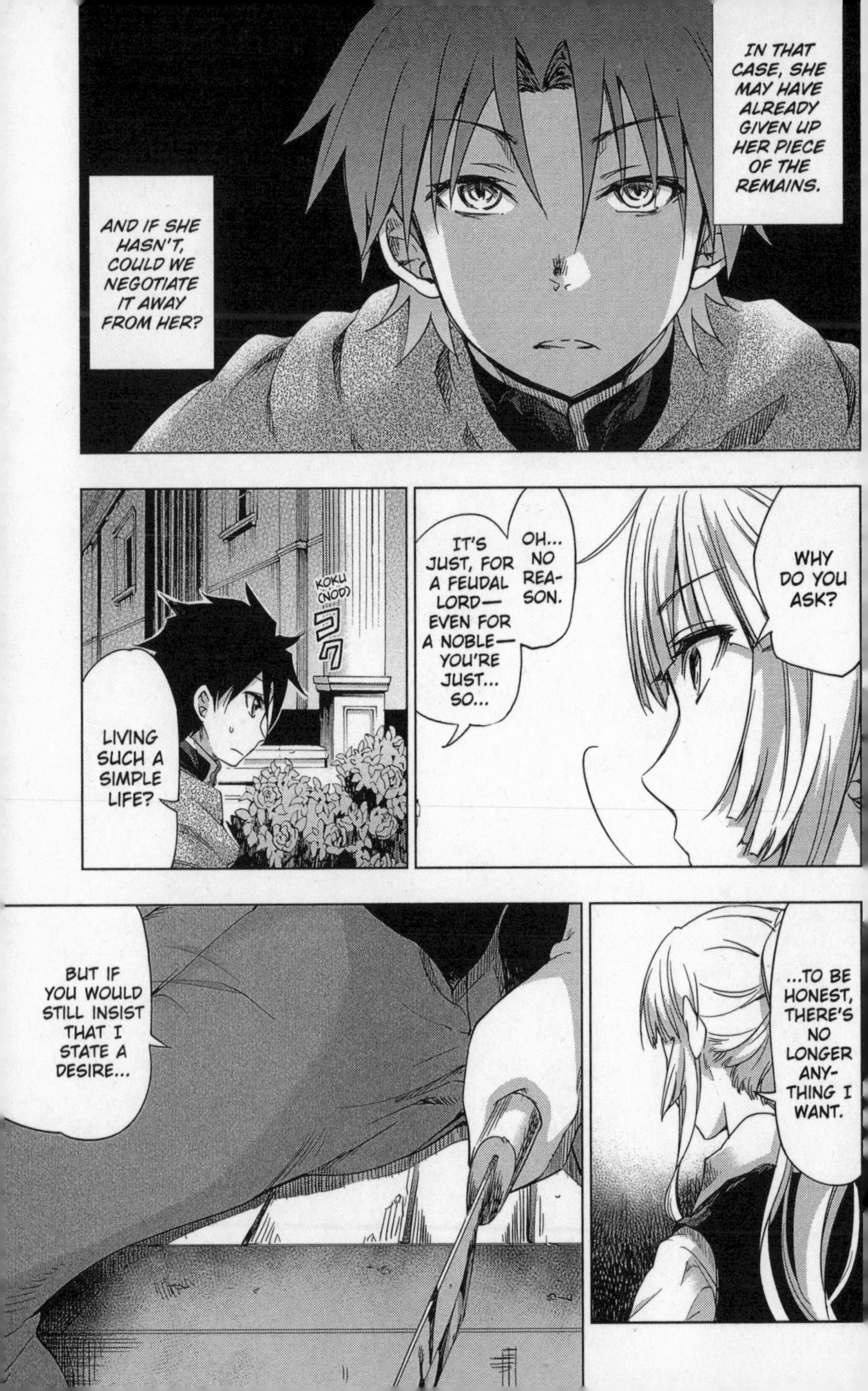
IN THAT CASE, SHE MAY HAVE ALREADY GIVEN UP HER PIECE OF THE REMAINS.
AND IF SHE HASN'T, COULD WE NEGOTIATE IT AWAY FROM HER?
WHY DO YOU ASK?
OH... NO REASON.
IT'S JUST, FOR A FEUDAL LORD—EVEN FOR A NOBLE—YOU'RE JUST... SO...
KOKU (NOD)
LIVING SUCH A SIMPLE LIFE?
...TO BE HONEST, THERE'S NO LONGER ANYTHING I WANT.
BUT IF YOU WOULD STILL INSIST THAT I STATE A DESIRE...

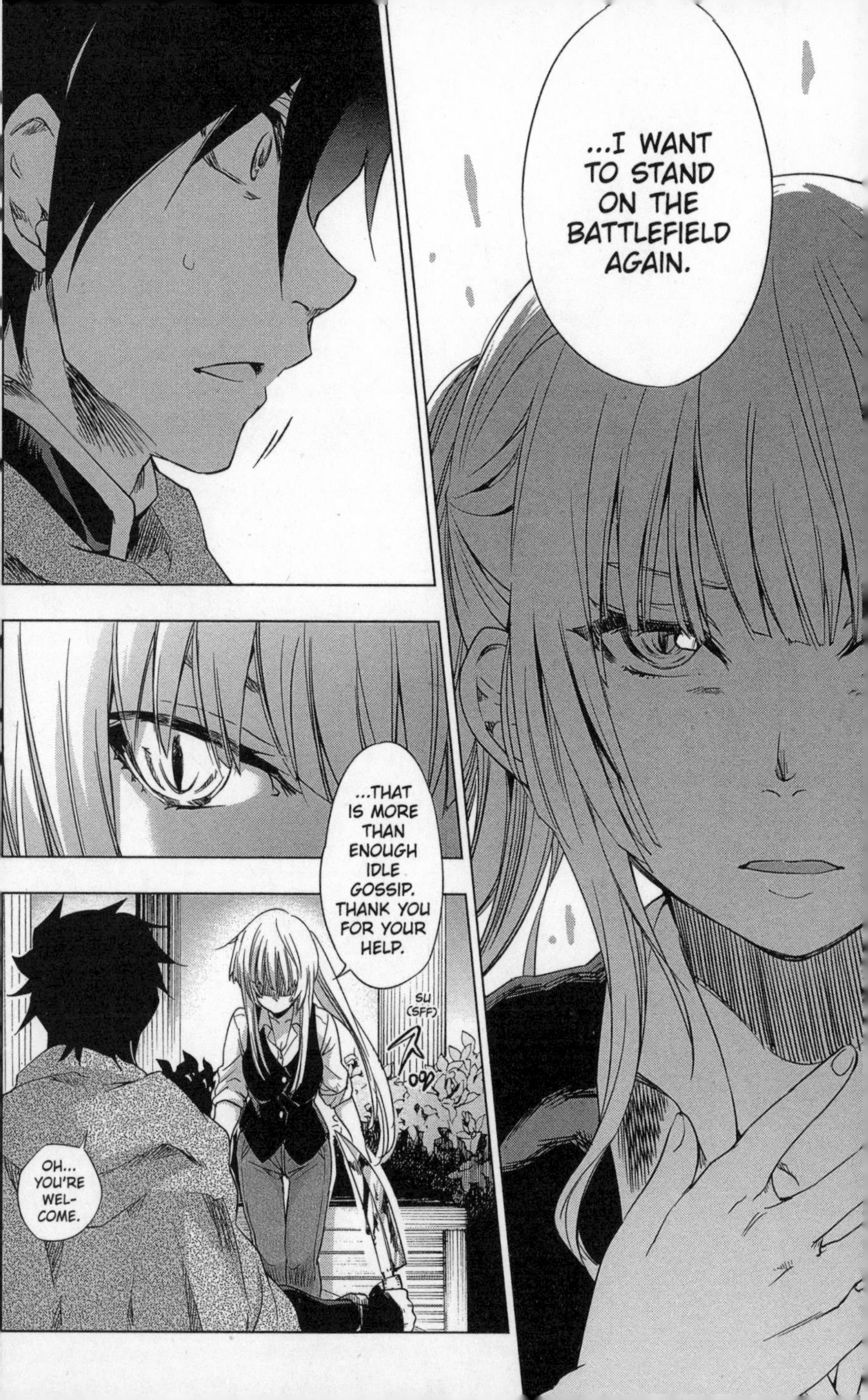
...I WANT TO STAND ON THE BATTLEFIELD AGAIN.
...THAT IS MORE THAN ENOUGH IDLE GOSSIP. THANK YOU FOR YOUR HELP.
SU (SFF)
OH... YOU'RE WEL-COME.

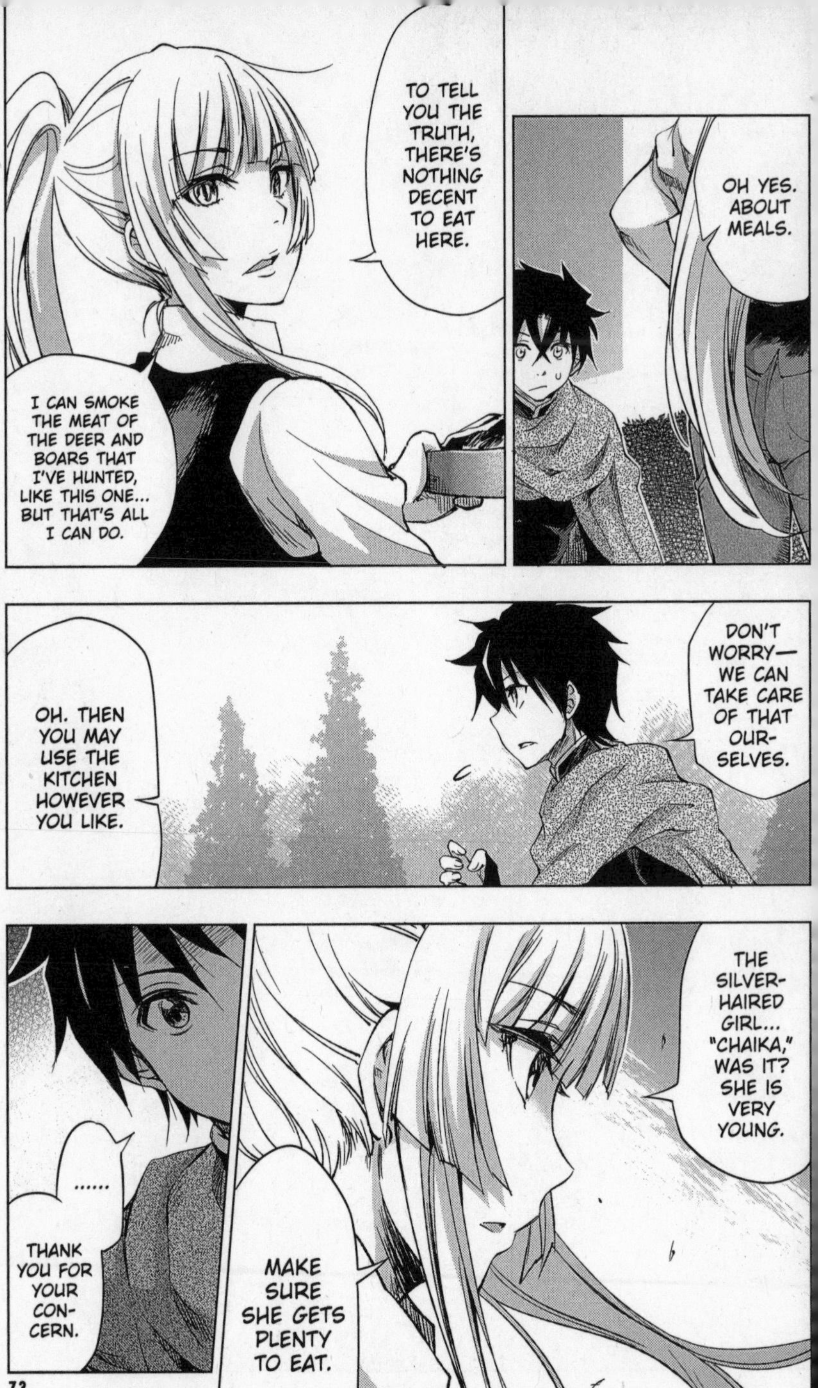
OH YES. ABOUT MEALS.
TO TELL YOU THE TRUTH, THERE'S NOTHING DECENT TO EAT HERE.
I CAN SMOKE THE MEAT OF THE DEER AND BOARS THAT I'VE HUNTED, LIKE THIS ONE... BUT THAT'S ALL I CAN DO.
DON'T WORRY— WE CAN TAKE CARE OF THAT OURSELVES.
OH. THEN YOU MAY USE THE KITCHEN HOWEVER YOU LIKE.
THE SILVER-HAIRED GIRL... "CHAIKA," WAS IT? SHE IS VERY YOUNG.
MAKE SURE SHE GETS PLENTY TO EAT.
......
THANK YOU FOR YOUR CONCERN.

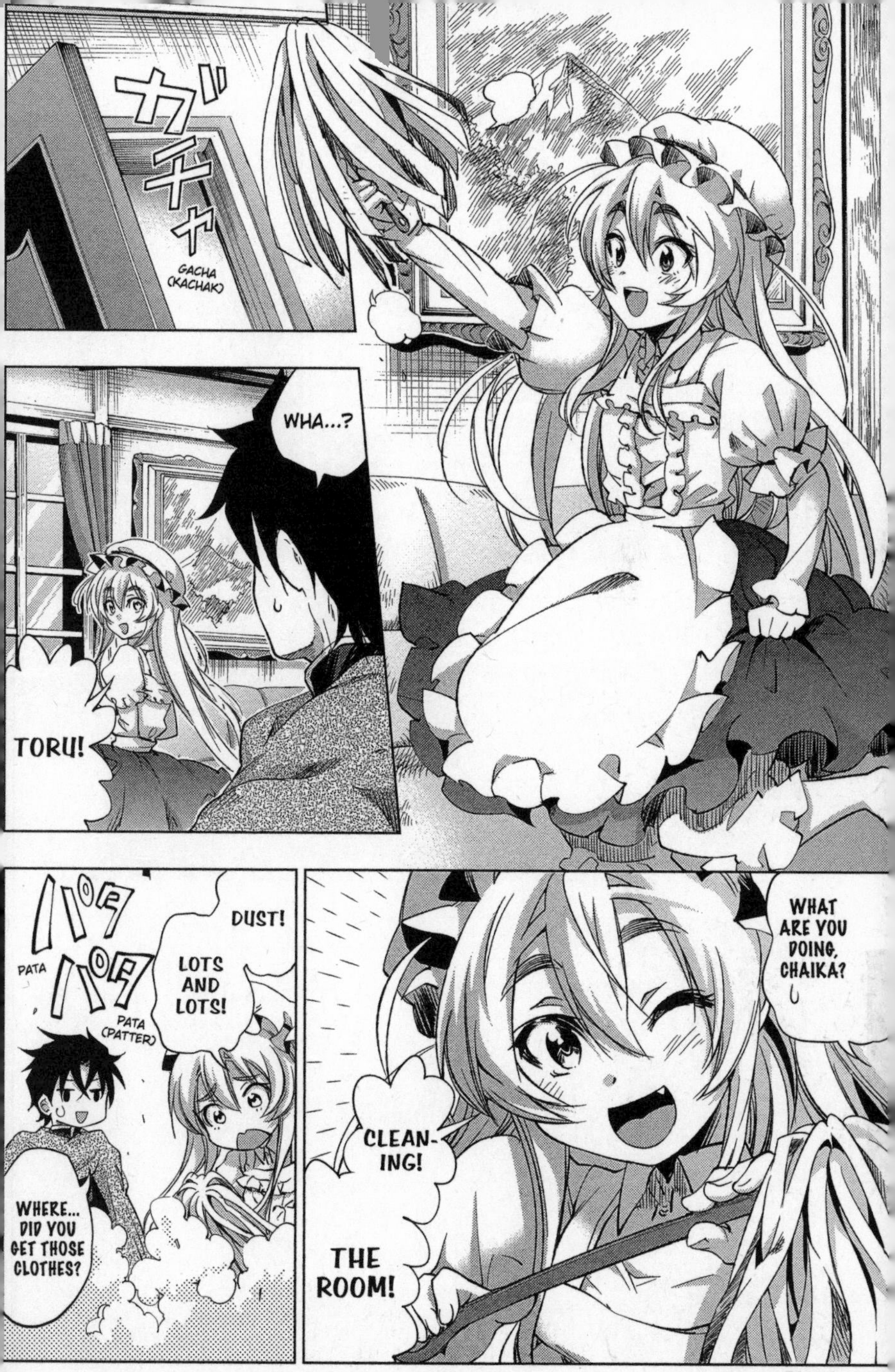
ガチャ
GACHA (KACHAK)
WHA...?
TORU!
WHAT ARE YOU DOING, CHAIKA?
CLEAN-ING!
THE ROOM!
DUST!
LOTS AND LOTS!
パタ
PATA
パタ
PATA (PATTER)
WHERE... DID YOU GET THOSE CLOTHES?

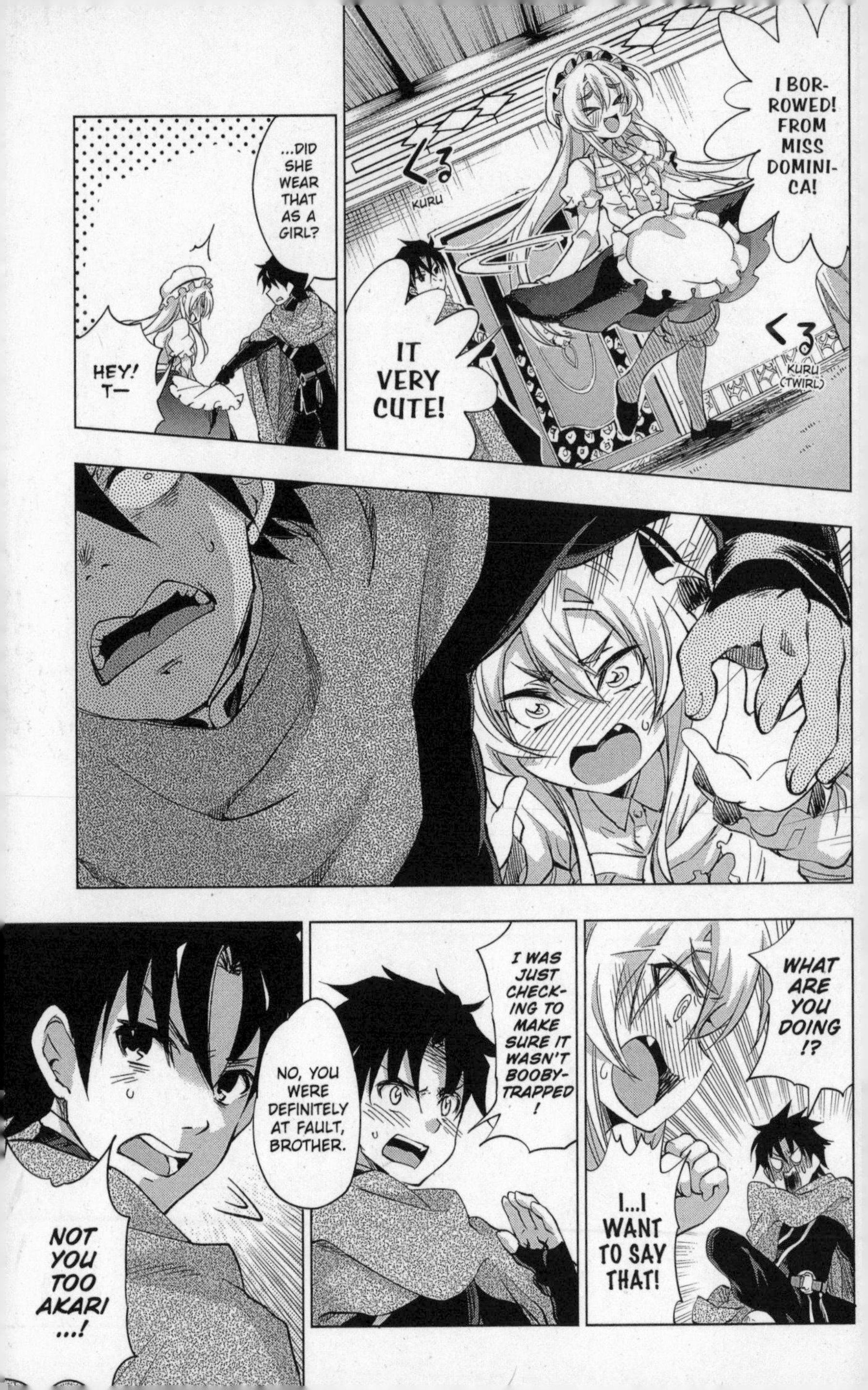
I BOR-ROWED! FROM MISS DOMINI-CA!
くる
KURU
くる
KURU (TWIRL)
IT VERY CUTE!
...DID SHE WEAR THAT AS A GIRL?
HEY! T—
WHAT ARE YOU DOING !?
I...I WANT TO SAY THAT!
I WAS JUST CHECK-ING TO MAKE SURE IT WASN'T BOOBY-TRAPPED!
NO, YOU WERE DEFINITELY AT FAULT, BROTHER.
NOT YOU TOO AKARI ...!

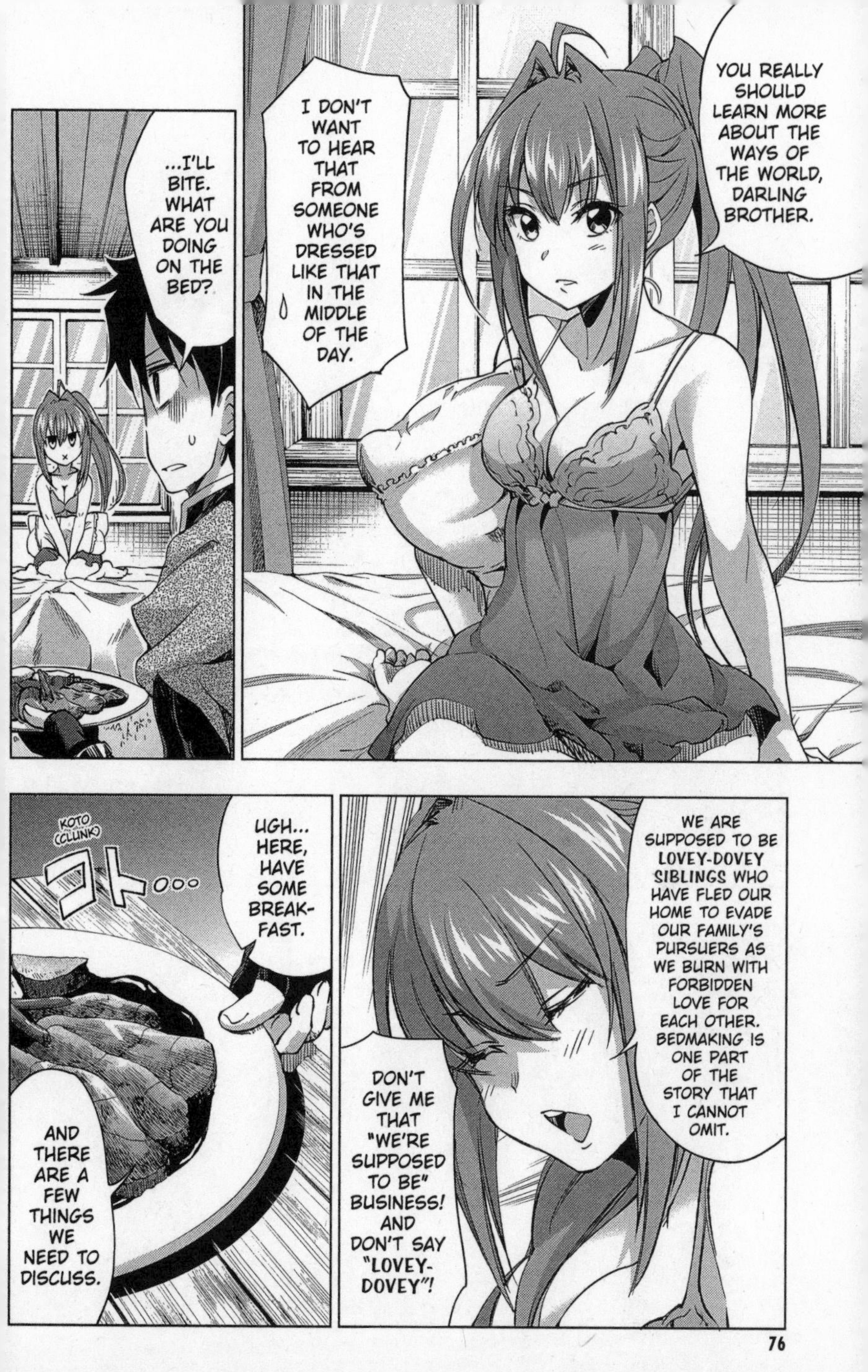
YOU REALLY SHOULD LEARN MORE ABOUT THE WAYS OF THE WORLD, DARLING BROTHER.
I DON'T WANT TO HEAR THAT FROM SOMEONE WHO'S DRESSED LIKE THAT IN THE MIDDLE OF THE DAY.
...I'LL BITE. WHAT ARE YOU DOING ON THE BED?
WE ARE SUPPOSED TO BE LOVEY-DOVEY SIBLINGS WHO HAVE FLED OUR HOME TO EVADE OUR FAMILY'S PURSUERS AS WE BURN WITH FORBIDDEN LOVE FOR EACH OTHER. BEDMAKING IS ONE PART OF THE STORY THAT I CANNOT OMIT.
DON'T GIVE ME THAT "WE'RE SUPPOSED TO BE" BUSINESS! AND DON'T SAY "LOVEY-DOVEY"!
KOTO (CLUNK)
UGH... HERE, HAVE SOME BREAKFAST.
AND THERE ARE A FEW THINGS WE NEED TO DISCUSS.

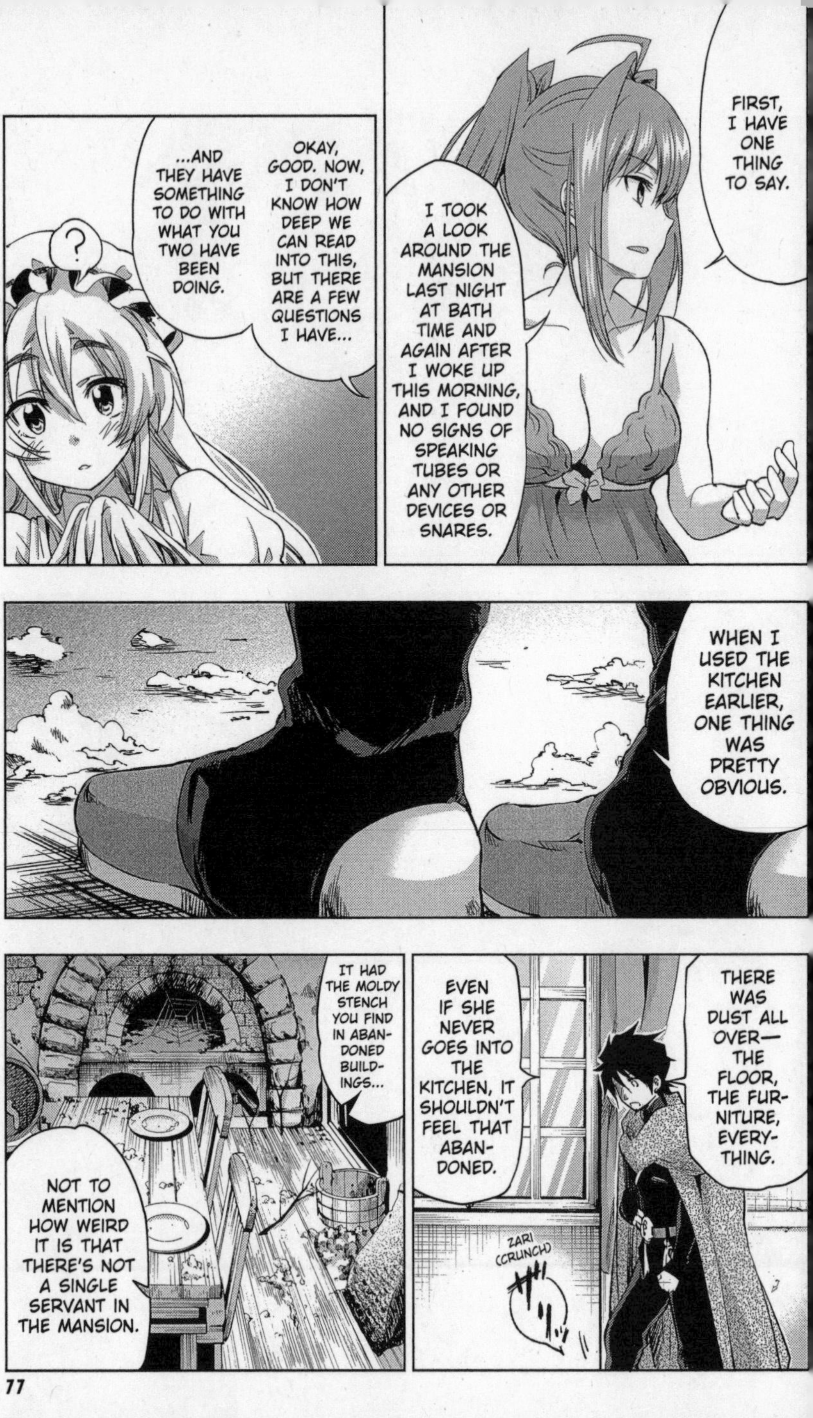
FIRST, I HAVE ONE THING TO SAY.
I TOOK A LOOK AROUND THE MANSION LAST NIGHT AT BATH TIME AND AGAIN AFTER I WOKE UP THIS MORNING, AND I FOUND NO SIGNS OF SPEAKING TUBES OR ANY OTHER DEVICES OR SNARES.
OKAY, GOOD. NOW, I DON'T KNOW HOW DEEP WE CAN READ INTO THIS, BUT THERE ARE A FEW QUESTIONS I HAVE...
...AND THEY HAVE SOMETHING TO DO WITH WHAT YOU TWO HAVE BEEN DOING.
?
WHEN I USED THE KITCHEN EARLIER, ONE THING WAS PRETTY OBVIOUS.
THERE WAS DUST ALL OVER— THE FLOOR, THE FURNITURE, EVERYTHING.
EVEN IF SHE NEVER GOES INTO THE KITCHEN, IT SHOULDN'T FEEL THAT ABANDONED.
ZARI (CRUNCH)
IT HAD THE MOLDY STENCH YOU FIND IN ABANDONED BUILDINGS...
NOT TO MENTION HOW WEIRD IT IS THAT THERE'S NOT A SINGLE SERVANT IN THE MANSION.

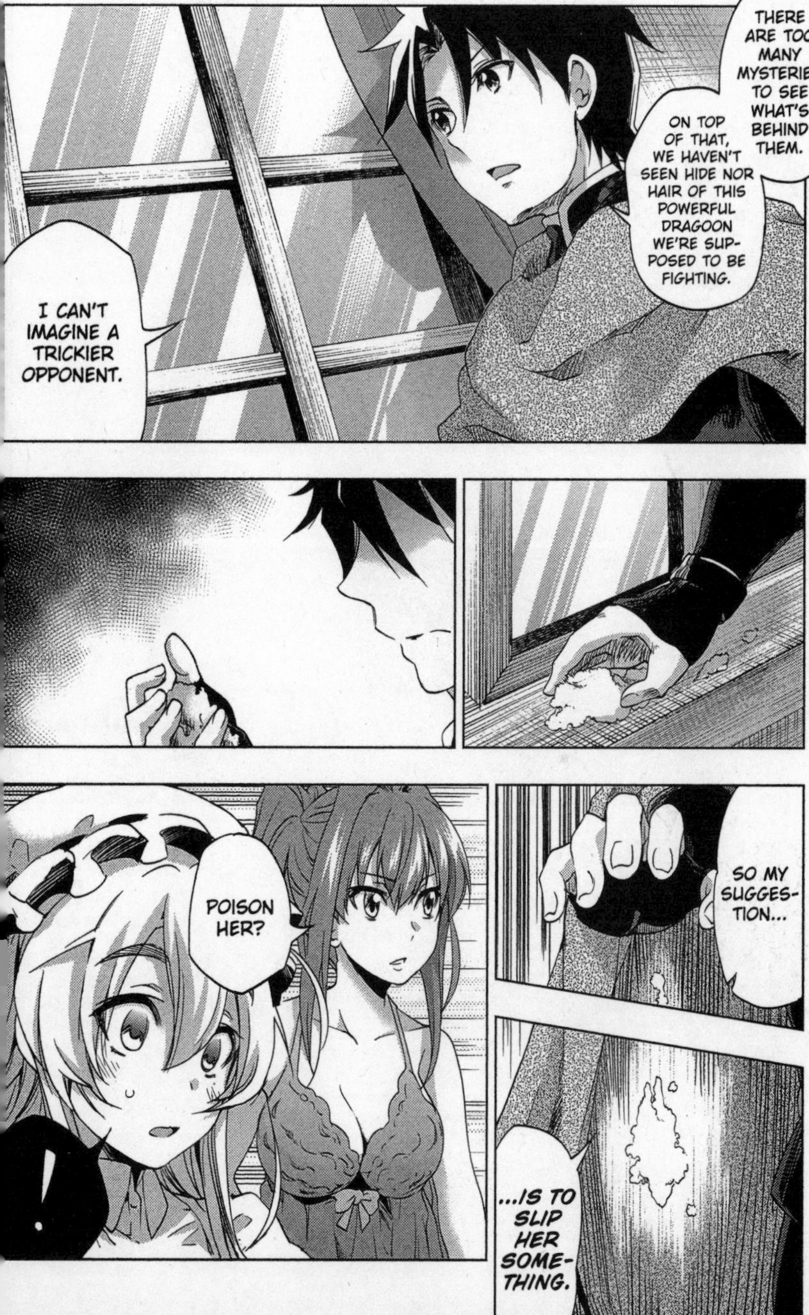
THERE ARE TOO MANY MYSTERIES TO SEE WHAT'S BEHIND THEM.
ON TOP OF THAT, WE HAVEN'T SEEN HIDE NOR HAIR OF THIS POWERFUL DRAGOON WE'RE SUPPOSED TO BE FIGHTING.
I CAN'T IMAGINE A TRICKIER OPPONENT.
SO MY SUGGESTION...
...IS TO SLIP HER SOMETHING.
POISON HER?

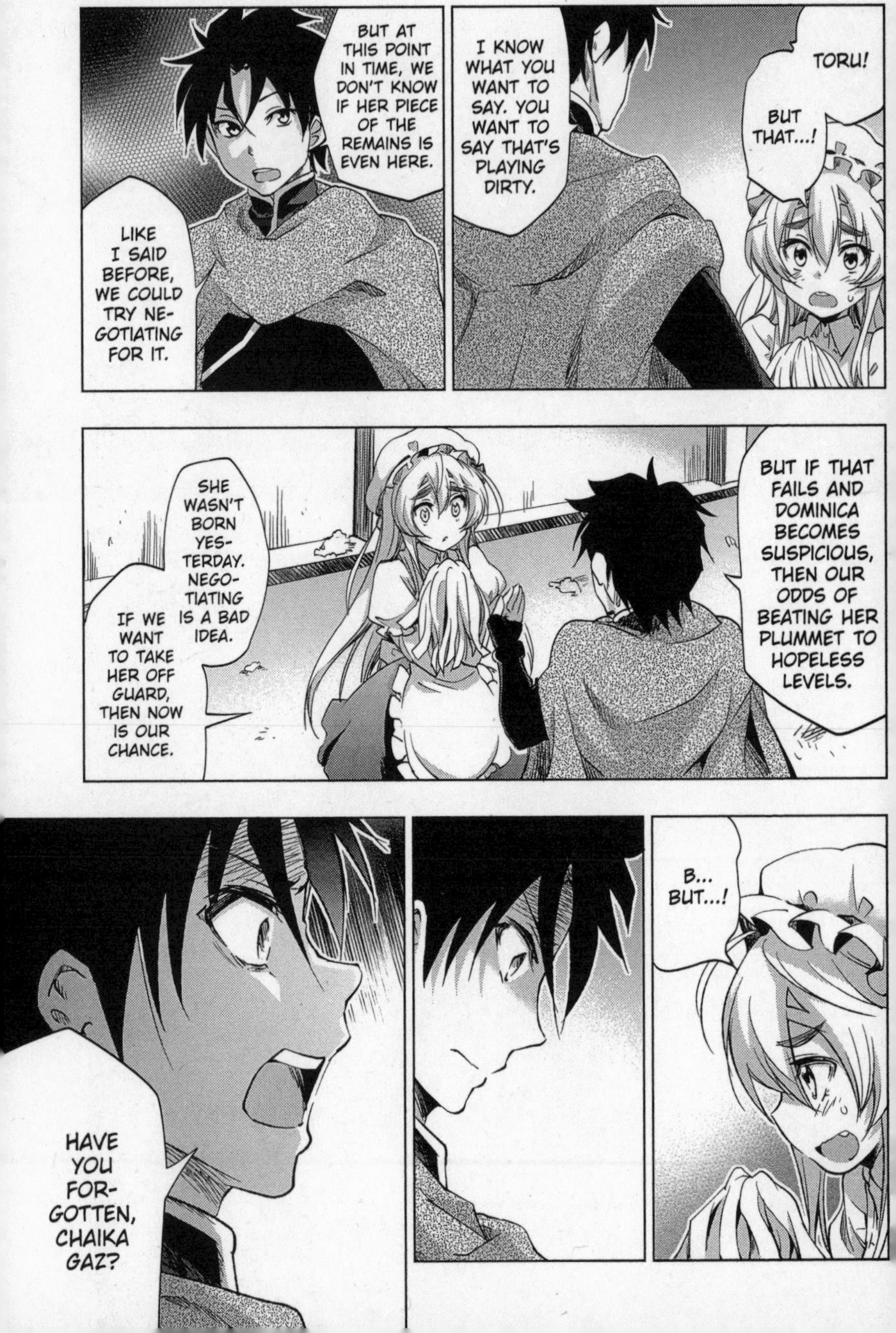
TORU!
BUT THAT...!
I KNOW WHAT YOU WANT TO SAY. YOU WANT TO SAY THAT'S PLAYING DIRTY.
BUT AT THIS POINT IN TIME, WE DON'T KNOW IF HER PIECE OF THE REMAINS IS EVEN HERE.
LIKE I SAID BEFORE, WE COULD TRY NEGOTIATING FOR IT.
BUT IF THAT FAILS AND DOMINICA BECOMES SUSPICIOUS, THEN OUR ODDS OF BEATING HER PLUMMET TO HOPELESS LEVELS.
SHE WASN'T BORN YESTERDAY. NEGOTIATING IS A BAD IDEA.
IF WE WANT TO TAKE HER OFF GUARD, THEN NOW IS OUR CHANCE.
B... BUT...!
HAVE YOU FORGOTTEN, CHAIKA GAZ?

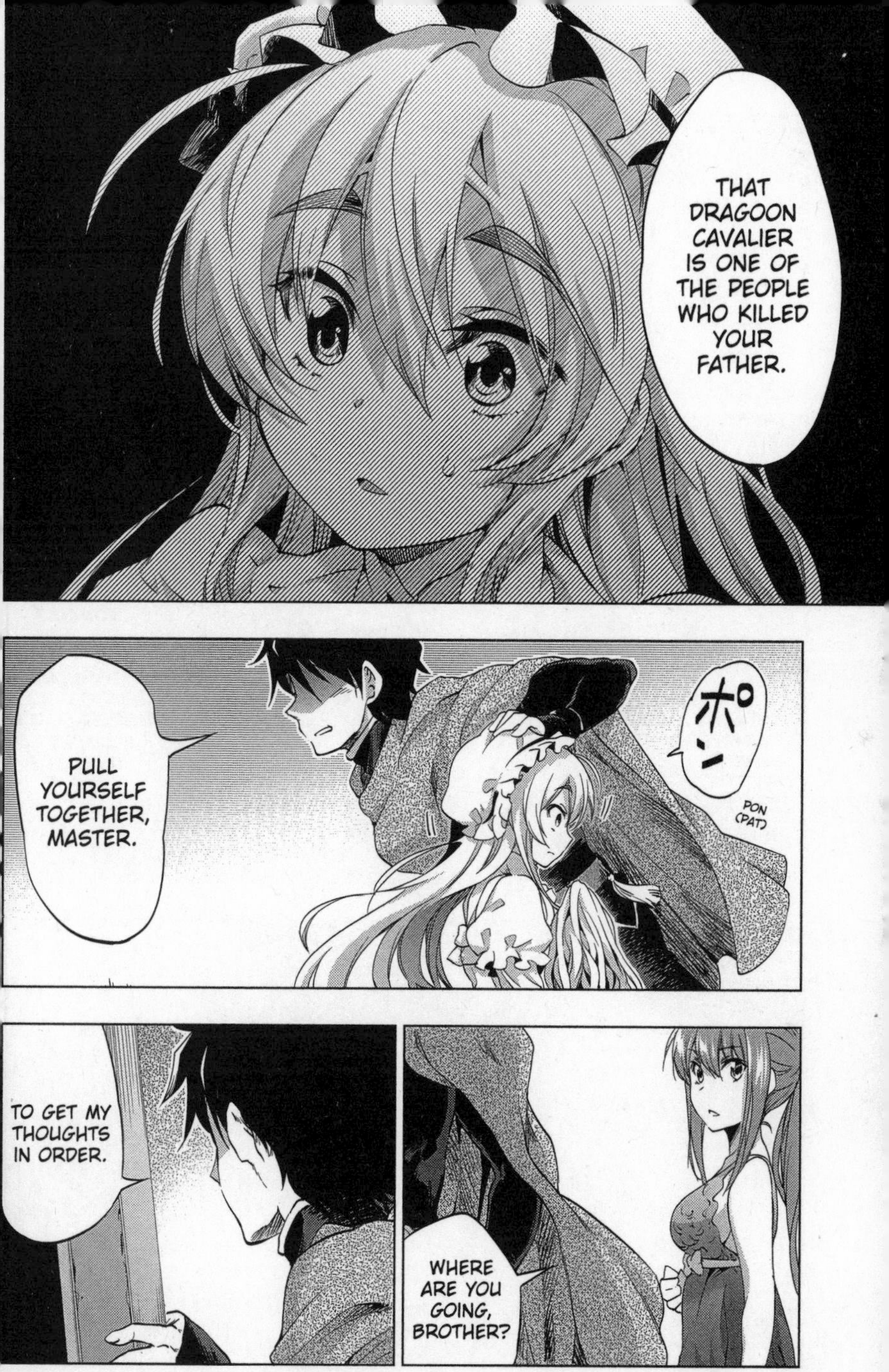
THAT DRAGOON CAVALIER IS ONE OF THE PEOPLE WHO KILLED YOUR FATHER.
ポン
PON (PAT)
PULL YOURSELF TOGETHER, MASTER.
WHERE ARE YOU GOING, BROTHER?
TO GET MY THOUGHTS IN ORDER.

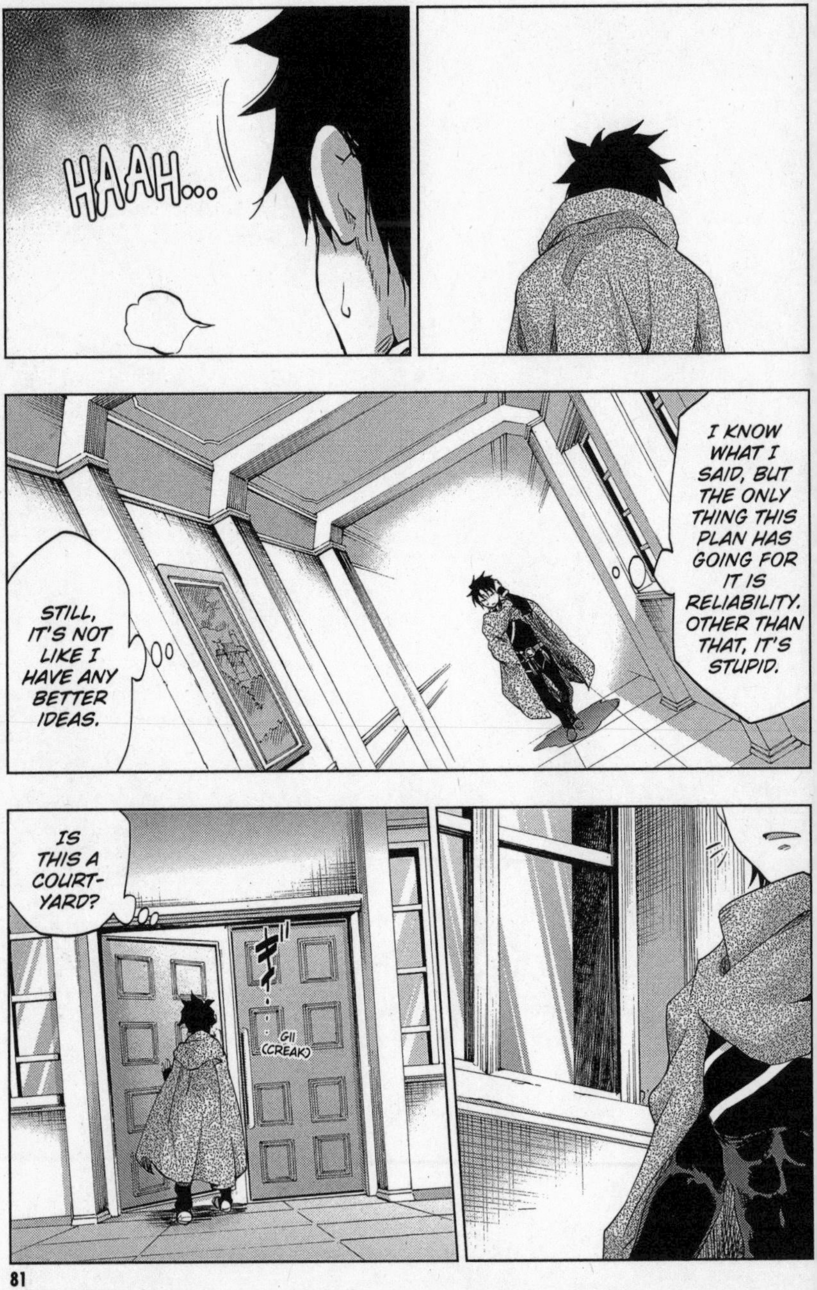
HAAH...
I KNOW WHAT I SAID, BUT THE ONLY THING THIS PLAN HAS GOING FOR IT IS RELIABILITY. OTHER THAN THAT, IT'S STUPID.
STILL, IT'S NOT LIKE I HAVE ANY BETTER IDEAS.
IS THIS A COURT-YARD?
GII (CREAK)

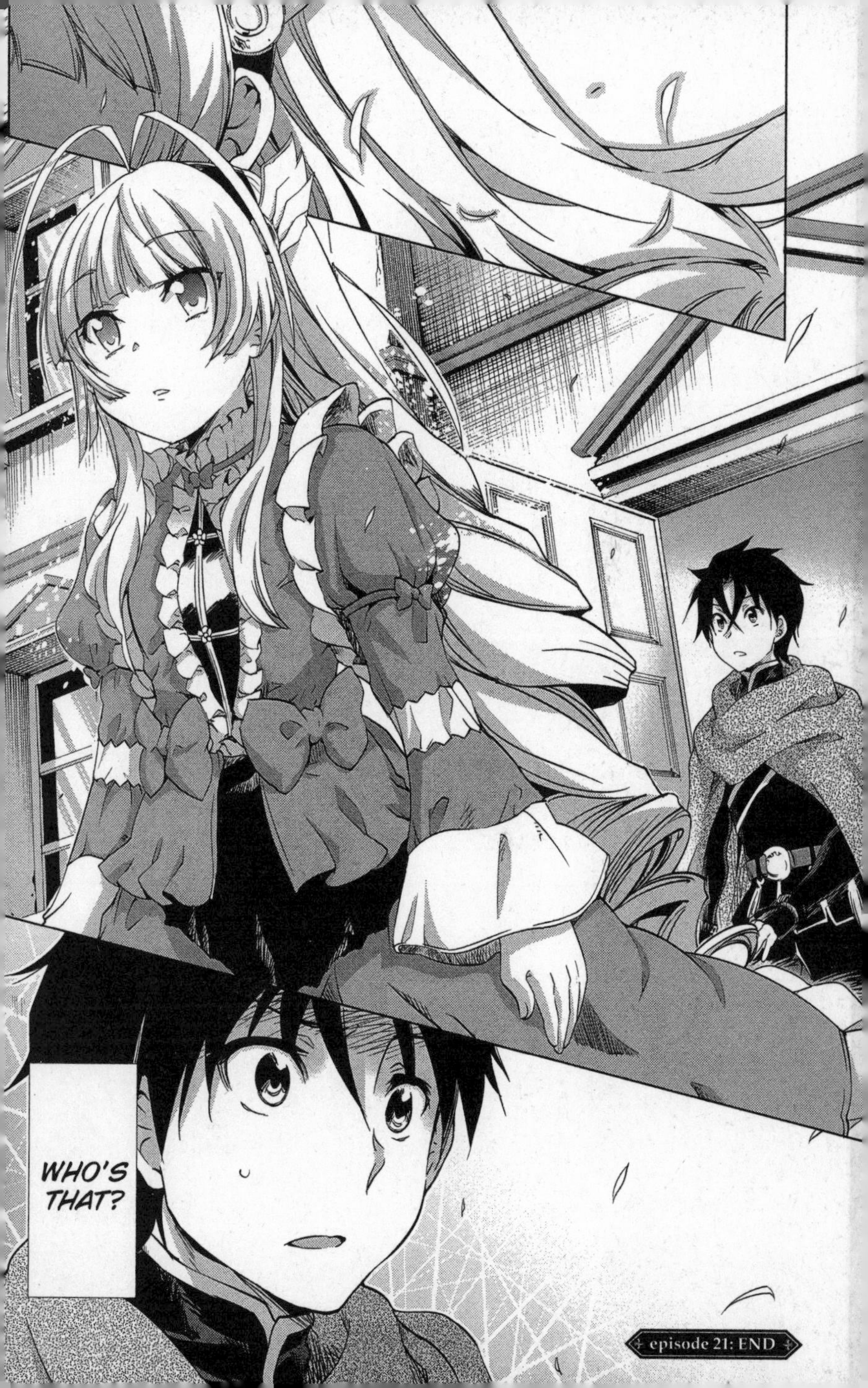
WHO'S THAT?
episode 21: END

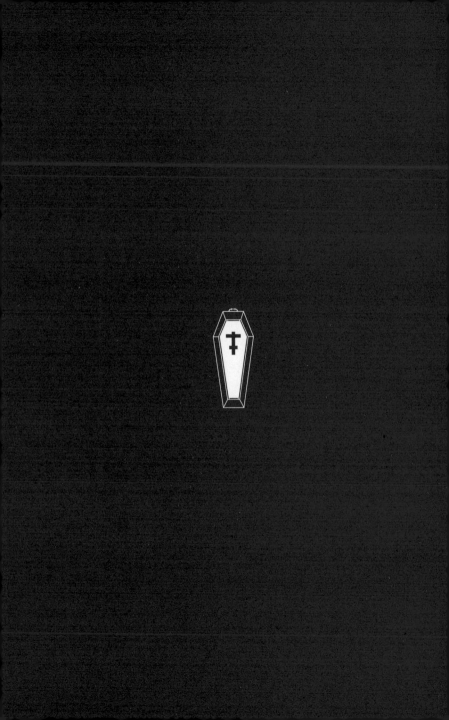

CHAIKA: THE COFFIN PRINCESS

episode 22: Lucie

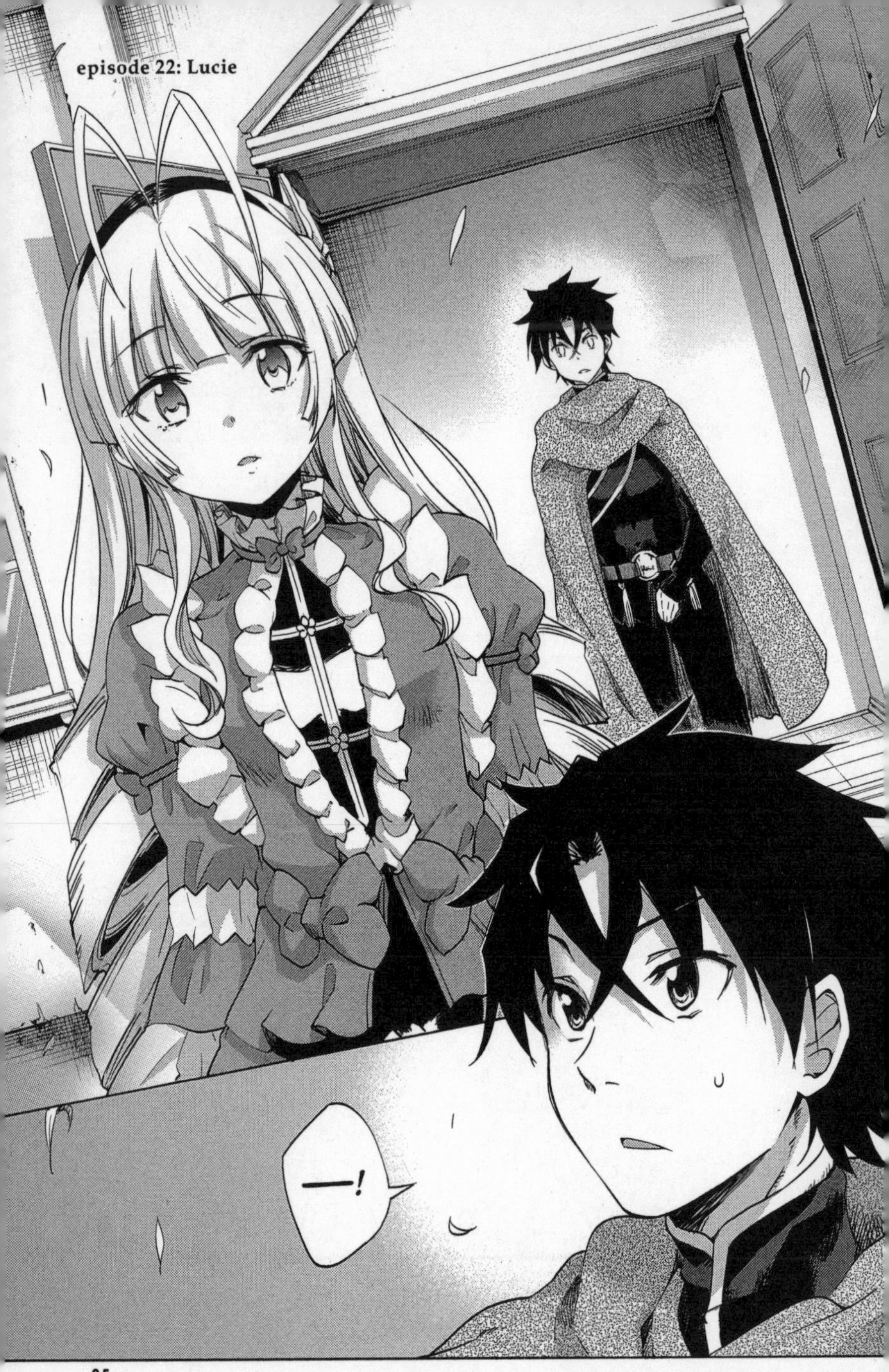
—!

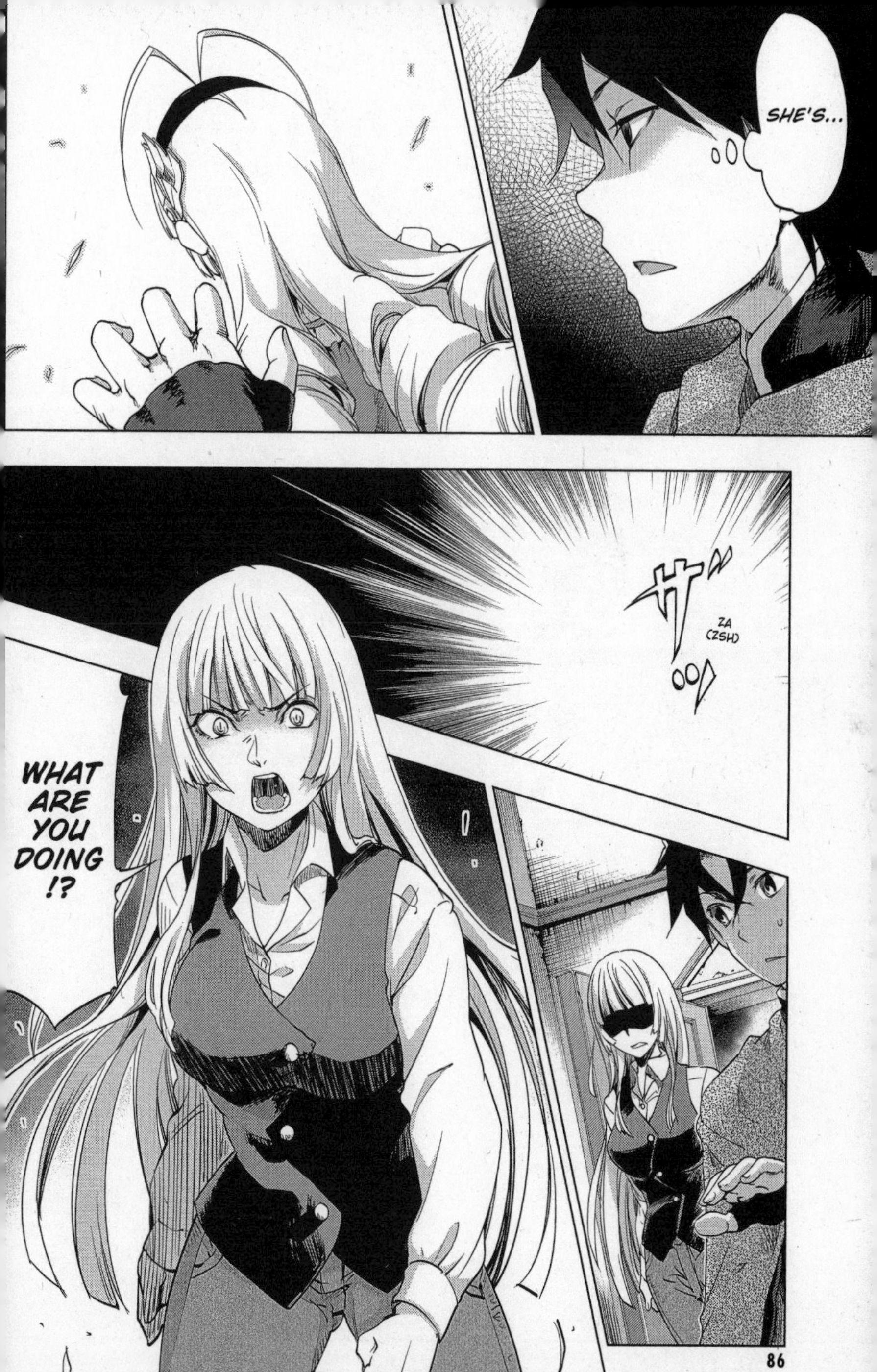
SHE'S...
ザッ
ZA (ZSH)
WHAT ARE YOU DOING !?

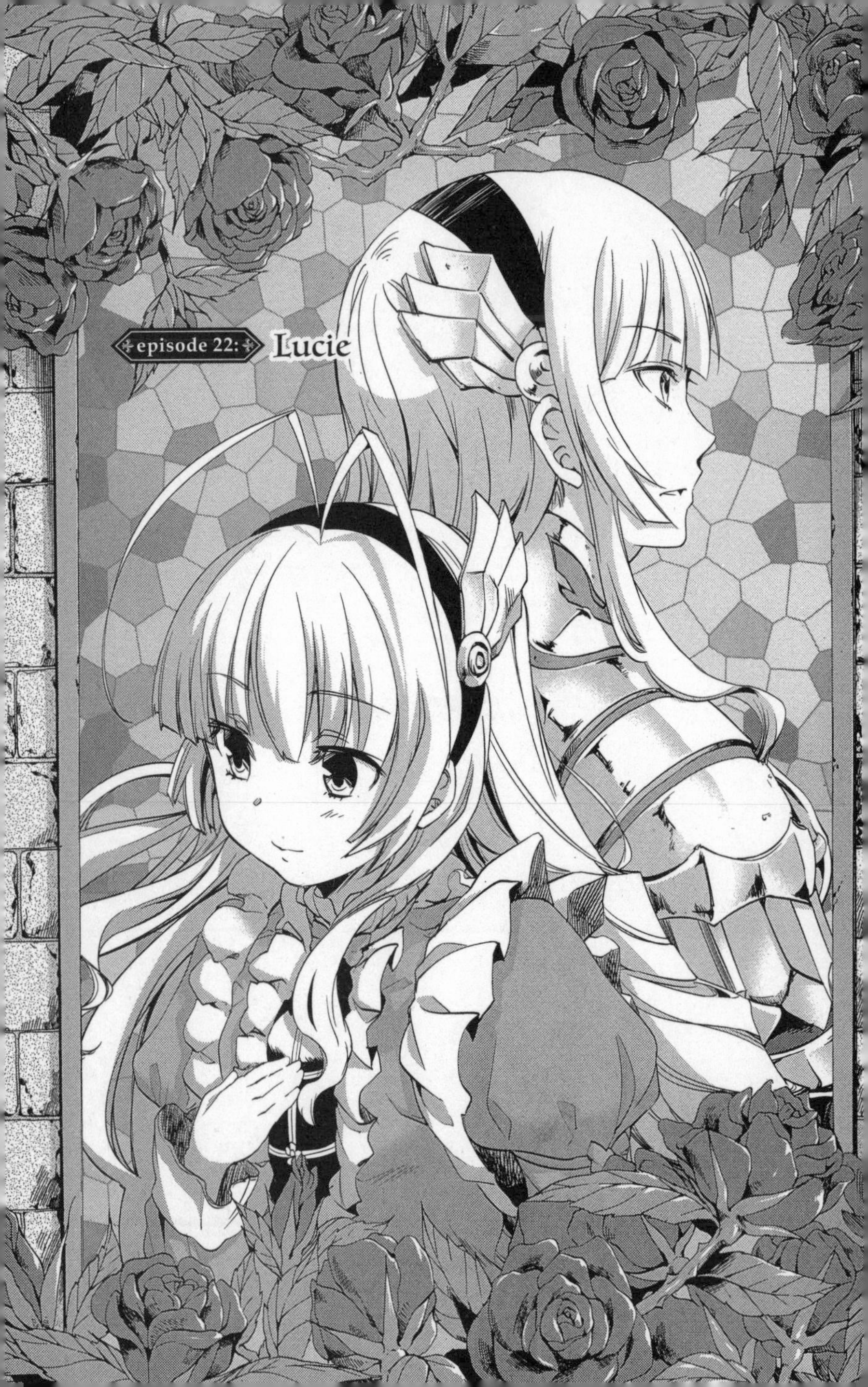
episode 22: Lucie

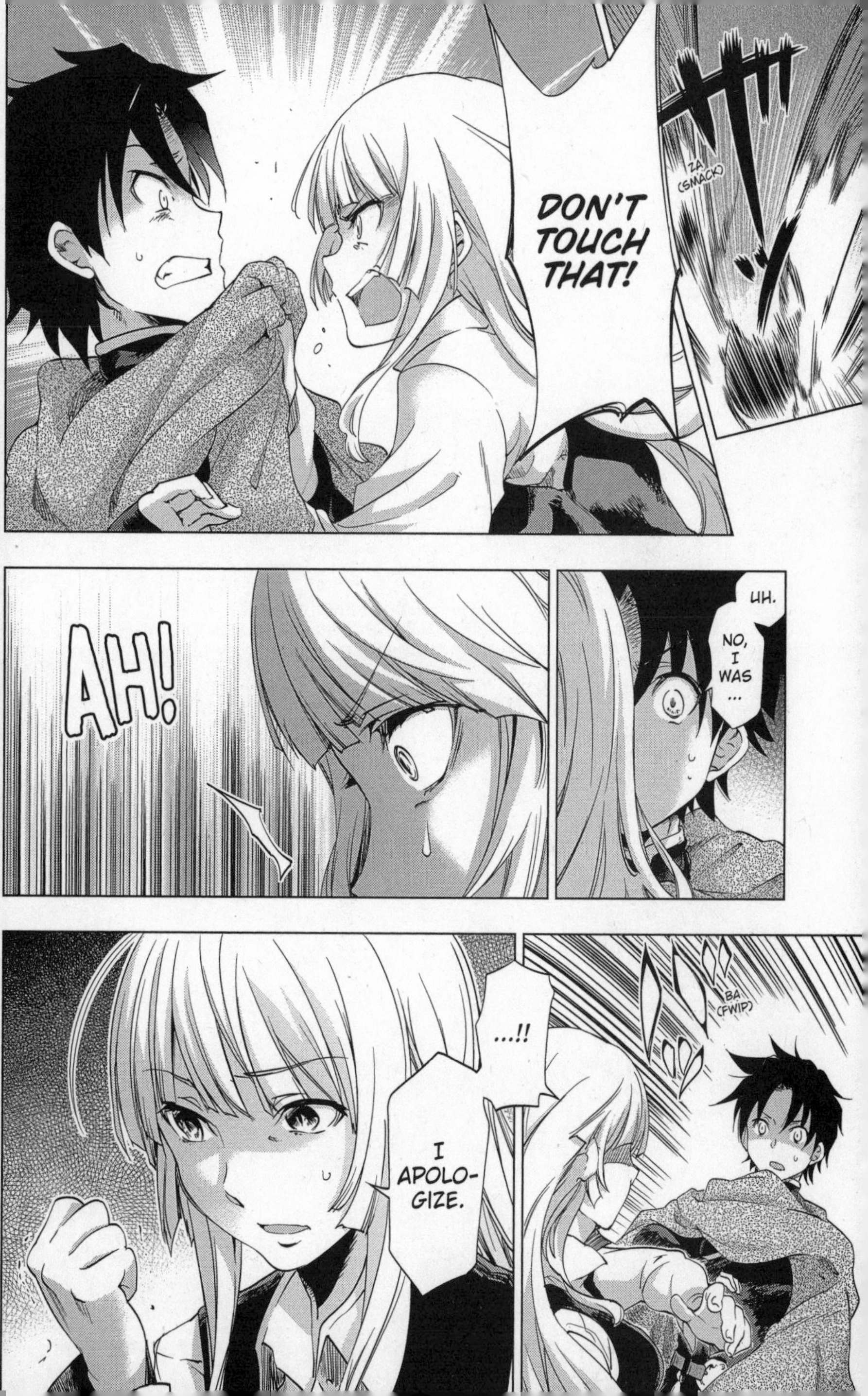
ZA (SMACK)
DON'T TOUCH THAT!
UH.
NO, I WAS ...
AH!
BA (FWIP)
...!!
I APOLOGIZE.

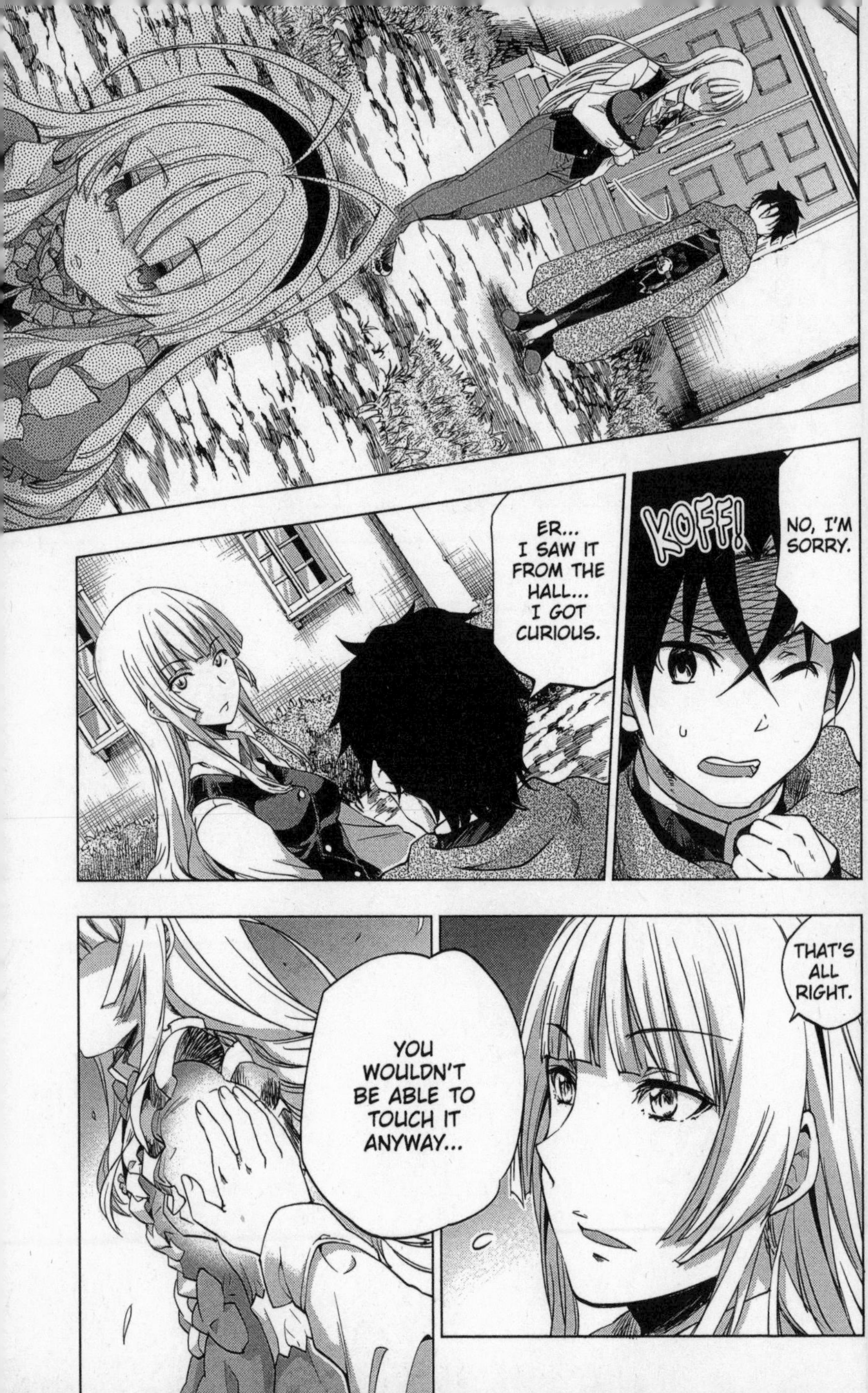
NO, I'M SORRY.
KOFF!
ER... I SAW IT FROM THE HALL... I GOT CURIOUS.
THAT'S ALL RIGHT.
YOU WOULDN'T BE ABLE TO TOUCH IT ANYWAY...

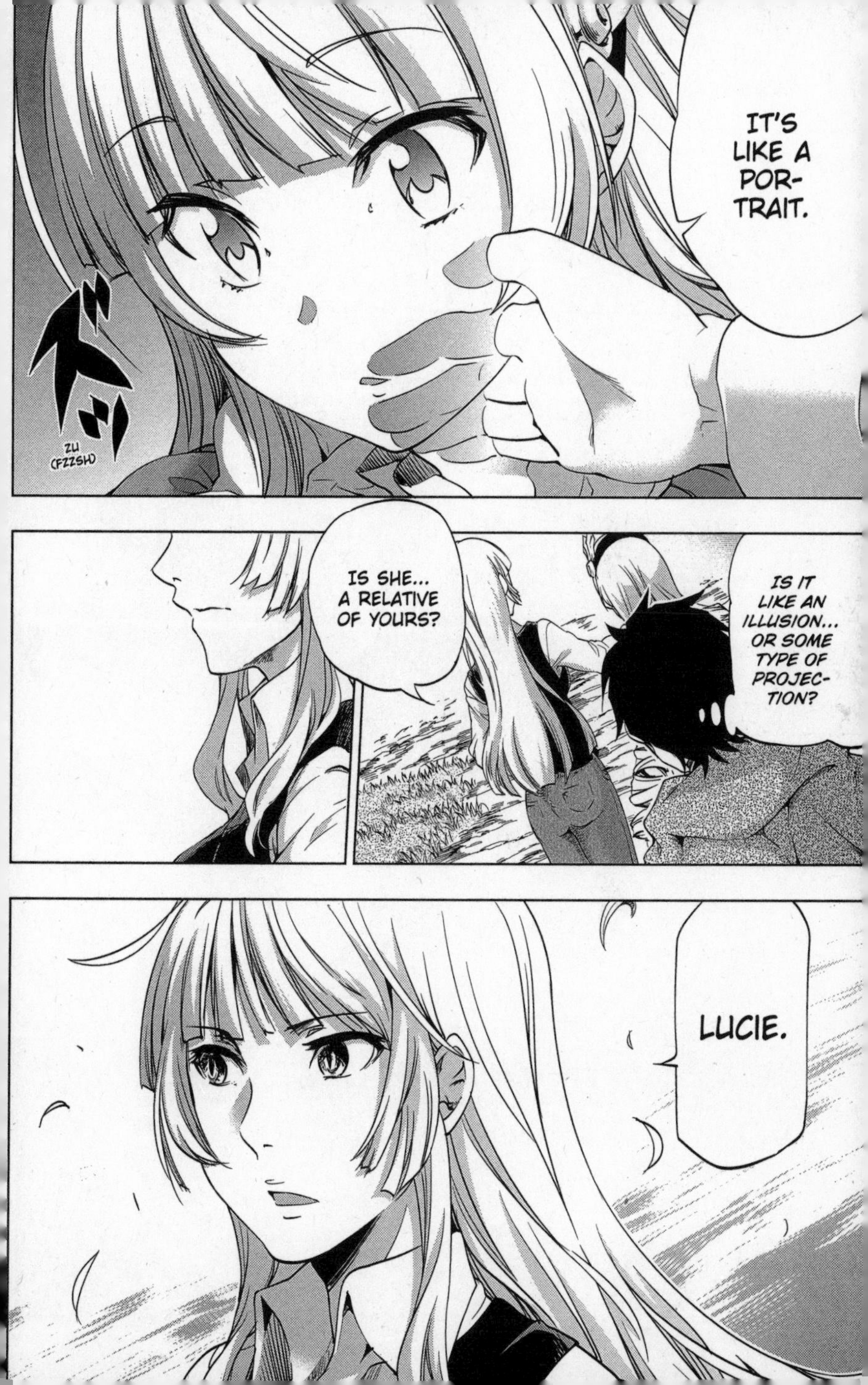
IT'S LIKE A POR-TRAIT.
ZU (FZZSH)
IS SHE... A RELATIVE OF YOURS?
IS IT LIKE AN ILLUSION... OR SOME TYPE OF PROJEC-TION?
LUCIE.

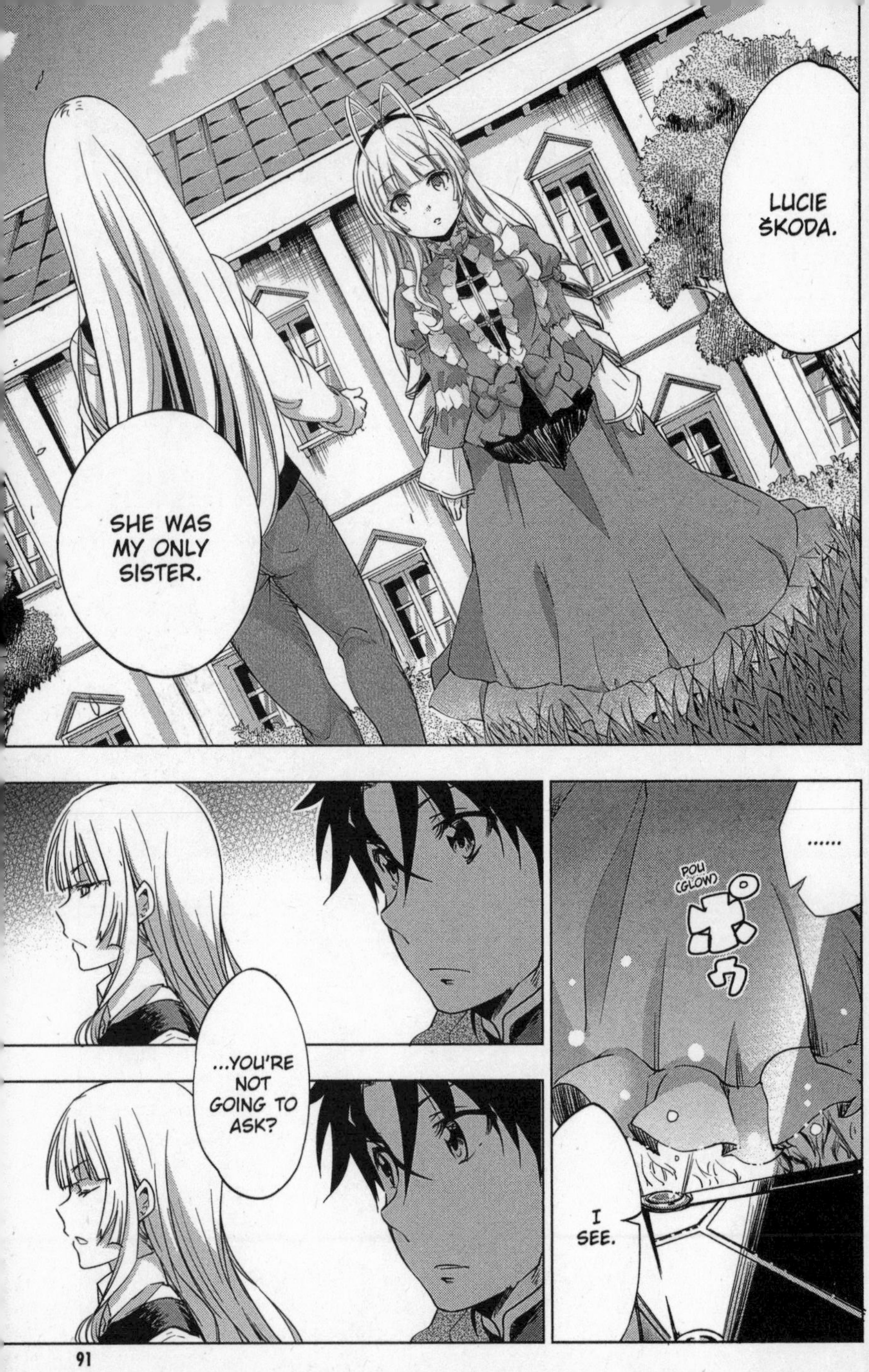
LUCIE ŠKODA.
SHE WAS MY ONLY SISTER.
......
POU (GLOW)
I SEE.
...YOU'RE NOT GOING TO ASK?

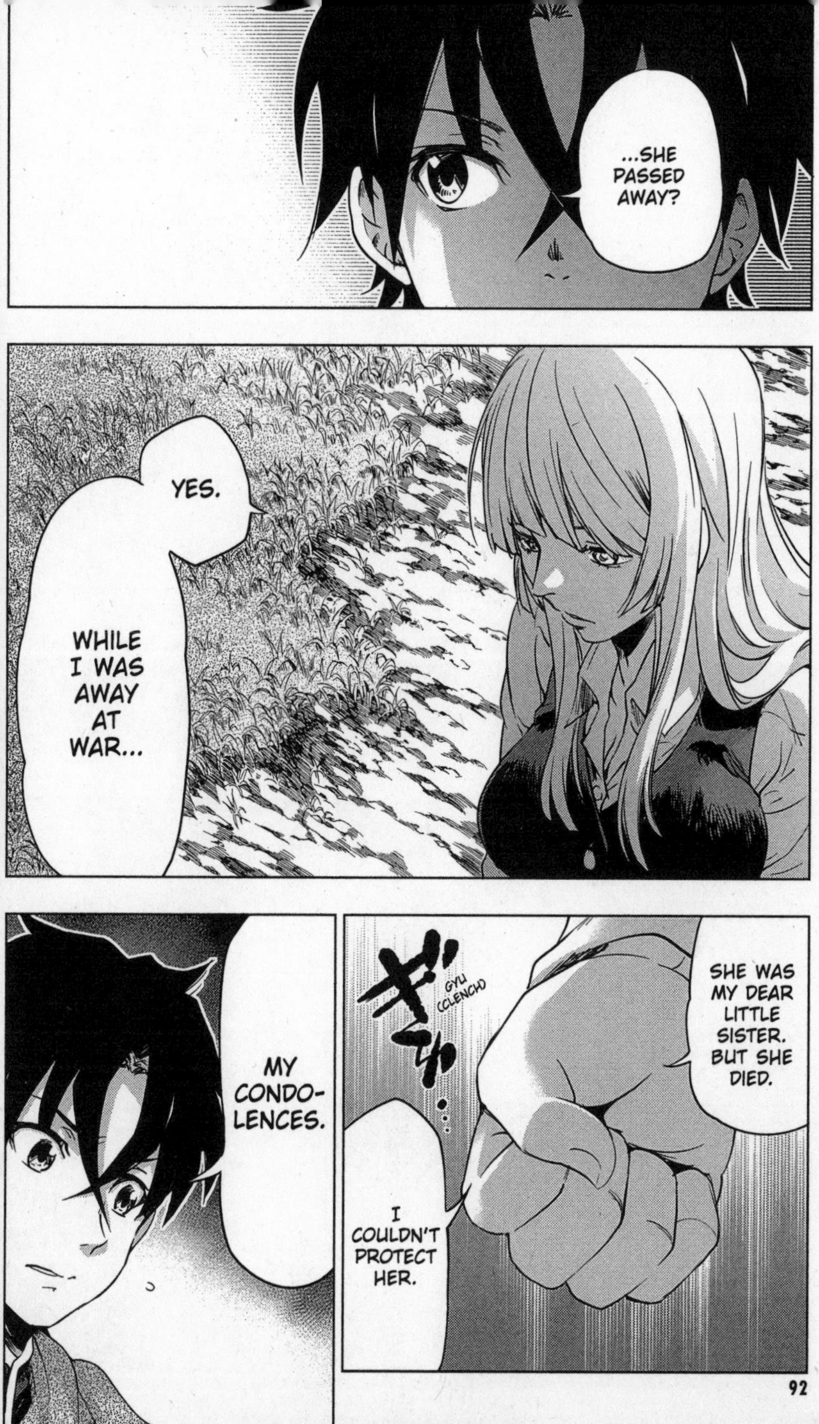
...SHE PASSED AWAY?
YES.
WHILE I WAS AWAY AT WAR...
SHE WAS MY DEAR LITTLE SISTER. BUT SHE DIED.
GYU (CLENCH)
I COULDN'T PROTECT HER.
MY CONDO-LENCES.

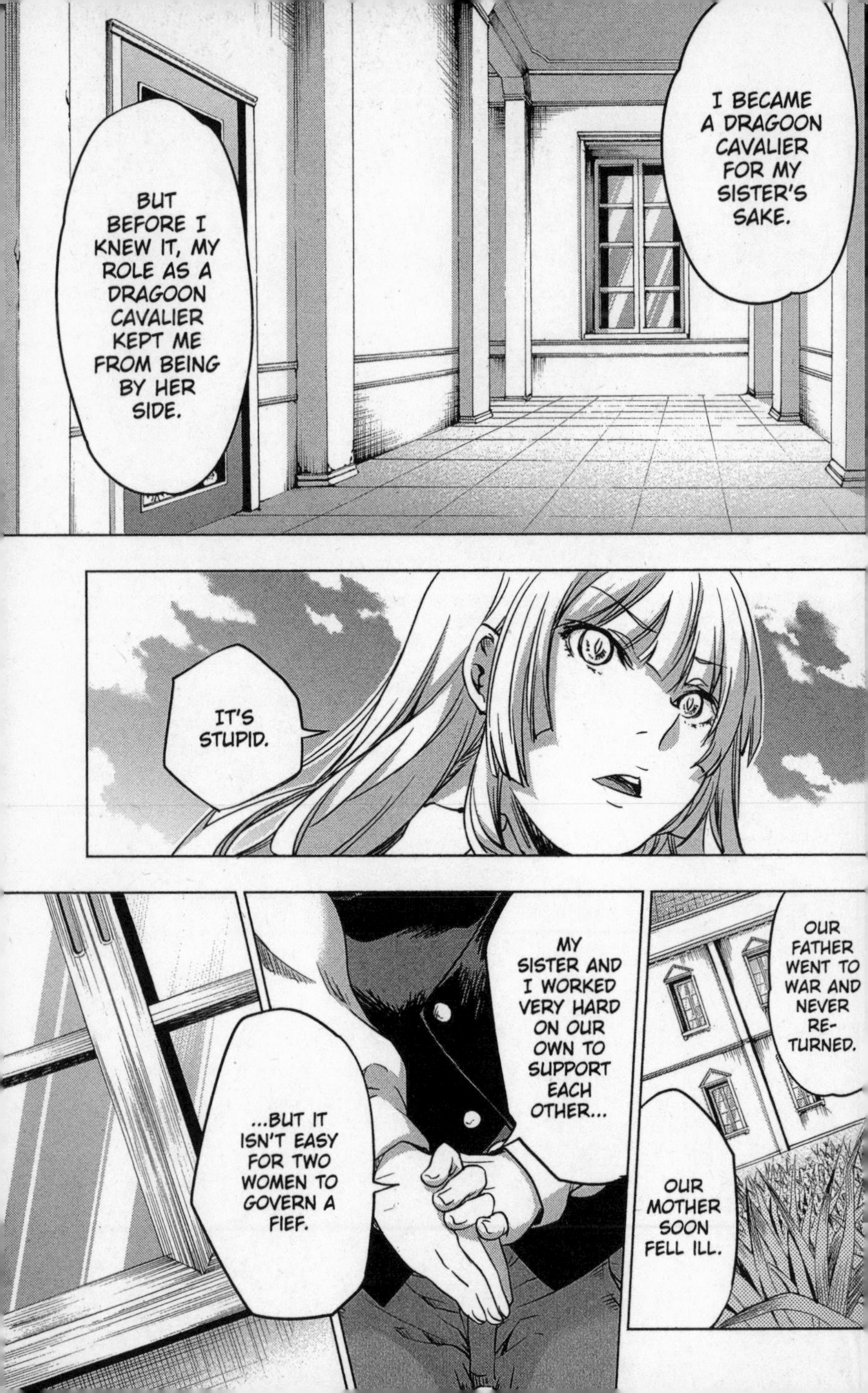
I BECAME A DRAGOON CAVALIER FOR MY SISTER'S SAKE.
BUT BEFORE I KNEW IT, MY ROLE AS A DRAGOON CAVALIER KEPT ME FROM BEING BY HER SIDE.
IT'S STUPID.
OUR FATHER WENT TO WAR AND NEVER RE-TURNED.
OUR MOTHER SOON FELL ILL.
MY SISTER AND I WORKED VERY HARD ON OUR OWN TO SUPPORT EACH OTHER...
...BUT IT ISN'T EASY FOR TWO WOMEN TO GOVERN A FIEF.

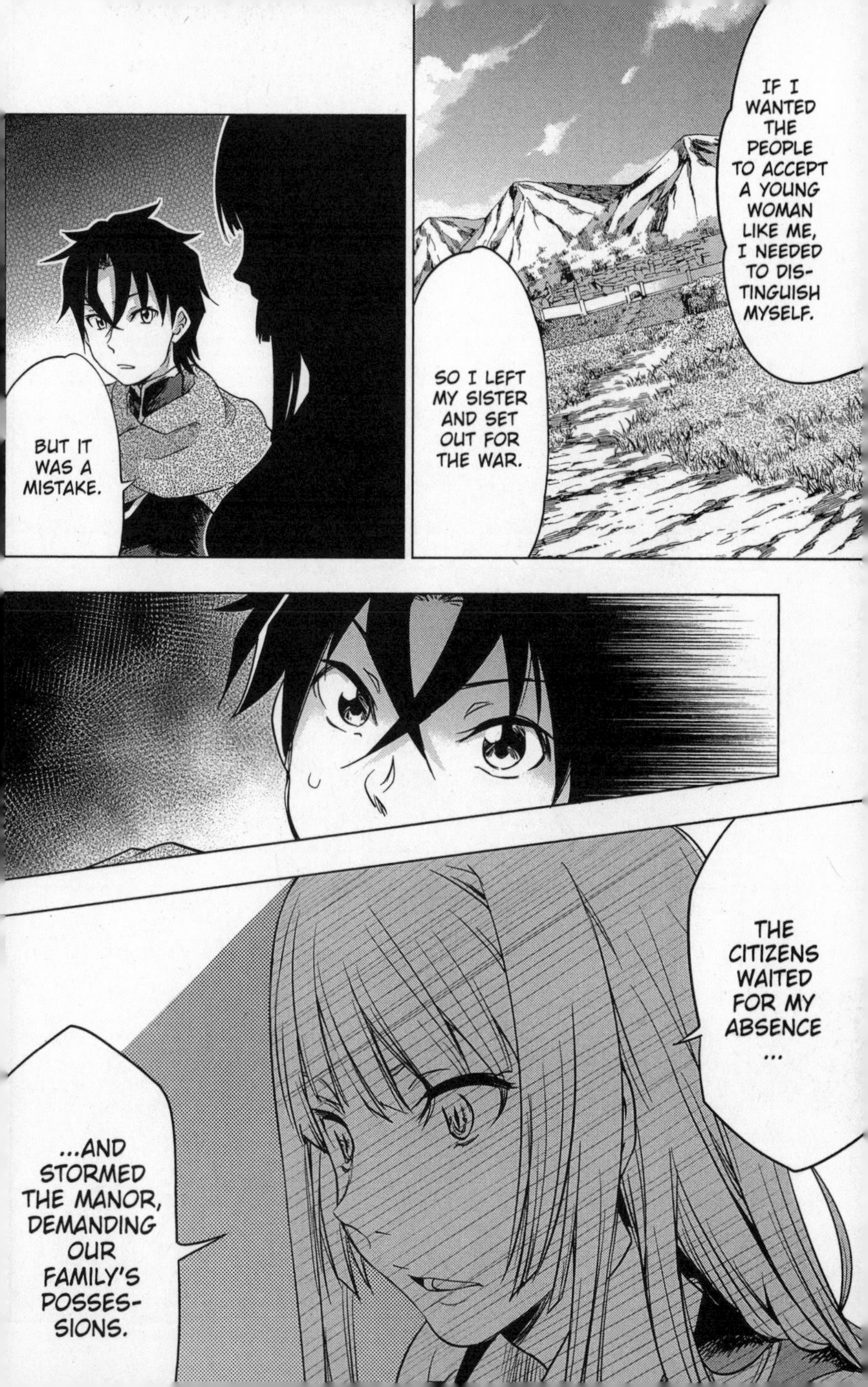
IF I WANTED THE PEOPLE TO ACCEPT A YOUNG WOMAN LIKE ME, I NEEDED TO DIS-TINGUISH MYSELF.
SO I LEFT MY SISTER AND SET OUT FOR THE WAR.
BUT IT WAS A MISTAKE.
THE CITIZENS WAITED FOR MY ABSENCE ...
...AND STORMED THE MANOR, DEMANDING OUR FAMILY'S POSSES-SIONS.

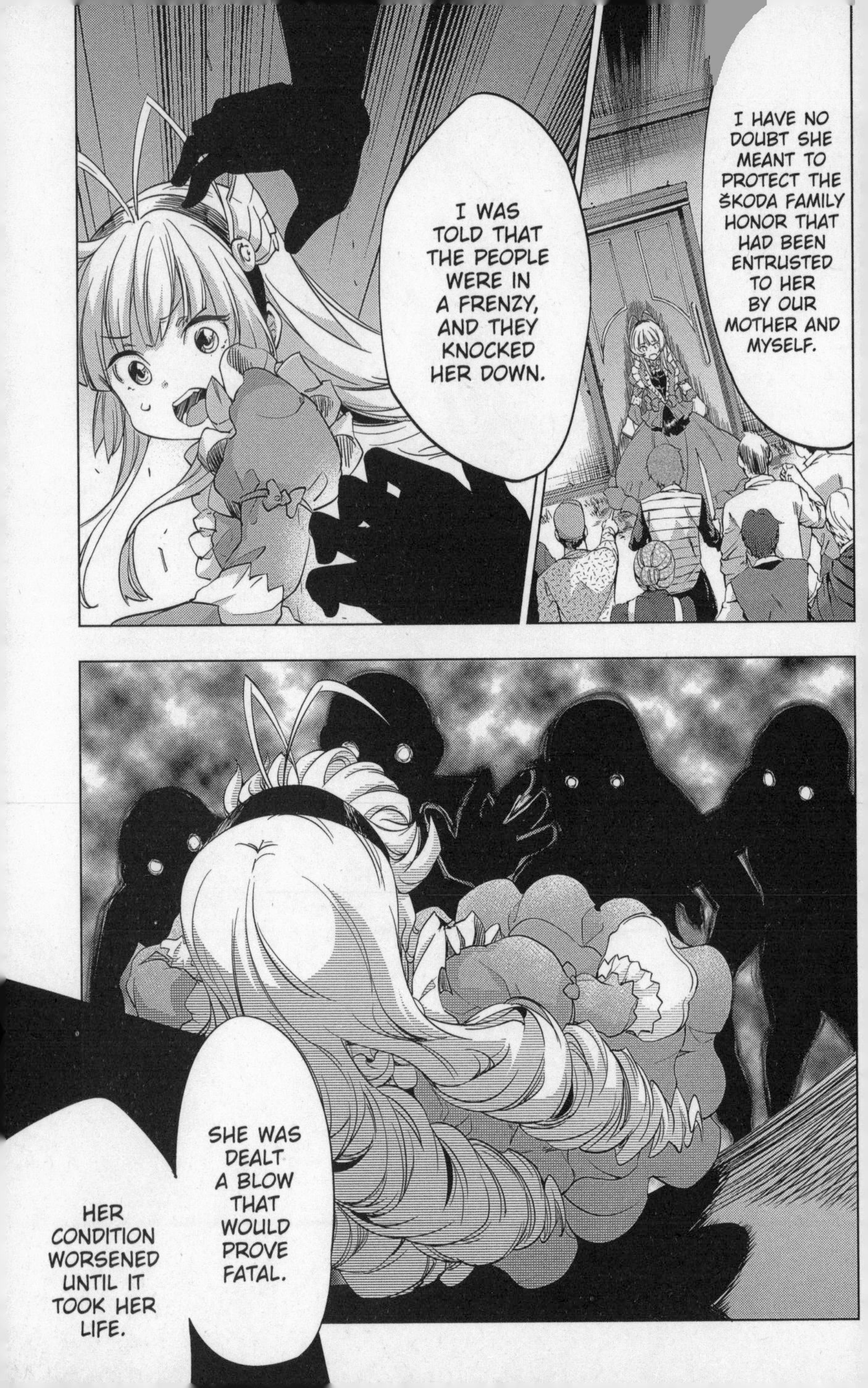
I HAVE NO DOUBT SHE MEANT TO PROTECT THE ŠKODA FAMILY HONOR THAT HAD BEEN ENTRUSTED TO HER BY OUR MOTHER AND MYSELF.
I WAS TOLD THAT THE PEOPLE WERE IN A FRENZY, AND THEY KNOCKED HER DOWN.
SHE WAS DEALT A BLOW THAT WOULD PROVE FATAL.
HER CONDITION WORSENED UNTIL IT TOOK HER LIFE.

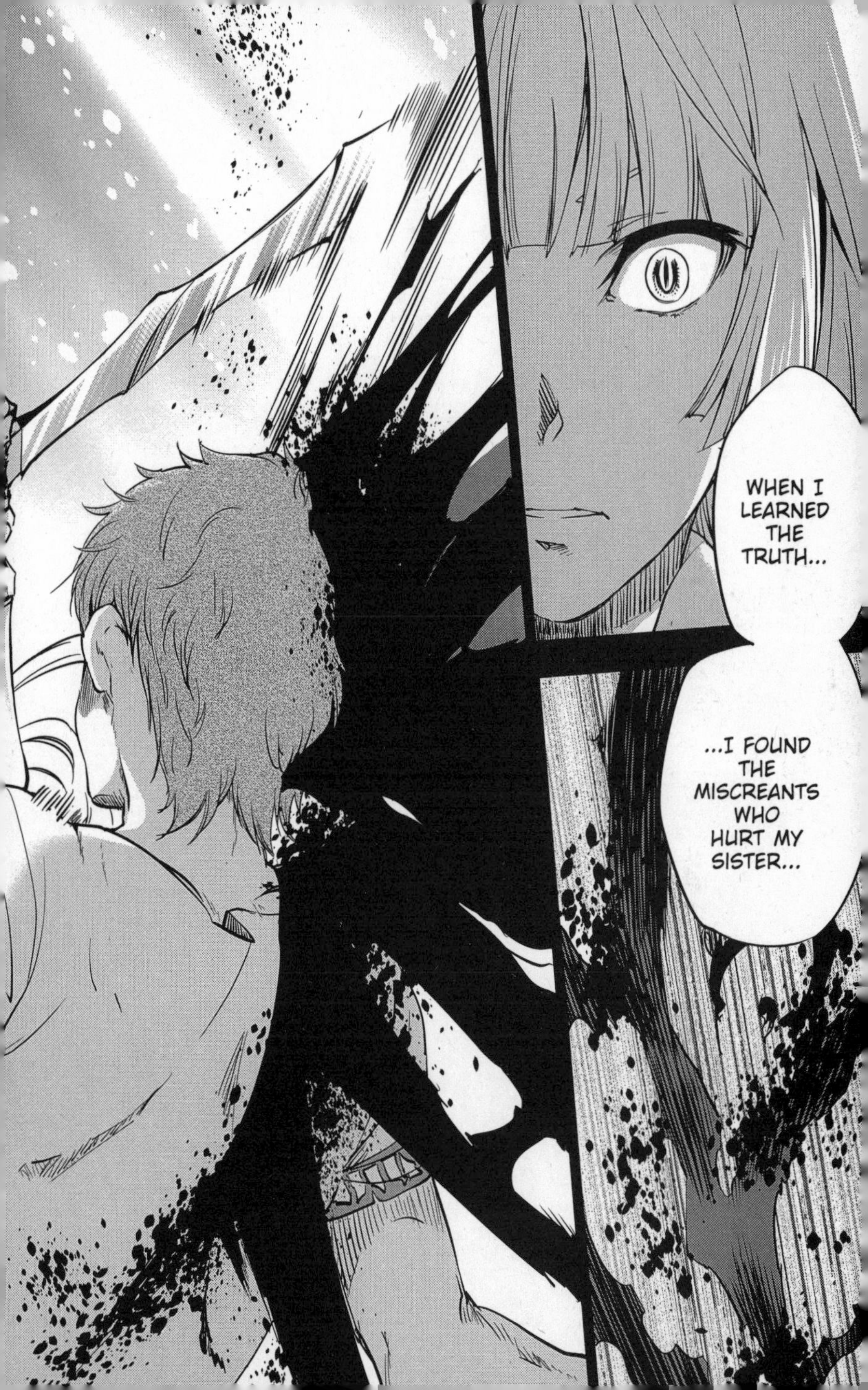
WHEN I LEARNED THE TRUTH...
...I FOUND THE MISCREANTS WHO HURT MY SISTER...

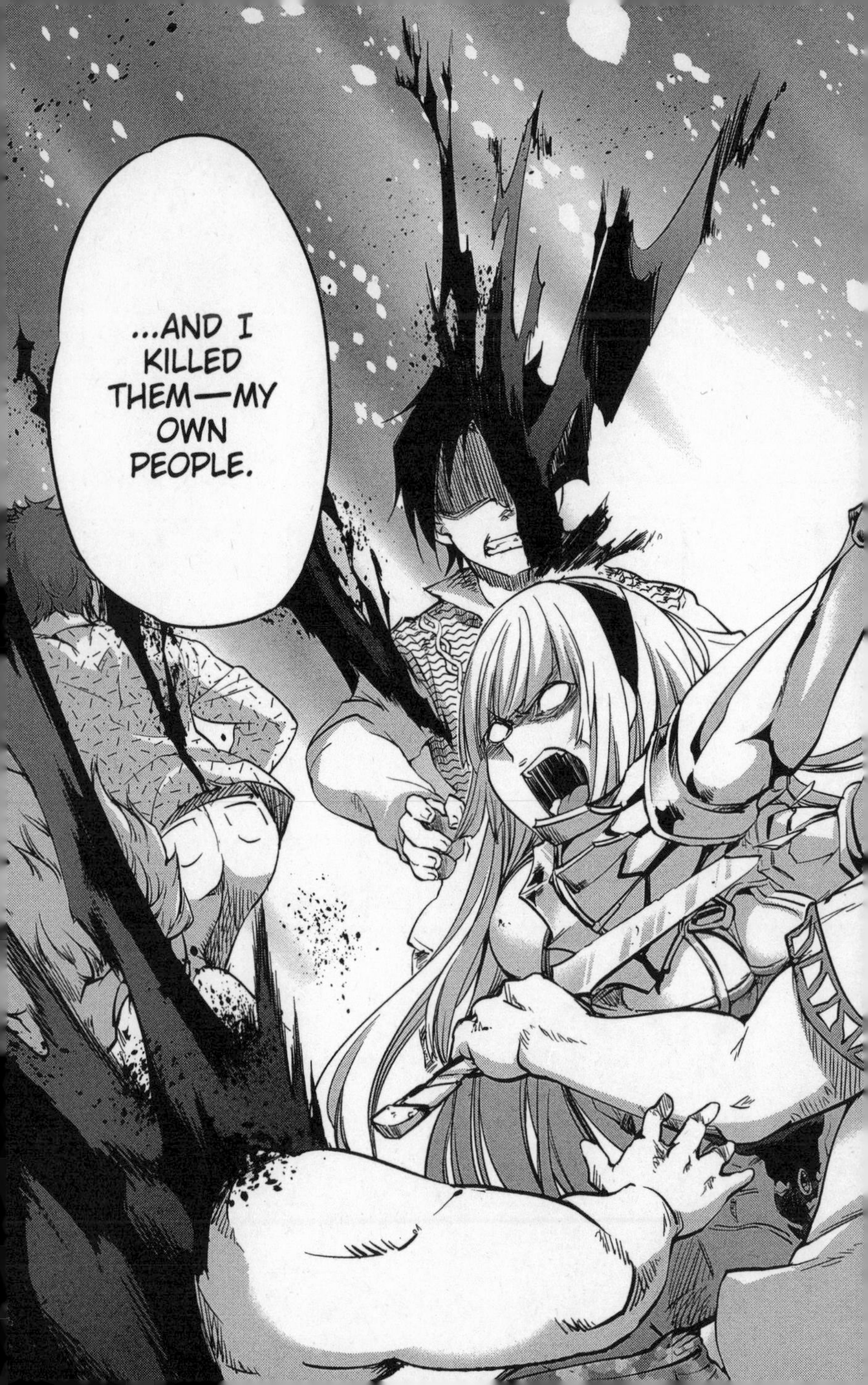
...AND I KILLED THEM—MY OWN PEOPLE.

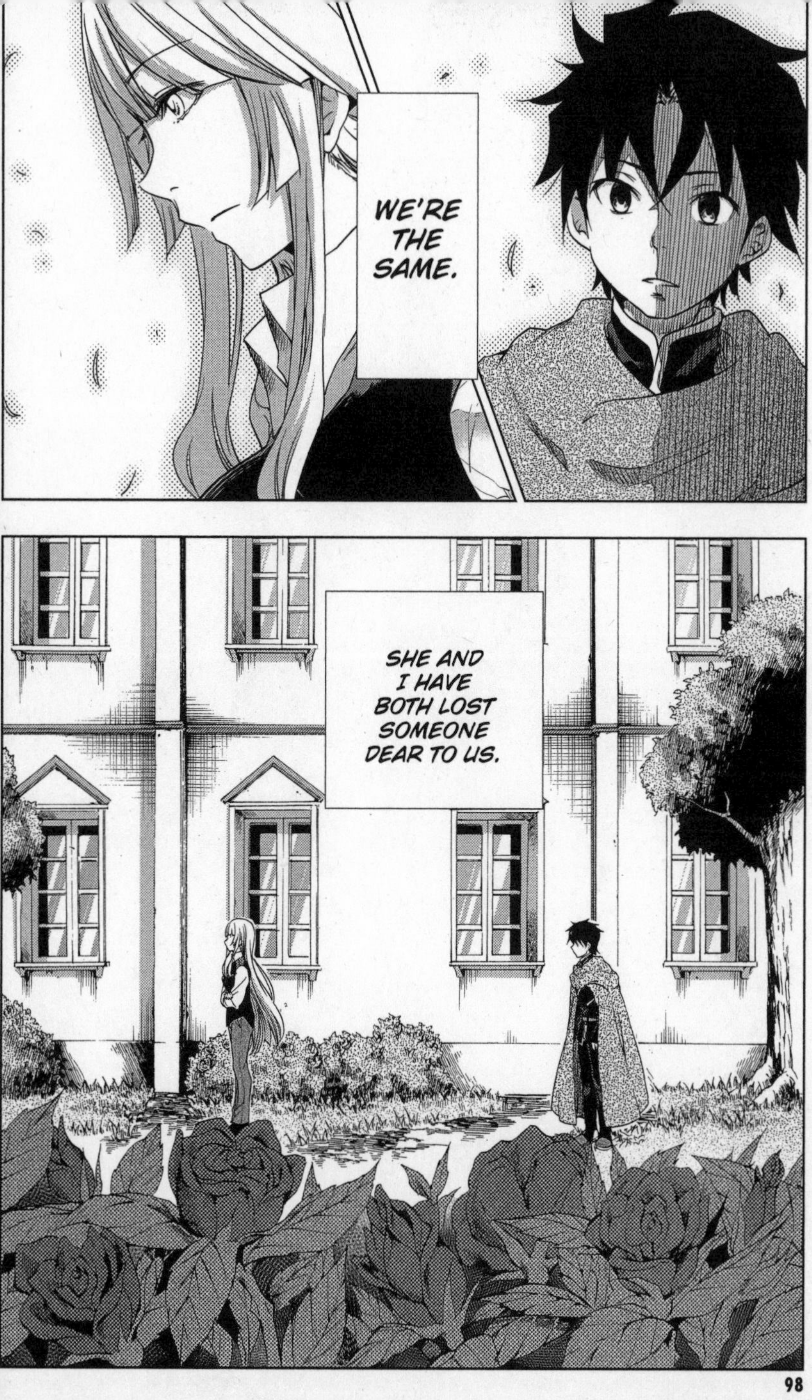
WE'RE THE SAME.
SHE AND I HAVE BOTH LOST SOMEONE DEAR TO US.

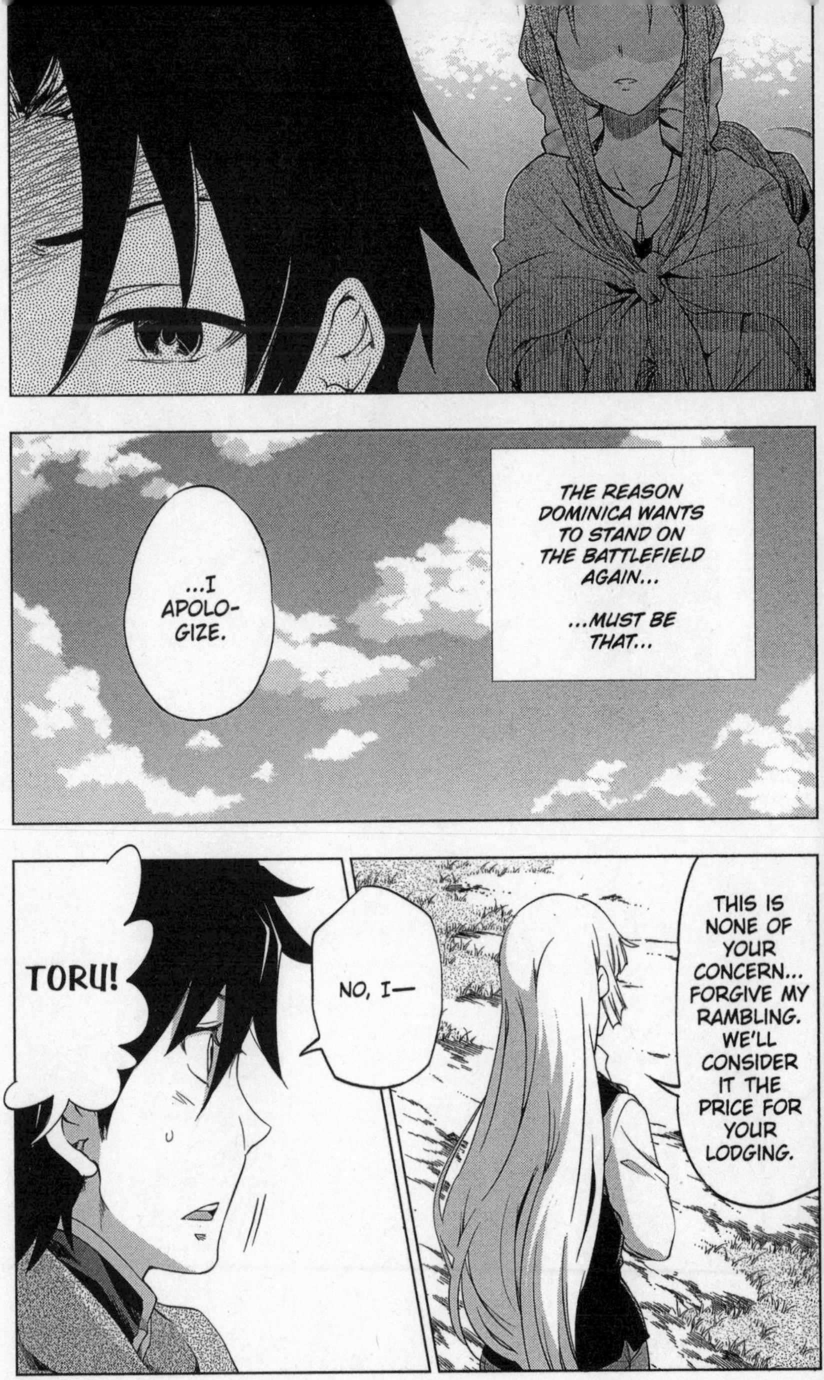
THE REASON DOMINICA WANTS TO STAND ON THE BATTLEFIELD AGAIN... ...MUST BE THAT...
...I APOLO-GIZE.
THIS IS NONE OF YOUR CONCERN... FORGIVE MY RAMBLING. WE'LL CONSIDER IT THE PRICE FOR YOUR LODGING.
NO, I—
TORU!

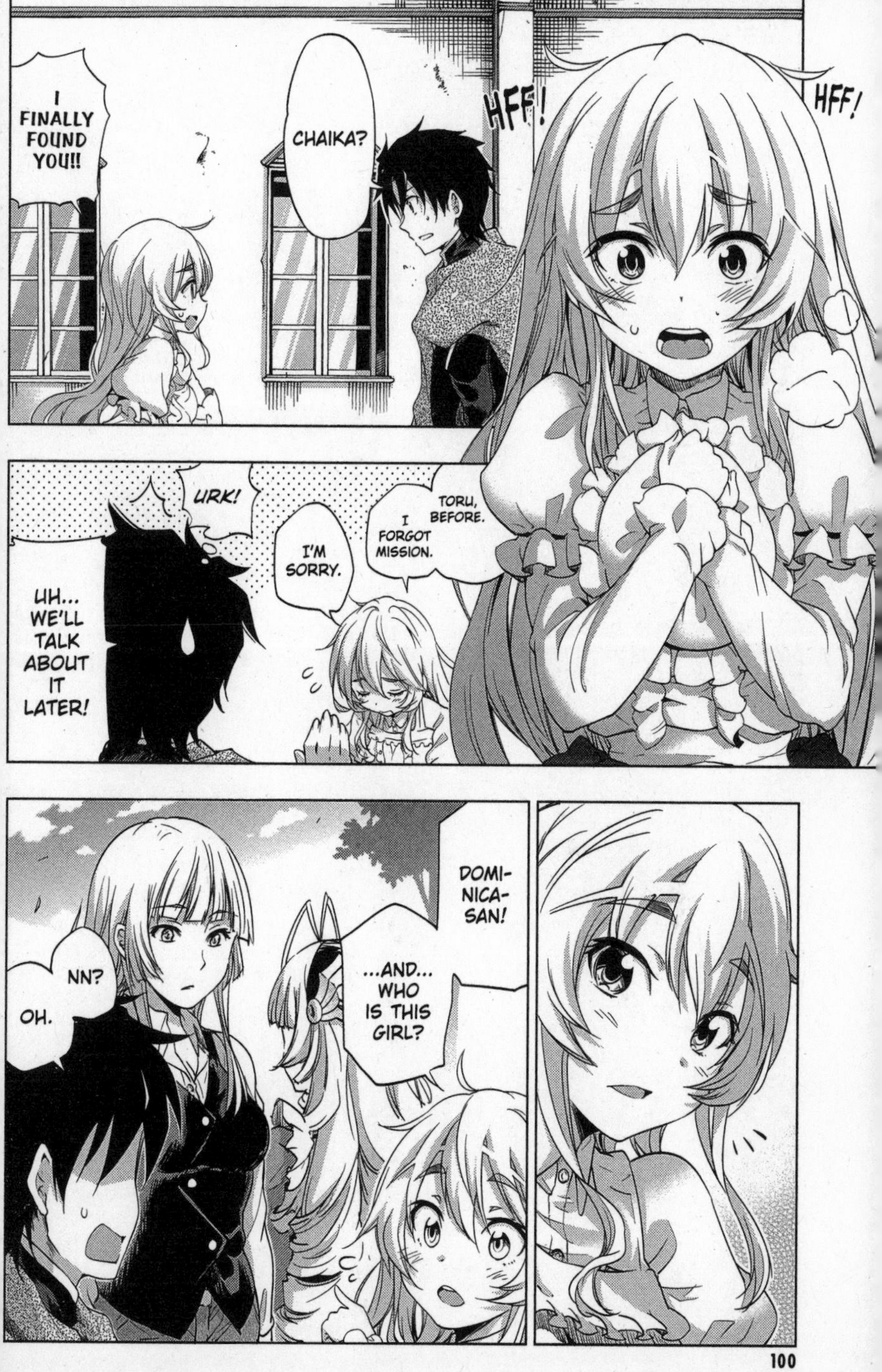
HFF!
HFF!
CHAIKA?
I FINALLY FOUND YOU!!
TORU, BEFORE. I FORGOT MISSION.
I'M SORRY.
URK!
UH... WE'LL TALK ABOUT IT LATER!
DOMINICA-SAN!
...AND... WHO IS THIS GIRL?
NN?
OH.

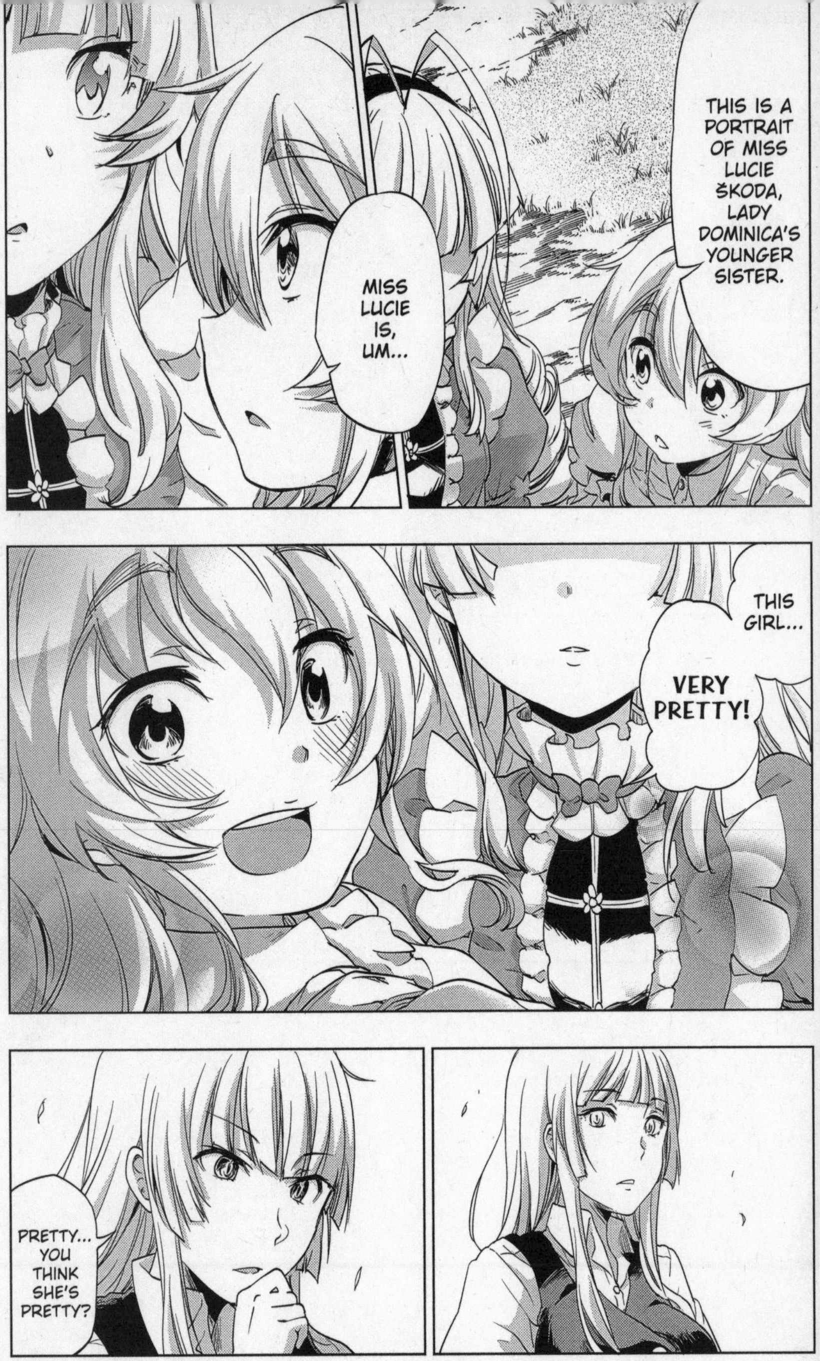
THIS IS A PORTRAIT OF MISS LUCIE ŠKODA, LADY DOMINICA'S YOUNGER SISTER.
MISS LUCIE IS, UM...
THIS GIRL...
VERY PRETTY!
PRETTY... YOU THINK SHE'S PRETTY?

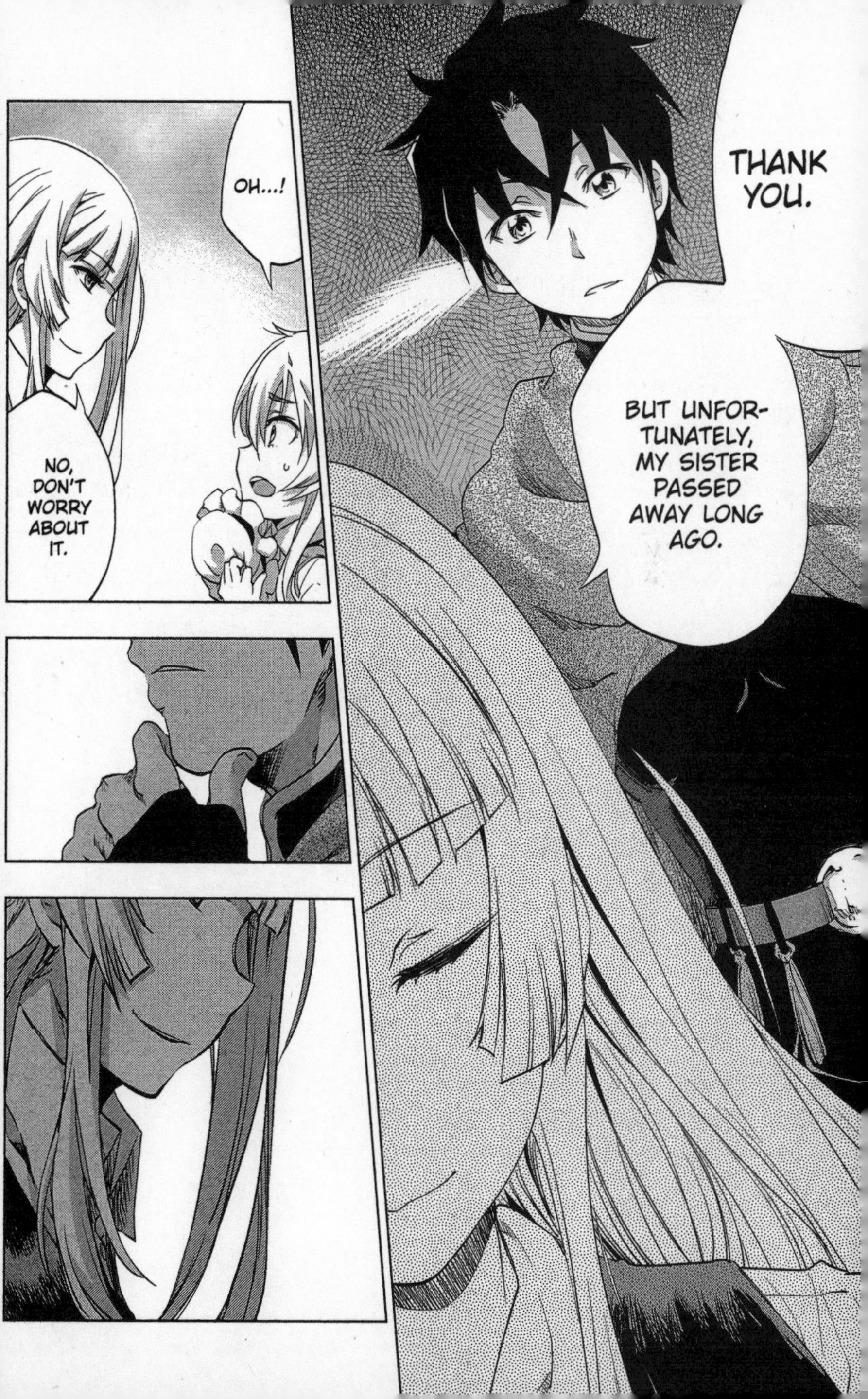
THANK YOU.
BUT UNFOR-TUNATELY, MY SISTER PASSED AWAY LONG AGO.
OH...!
NO, DON'T WORRY ABOUT IT.

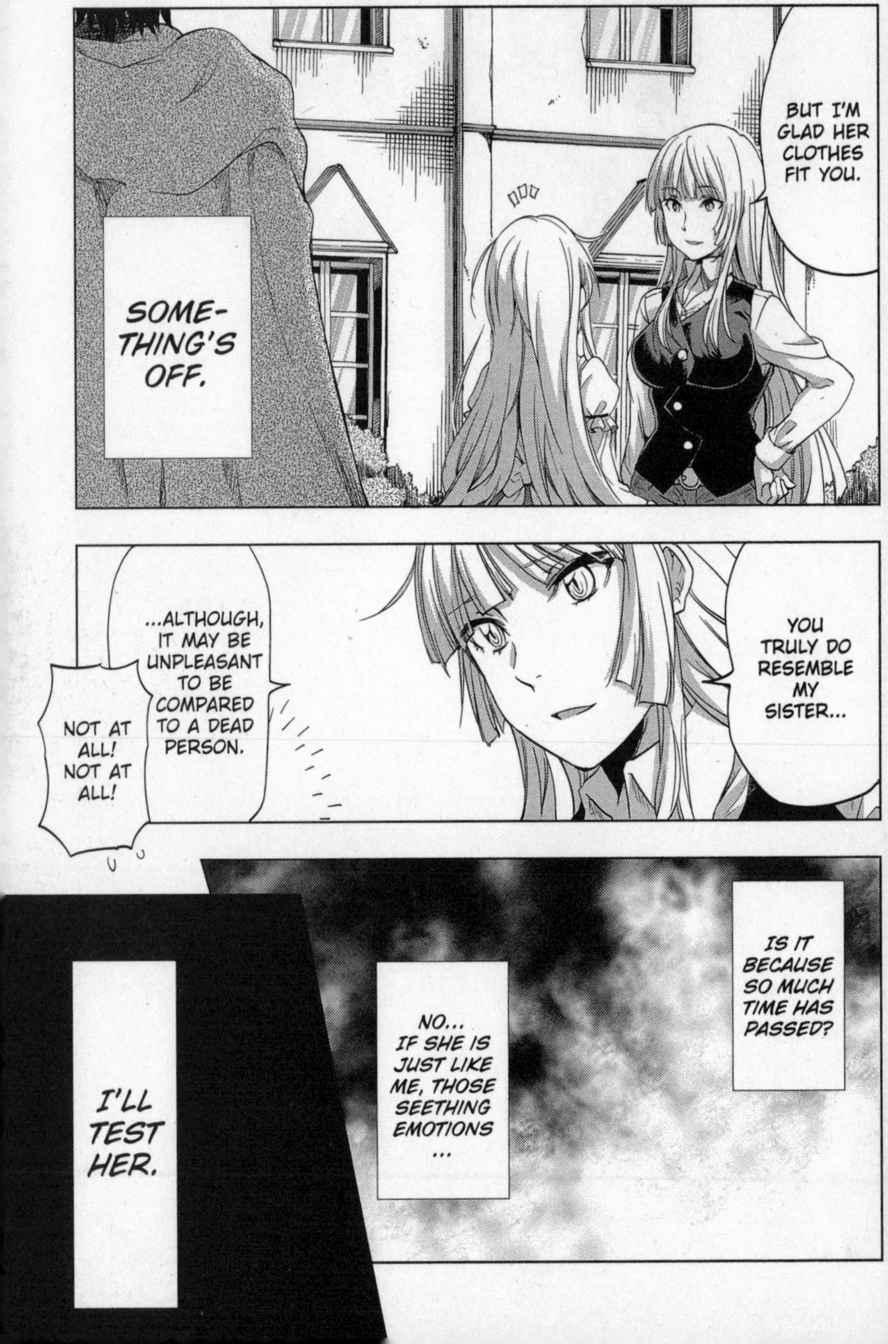
BUT I'M GLAD HER CLOTHES FIT YOU.
SOME-THING'S OFF.
YOU TRULY DO RESEMBLE MY SISTER...
...ALTHOUGH, IT MAY BE UNPLEASANT TO BE COMPARED TO A DEAD PERSON.
NOT AT ALL! NOT AT ALL!
IS IT BECAUSE SO MUCH TIME HAS PASSED?
NO... IF SHE IS JUST LIKE ME, THOSE SEETHING EMOTIONS ...
I'LL TEST HER.

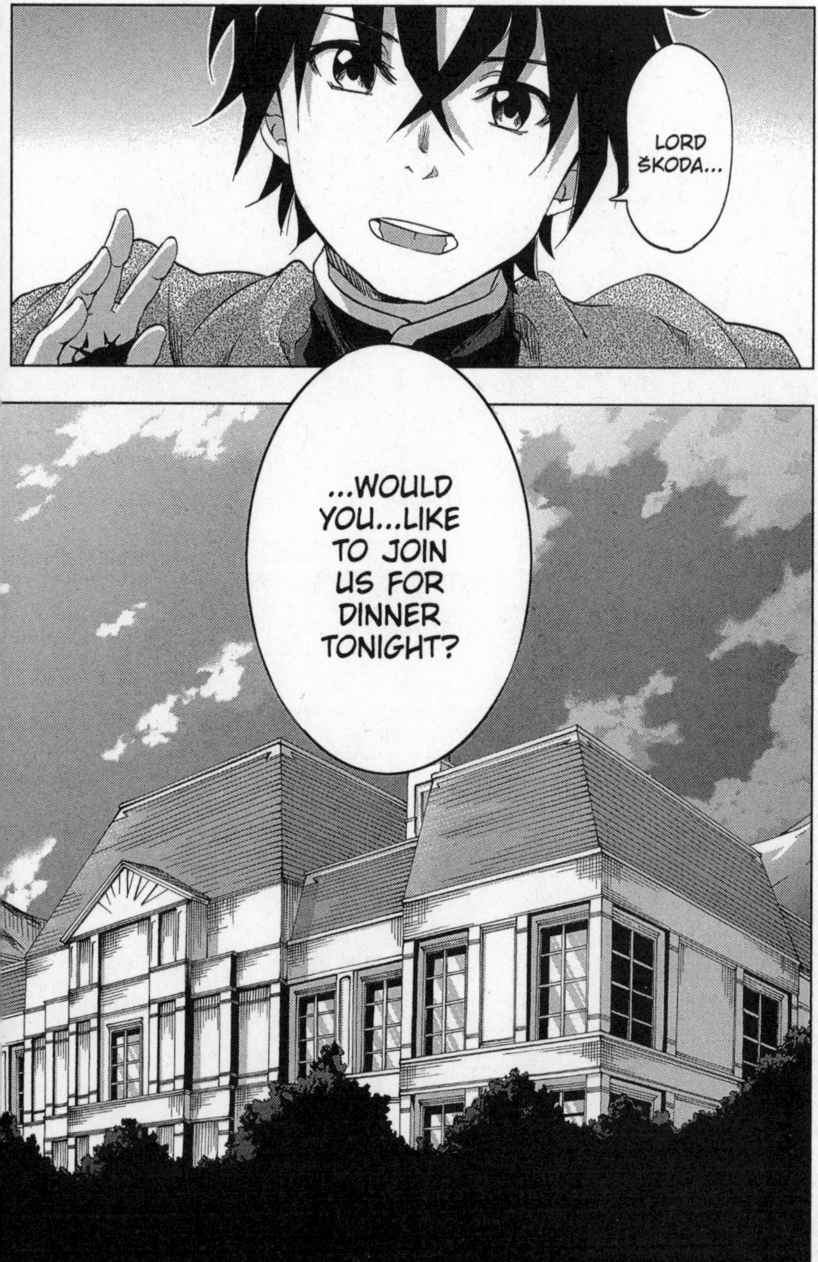
LORD ŠKODA...
...WOULD YOU...LIKE TO JOIN US FOR DINNER TONIGHT?

episode 22: END

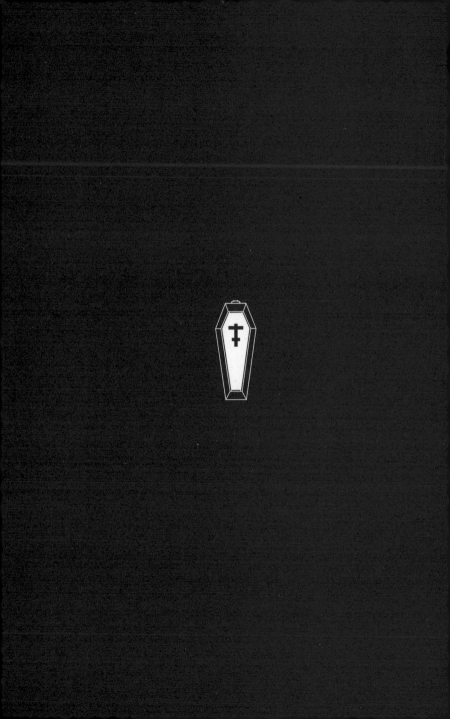

CHAIKA: THE COFFIN PRINCESS

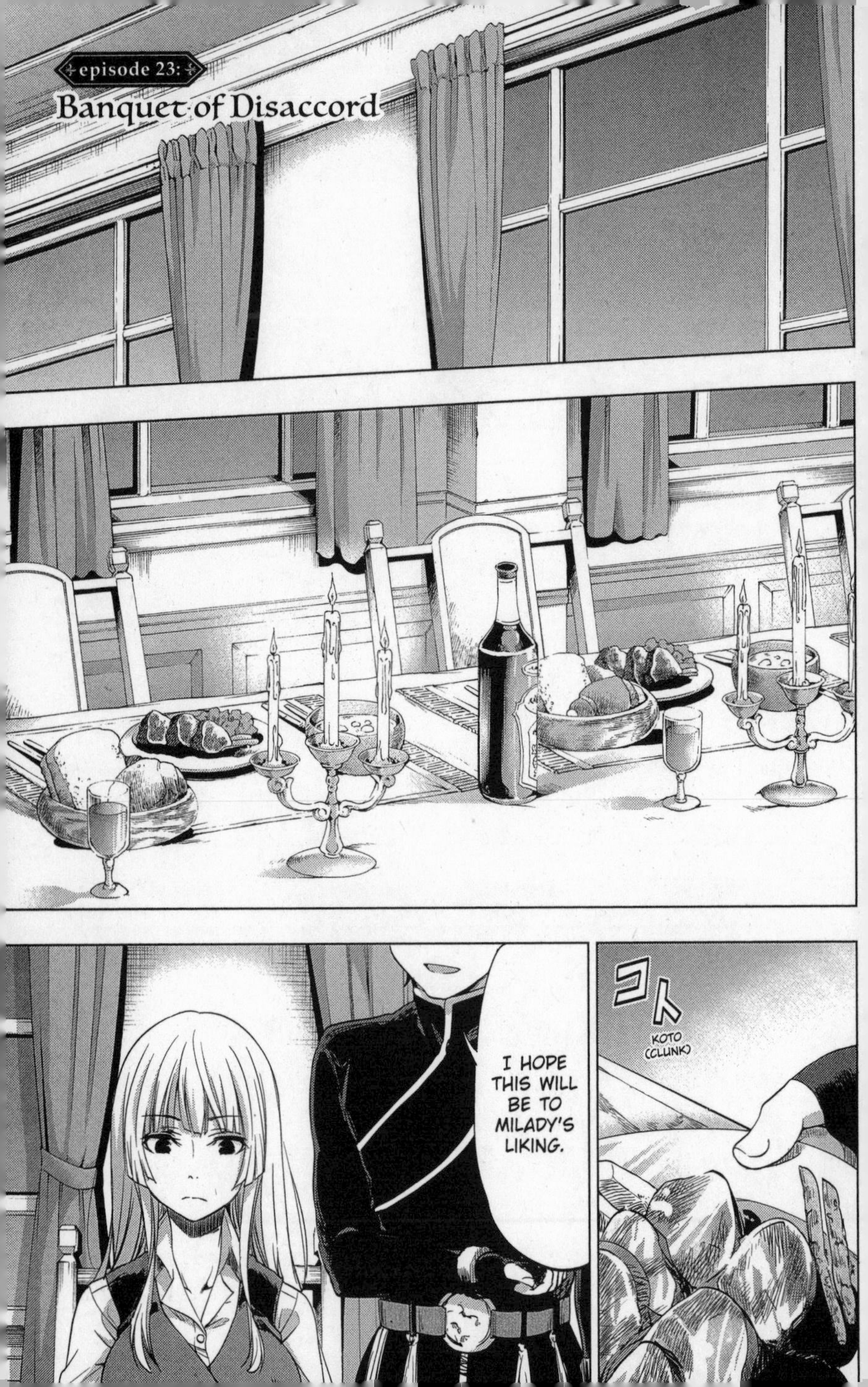
episode 23:
Banquet of Disaccord
コト
KOTO (CLUNK)
I HOPE THIS WILL BE TO MILADY'S LIKING.

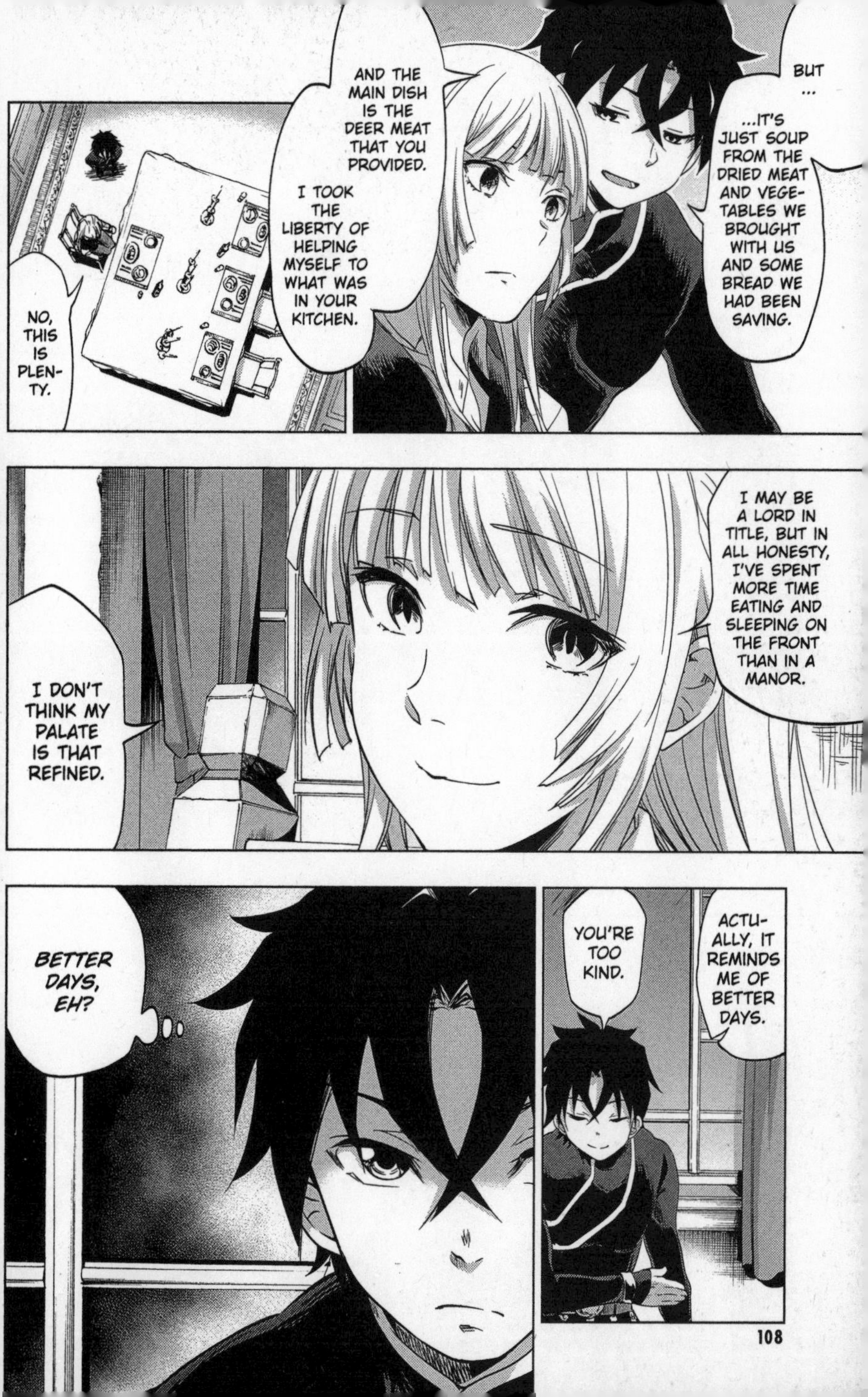
BUT ...
...IT'S JUST SOUP FROM THE DRIED MEAT AND VEGE-TABLES WE BROUGHT WITH US AND SOME BREAD WE HAD BEEN SAVING.
AND THE MAIN DISH IS THE DEER MEAT THAT YOU PROVIDED.
I TOOK THE LIBERTY OF HELPING MYSELF TO WHAT WAS IN YOUR KITCHEN.
NO, THIS IS PLEN-TY.
I MAY BE A LORD IN TITLE, BUT IN ALL HONESTY, I'VE SPENT MORE TIME EATING AND SLEEPING ON THE FRONT THAN IN A MANOR.
I DON'T THINK MY PALATE IS THAT REFINED.
ACTU-ALLY, IT REMINDS ME OF BETTER DAYS.
YOU'RE TOO KIND.
BETTER DAYS, EH?

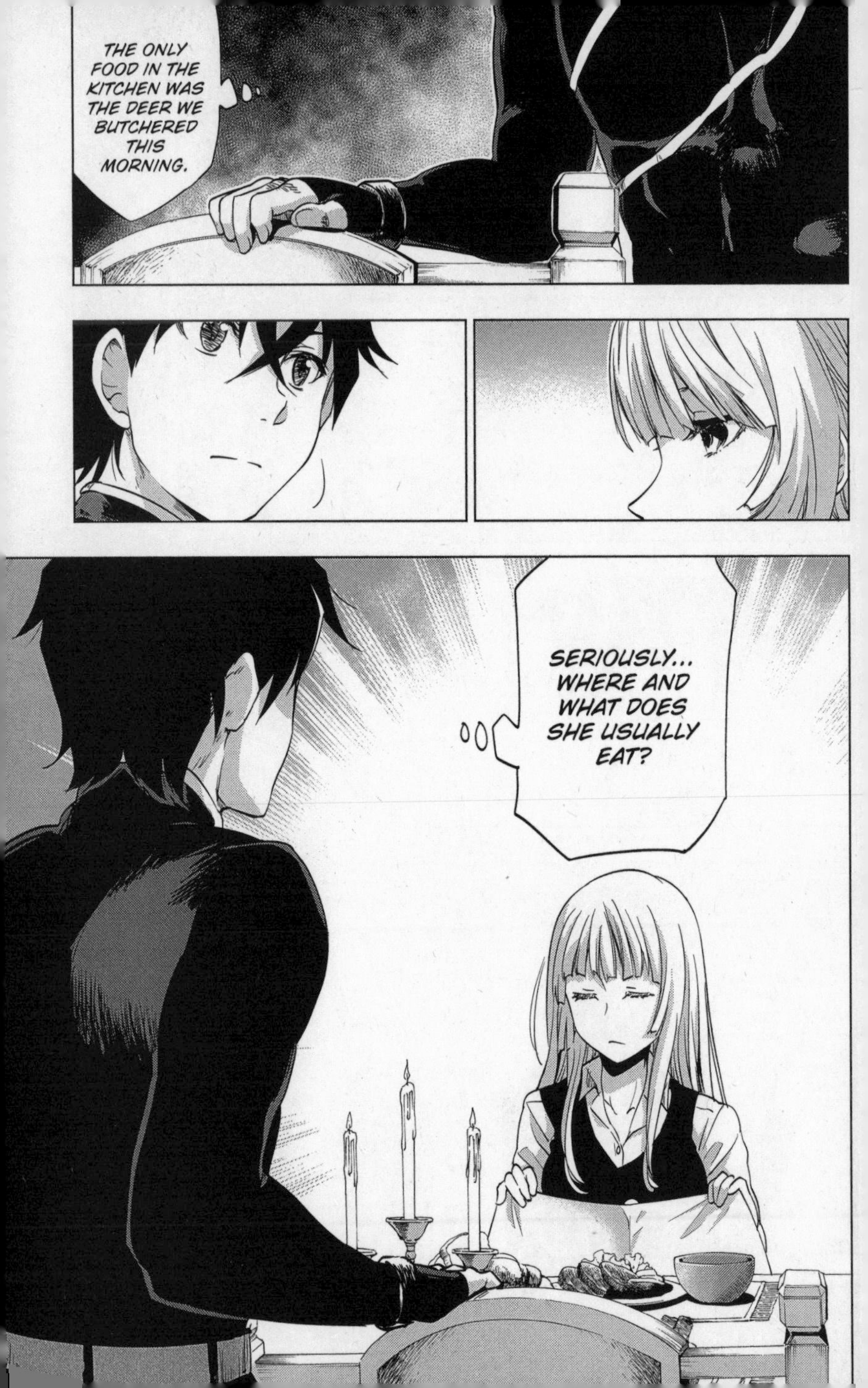
THE ONLY FOOD IN THE KITCHEN WAS THE DEER WE BUTCHERED THIS MORNING.
SERIOUSLY... WHERE AND WHAT DOES SHE USUALLY EAT?

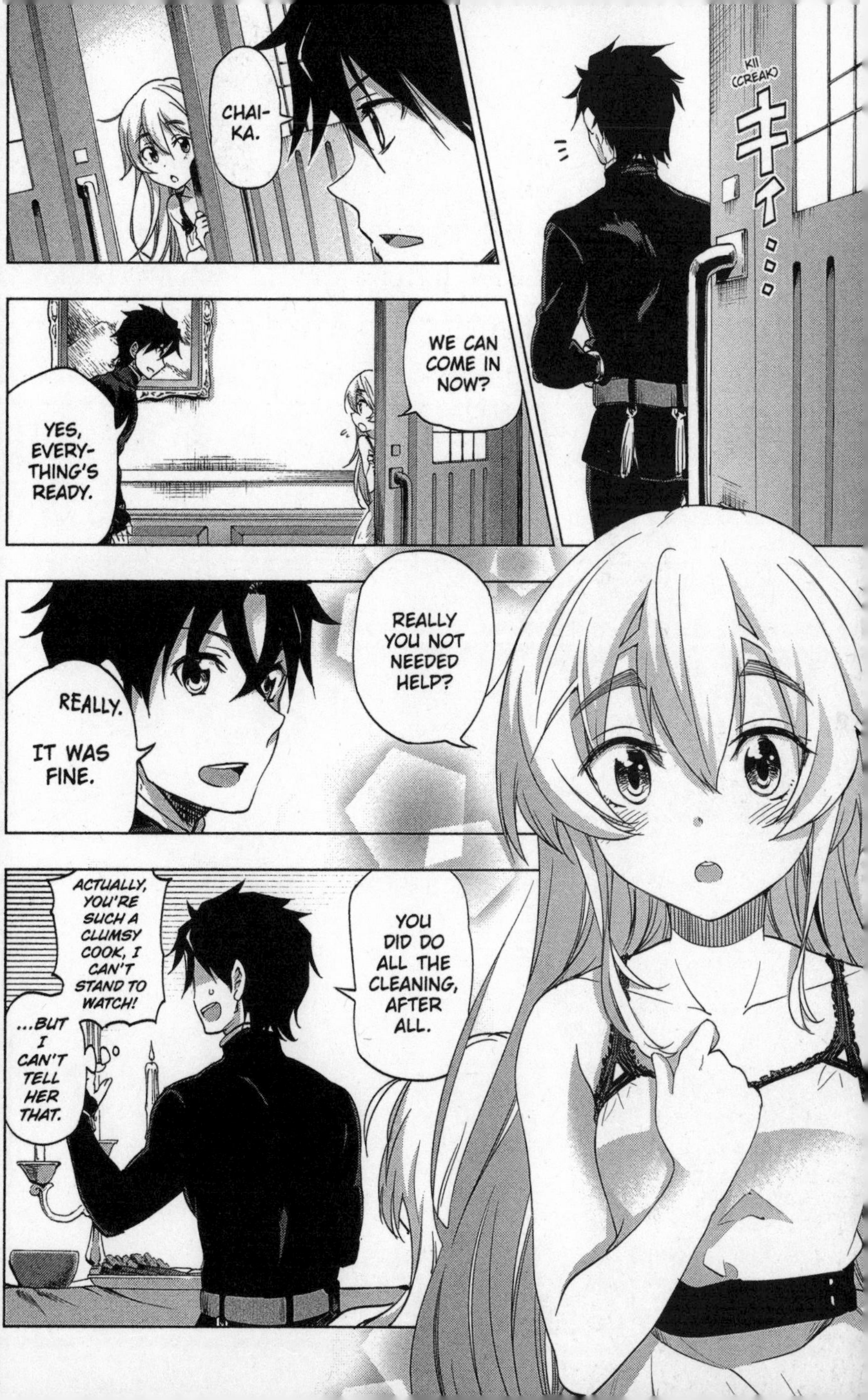
KII (CREAK)
キィ
CHAI-KA.
WE CAN COME IN NOW?
YES, EVERYTHING'S READY.
REALLY YOU NOT NEEDED HELP?
REALLY.
IT WAS FINE.
YOU DID DO ALL THE CLEANING, AFTER ALL.
ACTUALLY, YOU'RE SUCH A CLUMSY COOK, I CAN'T STAND TO WATCH!
...BUT I CAN'T TELL HER THAT.

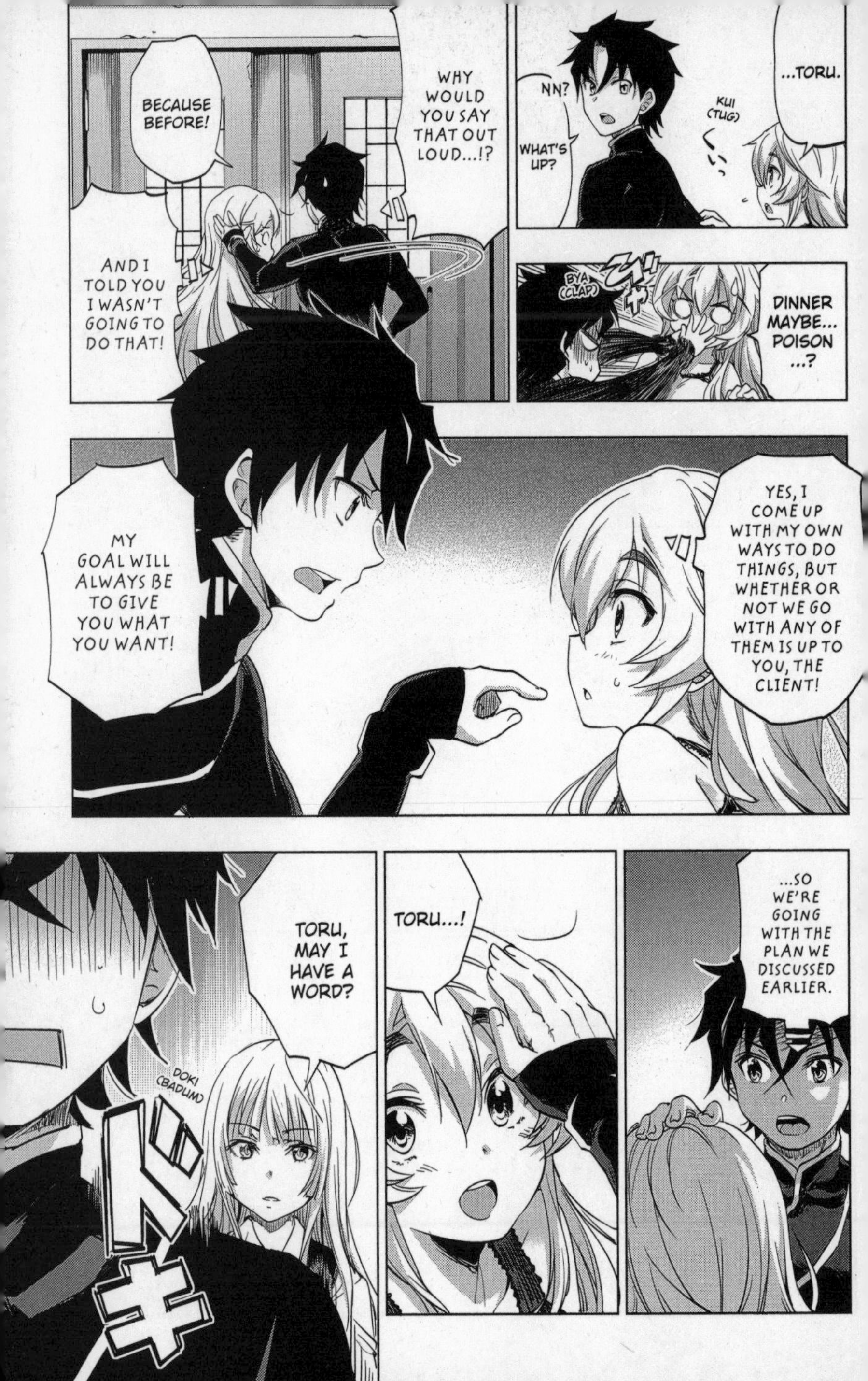
...TORU.
KUI (TUG)
NN?
WHAT'S UP?
DINNER MAYBE... POISON ...?
BYA (CLAP)
WHY WOULD YOU SAY THAT OUT LOUD...!?
BECAUSE BEFORE!
AND I TOLD YOU I WASN'T GOING TO DO THAT!
YES, I COME UP WITH MY OWN WAYS TO DO THINGS, BUT WHETHER OR NOT WE GO WITH ANY OF THEM IS UP TO YOU, THE CLIENT!
MY GOAL WILL ALWAYS BE TO GIVE YOU WHAT YOU WANT!
...SO WE'RE GOING WITH THE PLAN WE DISCUSSED EARLIER.
TORU...!
TORU, MAY I HAVE A WORD?
DOKI (BADUM)

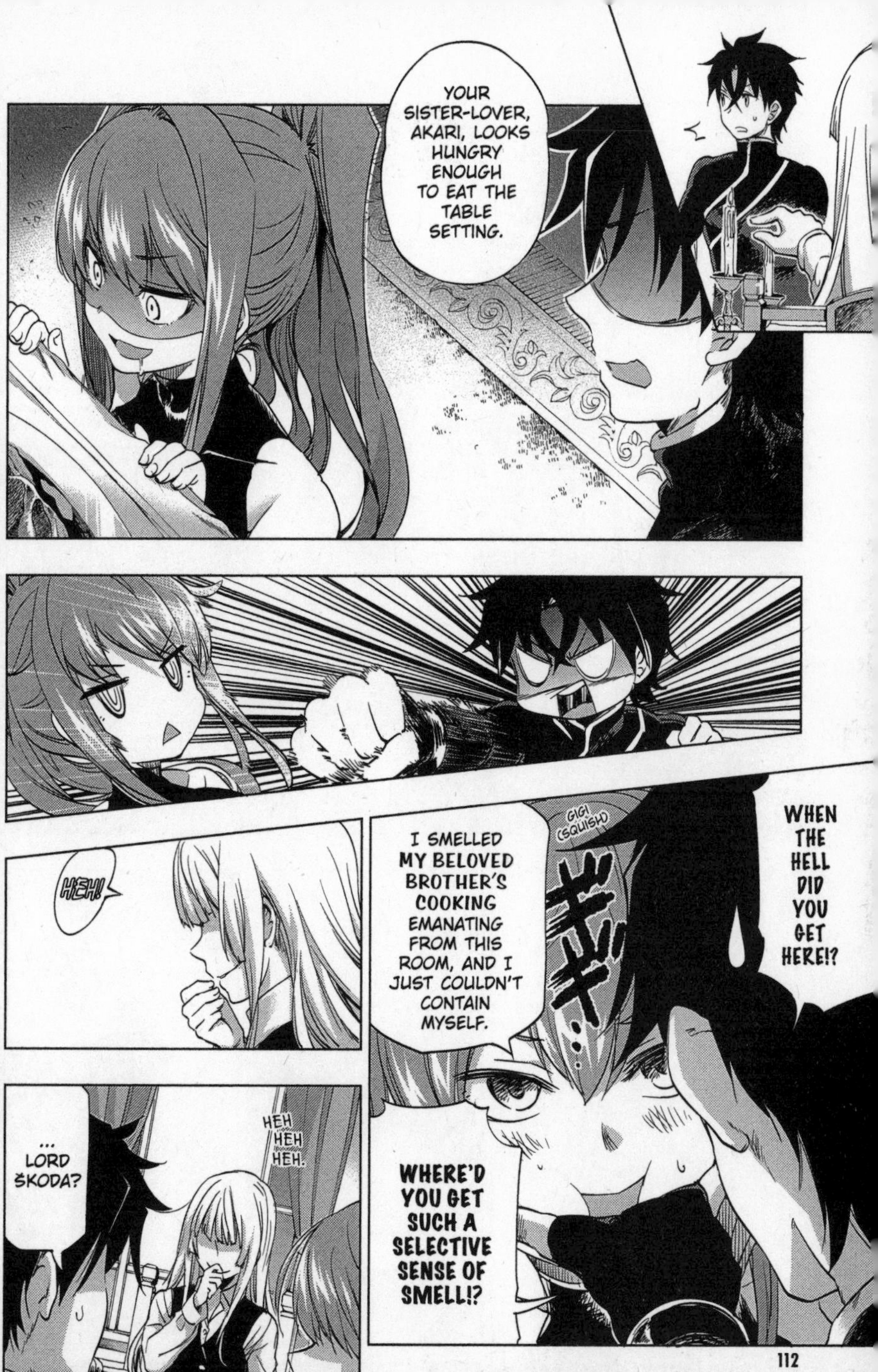
YOUR SISTER-LOVER, AKARI, LOOKS HUNGRY ENOUGH TO EAT THE TABLE SETTING.
WHEN THE HELL DID YOU GET HERE!?
GIGI (SQUISH)
I SMELLED MY BELOVED BROTHER'S COOKING EMANATING FROM THIS ROOM, AND I JUST COULDN'T CONTAIN MYSELF.
WHERE'D YOU GET SUCH A SELECTIVE SENSE OF SMELL!?
HEH!
HEH HEH HEH.
... LORD ŠKODA?

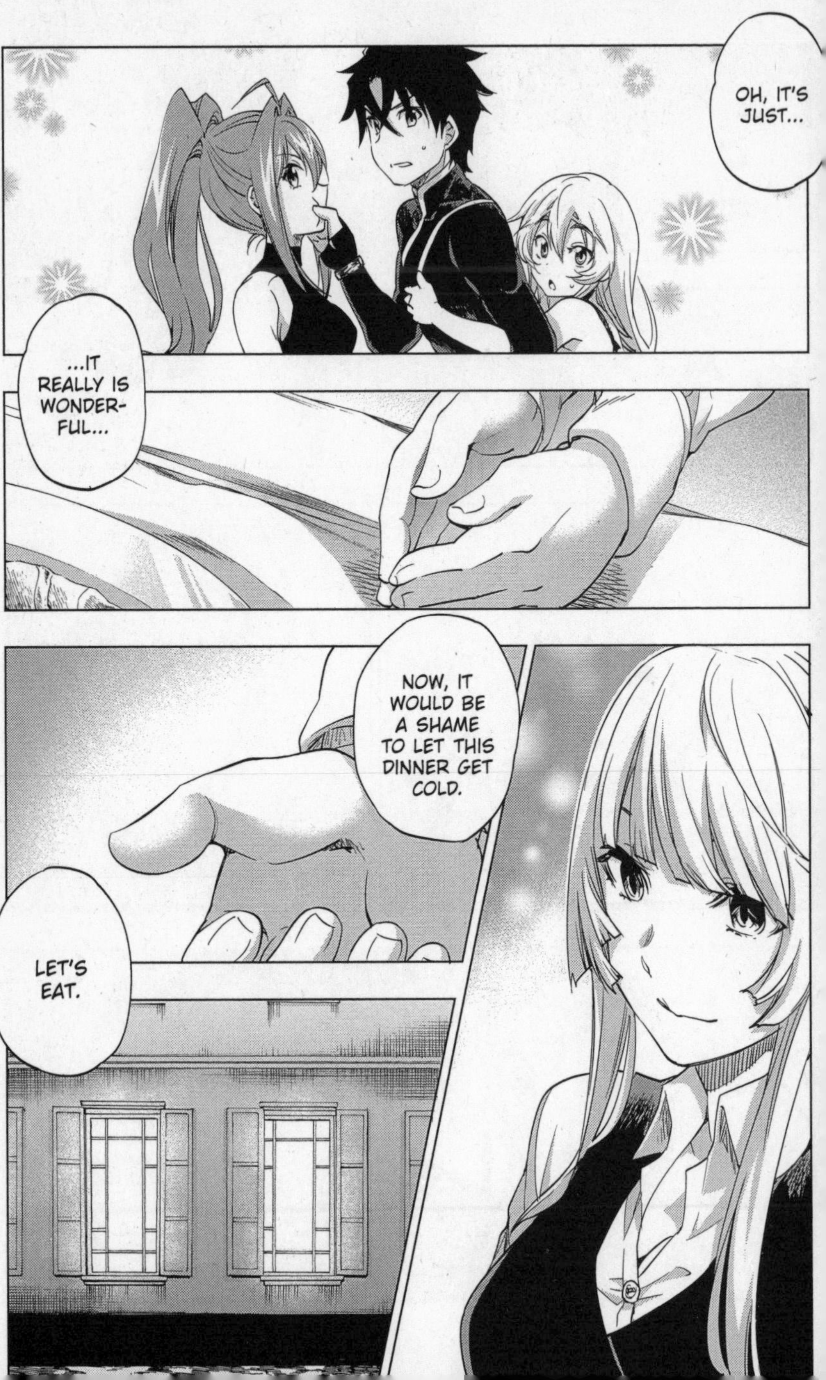
OH, IT'S JUST...
...IT REALLY IS WONDERFUL...
NOW, IT WOULD BE A SHAME TO LET THIS DINNER GET COLD.
LET'S EAT.

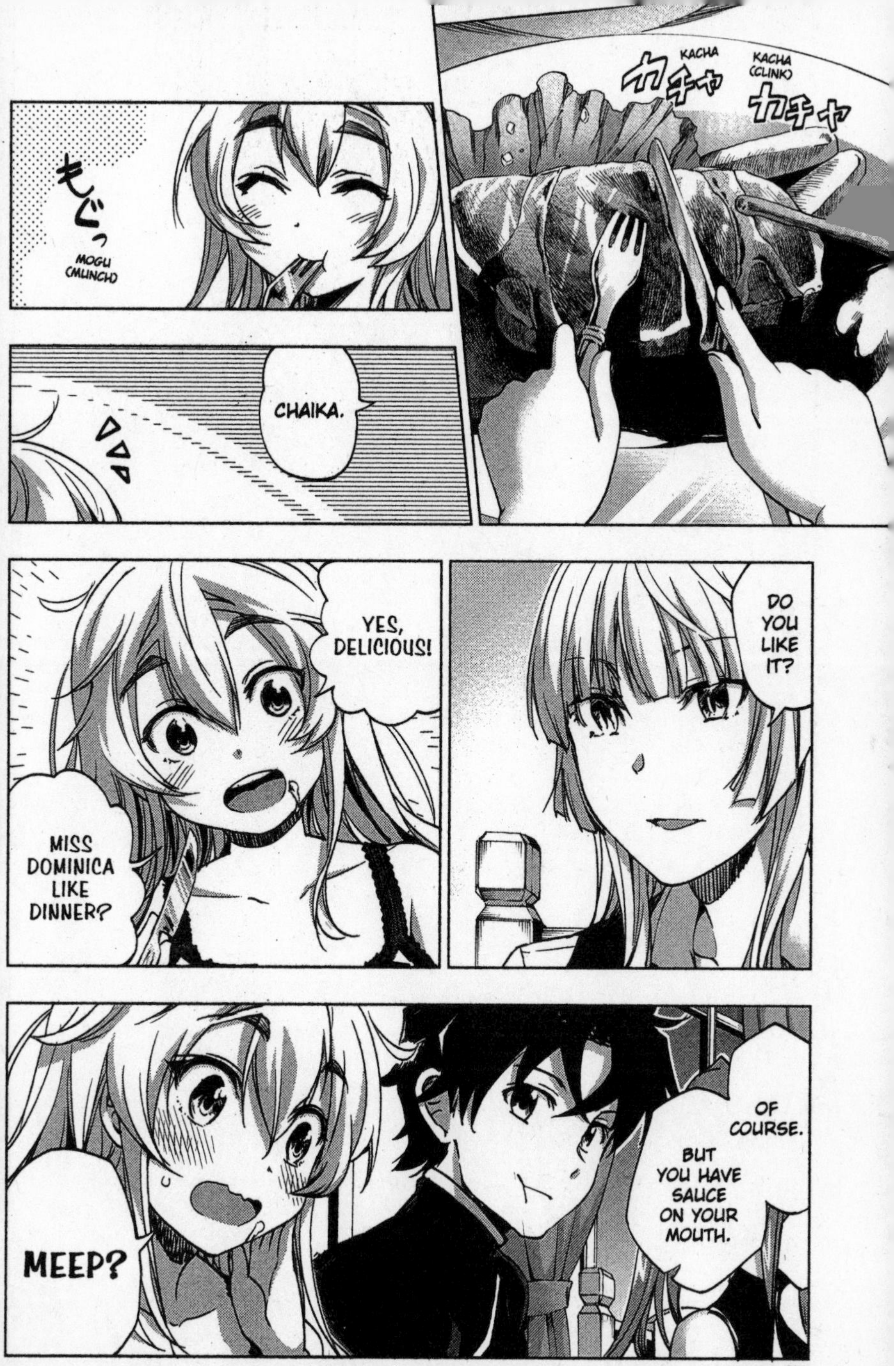
カチャ
KACHA
カチャ
KACHA (CLINK)
もぐっ
MOGU (MUNCH)
CHAIKA.
DO YOU LIKE IT?
YES, DELICIOUS!
MISS DOMINICA LIKE DINNER?
OF COURSE.
BUT YOU HAVE SAUCE ON YOUR MOUTH.
MEEP?

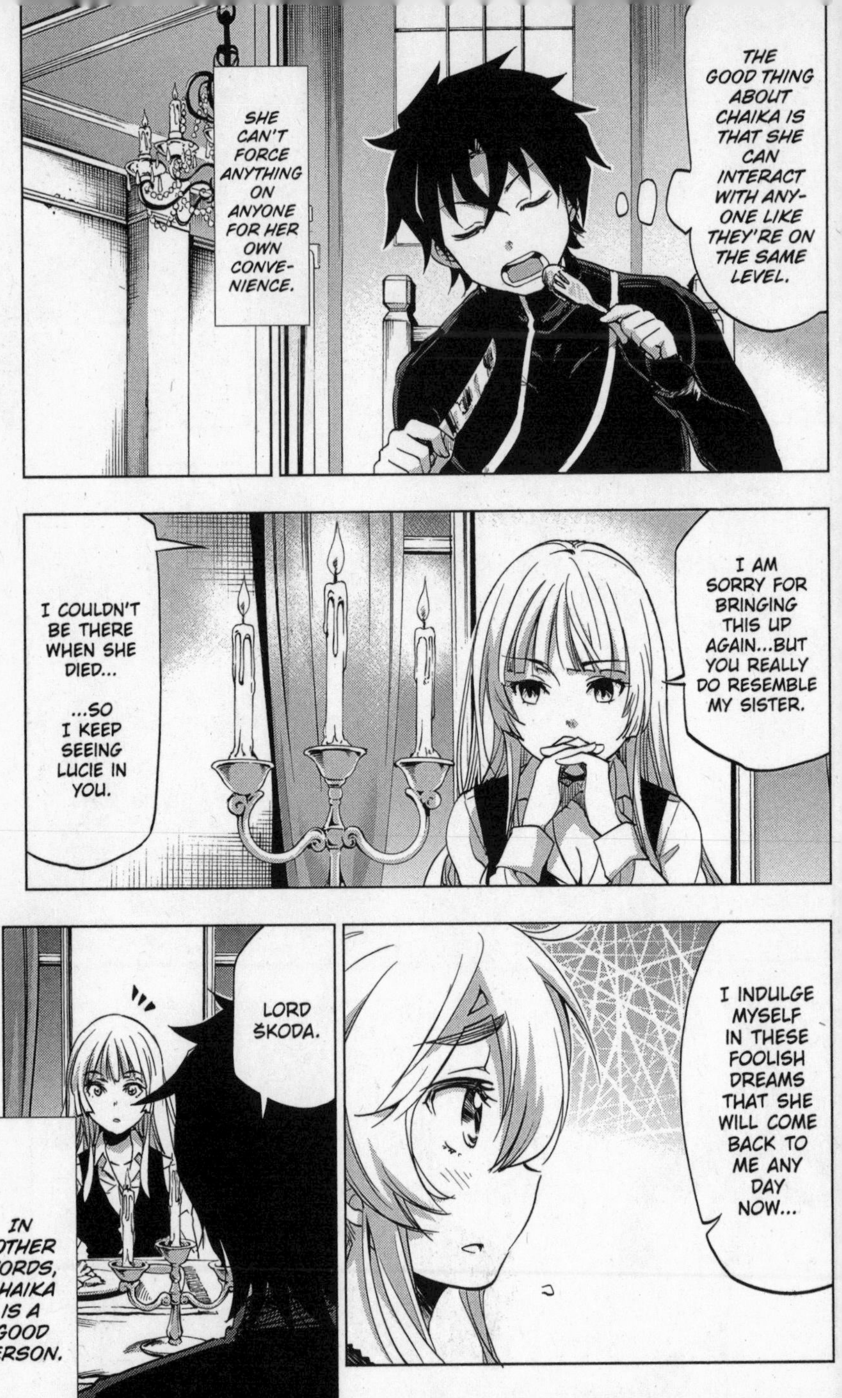
THE GOOD THING ABOUT CHAIKA IS THAT SHE CAN INTERACT WITH ANY-ONE LIKE THEY'RE ON THE SAME LEVEL.
SHE CAN'T FORCE ANYTHING ON ANYONE FOR HER OWN CONVE-NIENCE.
I AM SORRY FOR BRINGING THIS UP AGAIN...BUT YOU REALLY DO RESEMBLE MY SISTER.
I COULDN'T BE THERE WHEN SHE DIED...
...SO I KEEP SEEING LUCIE IN YOU.
I INDULGE MYSELF IN THESE FOOLISH DREAMS THAT SHE WILL COME BACK TO ME ANY DAY NOW...
LORD ŠKODA.
IN OTHER WORDS, CHAIKA IS A GOOD PERSON.

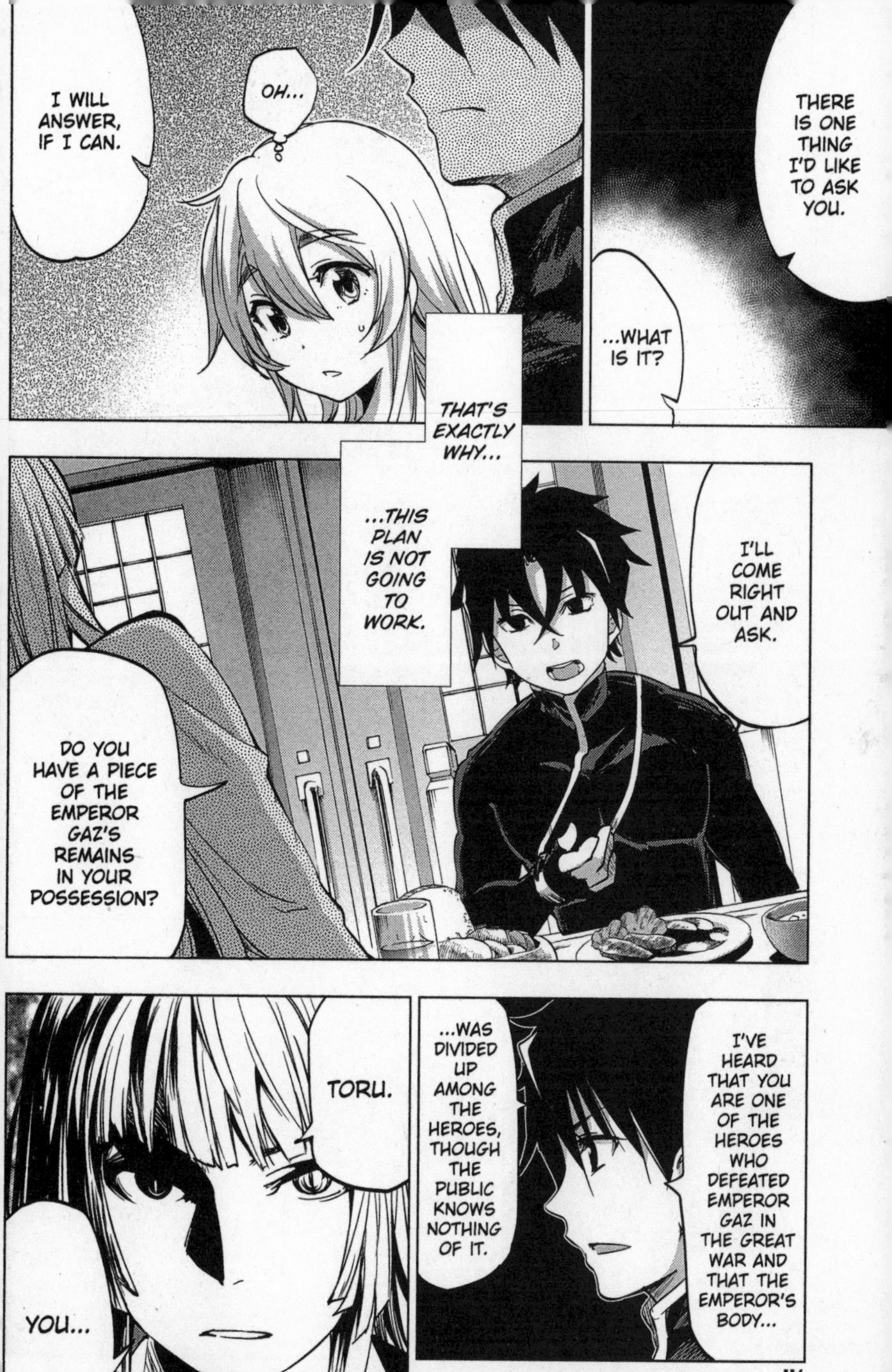
THERE IS ONE THING I'D LIKE TO ASK YOU.
...WHAT IS IT?
OH...
I WILL ANSWER, IF I CAN.
THAT'S EXACTLY WHY...
...THIS PLAN IS NOT GOING TO WORK.
I'LL COME RIGHT OUT AND ASK.
DO YOU HAVE A PIECE OF THE EMPEROR GAZ'S REMAINS IN YOUR POSSESSION?
I'VE HEARD THAT YOU ARE ONE OF THE HEROES WHO DEFEATED EMPEROR GAZ IN THE GREAT WAR AND THAT THE EMPEROR'S BODY...
...WAS DIVIDED UP AMONG THE HEROES, THOUGH THE PUBLIC KNOWS NOTHING OF IT.
TORU.
YOU...

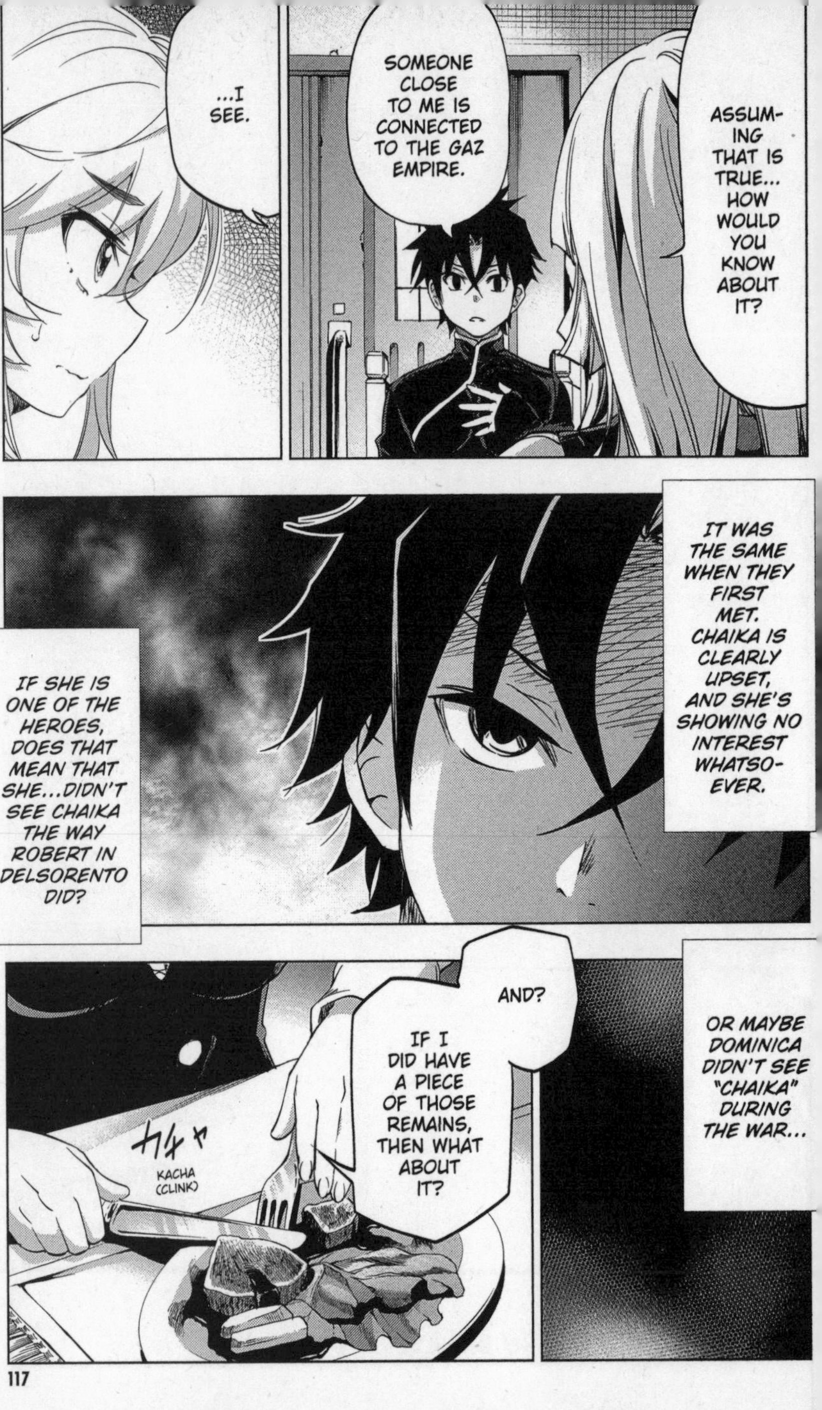
ASSUMING THAT IS TRUE... HOW WOULD YOU KNOW ABOUT IT?
SOMEONE CLOSE TO ME IS CONNECTED TO THE GAZ EMPIRE.
...I SEE.
IT WAS THE SAME WHEN THEY FIRST MET. CHAIKA IS CLEARLY UPSET, AND SHE'S SHOWING NO INTEREST WHATSOEVER.
IF SHE IS ONE OF THE HEROES, DOES THAT MEAN THAT SHE...DIDN'T SEE CHAIKA THE WAY ROBERT IN DELSORENTO DID?
OR MAYBE DOMINICA DIDN'T SEE "CHAIKA" DURING THE WAR...
AND?
IF I DID HAVE A PIECE OF THOSE REMAINS, THEN WHAT ABOUT IT?
カチャ
KACHA (CLINK)

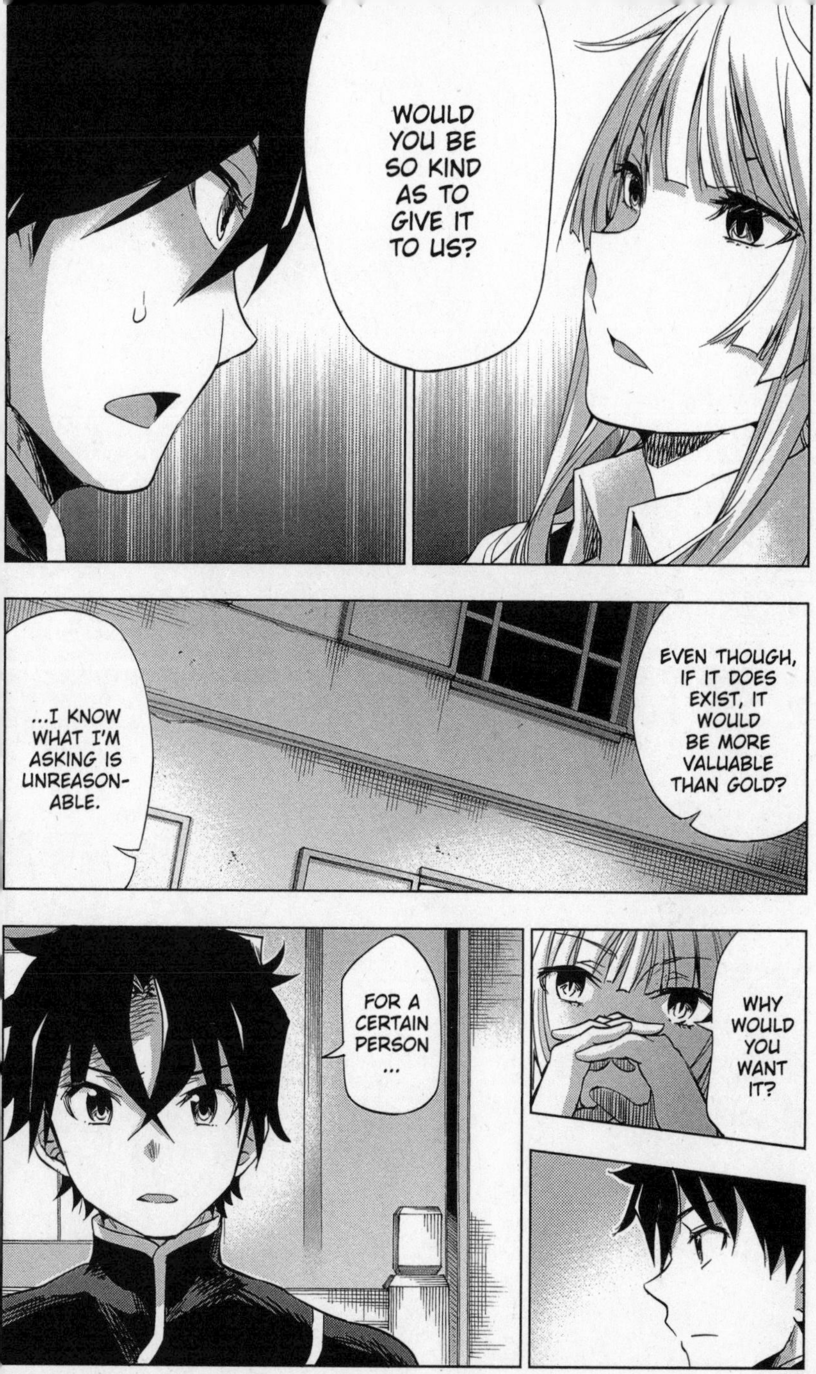
WOULD YOU BE SO KIND AS TO GIVE IT TO US?
EVEN THOUGH, IF IT DOES EXIST, IT WOULD BE MORE VALUABLE THAN GOLD?
...I KNOW WHAT I'M ASKING IS UNREASON-ABLE.
WHY WOULD YOU WANT IT?
FOR A CERTAIN PERSON ...

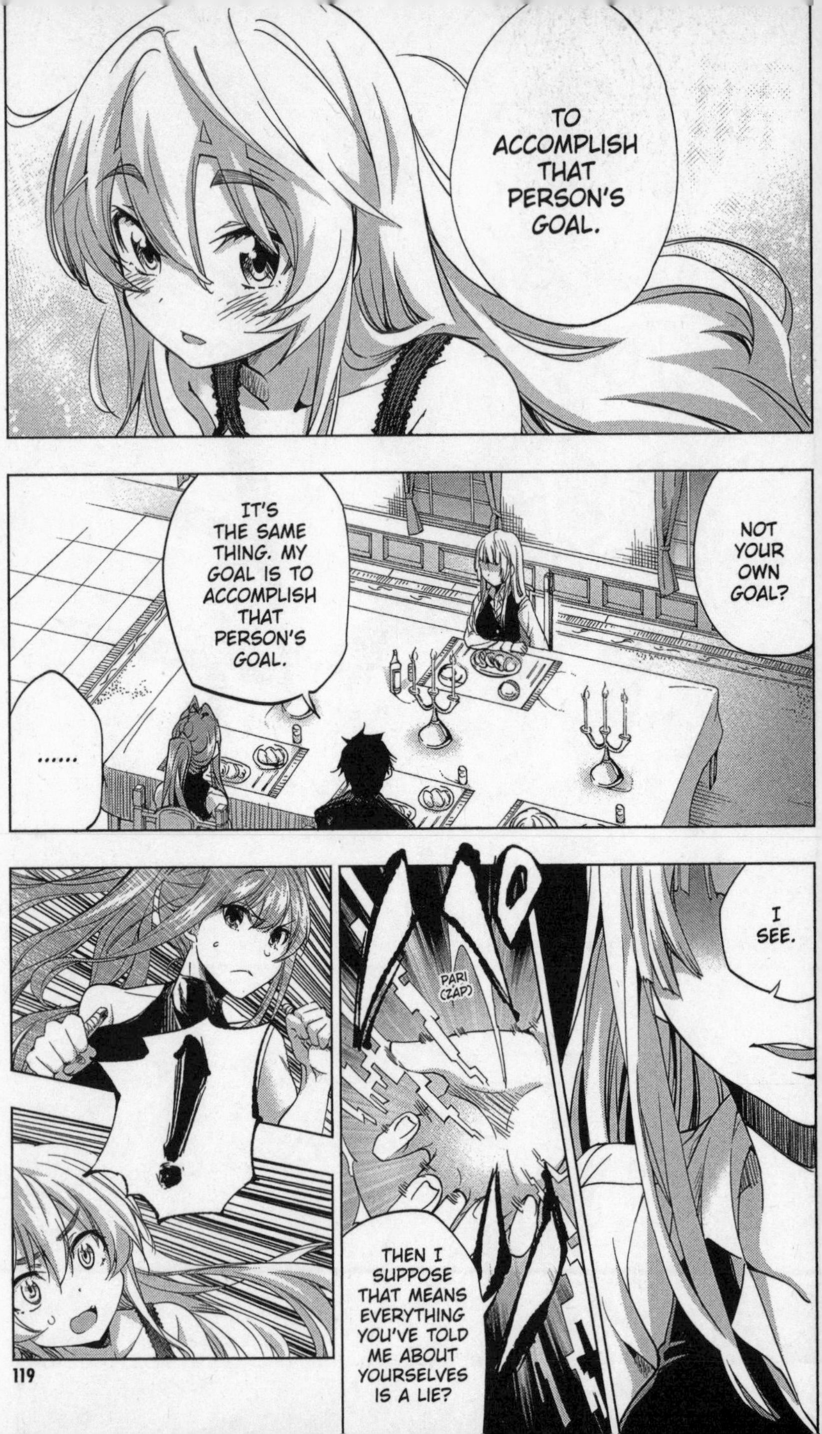
TO ACCOMPLISH THAT PERSON'S GOAL.
NOT YOUR OWN GOAL?
IT'S THE SAME THING. MY GOAL IS TO ACCOMPLISH THAT PERSON'S GOAL.
......
I SEE.
PARI (ZAP)
THEN I SUPPOSE THAT MEANS EVERYTHING YOU'VE TOLD ME ABOUT YOURSELVES IS A LIE?
!

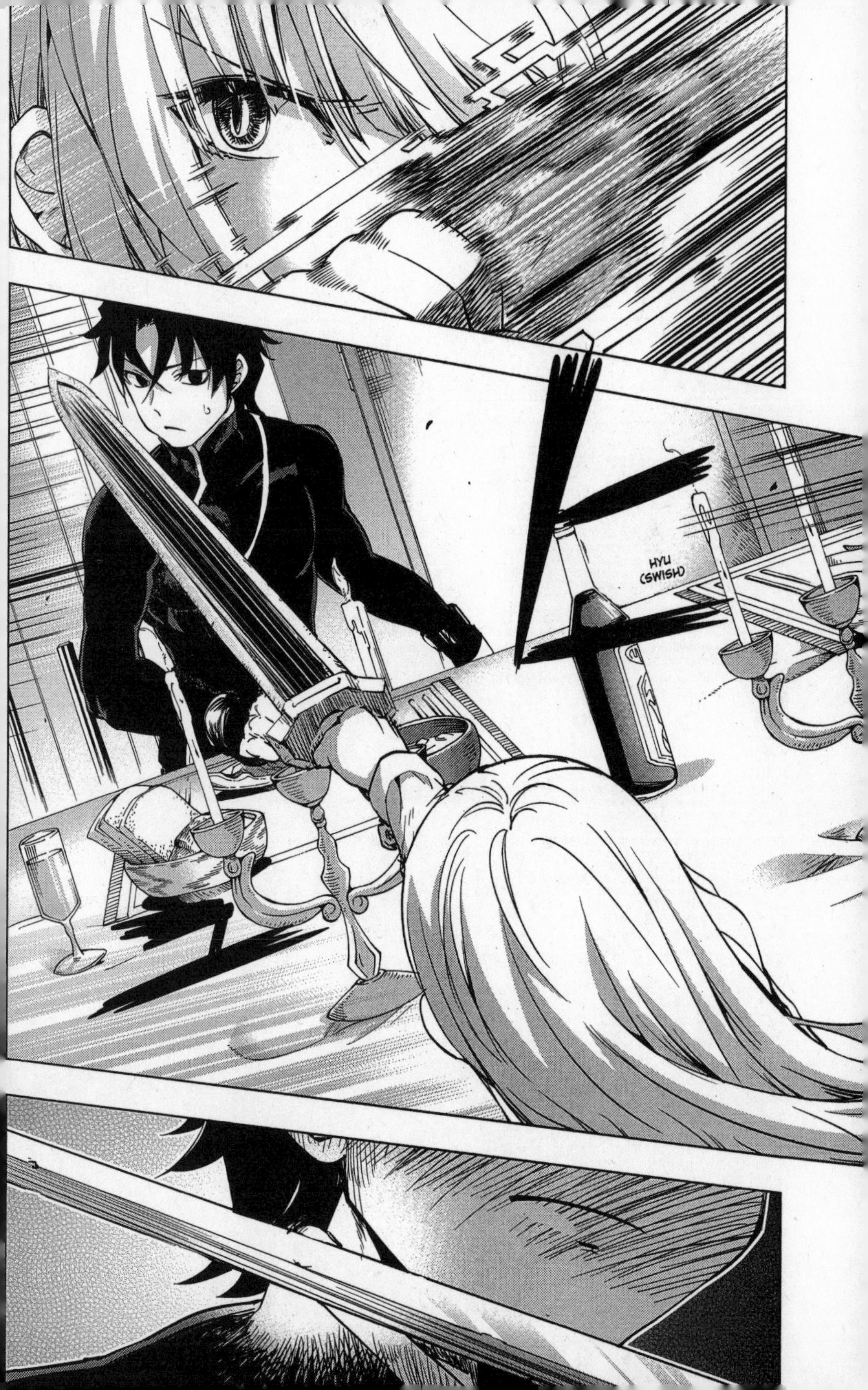
HYU
(SWISH)

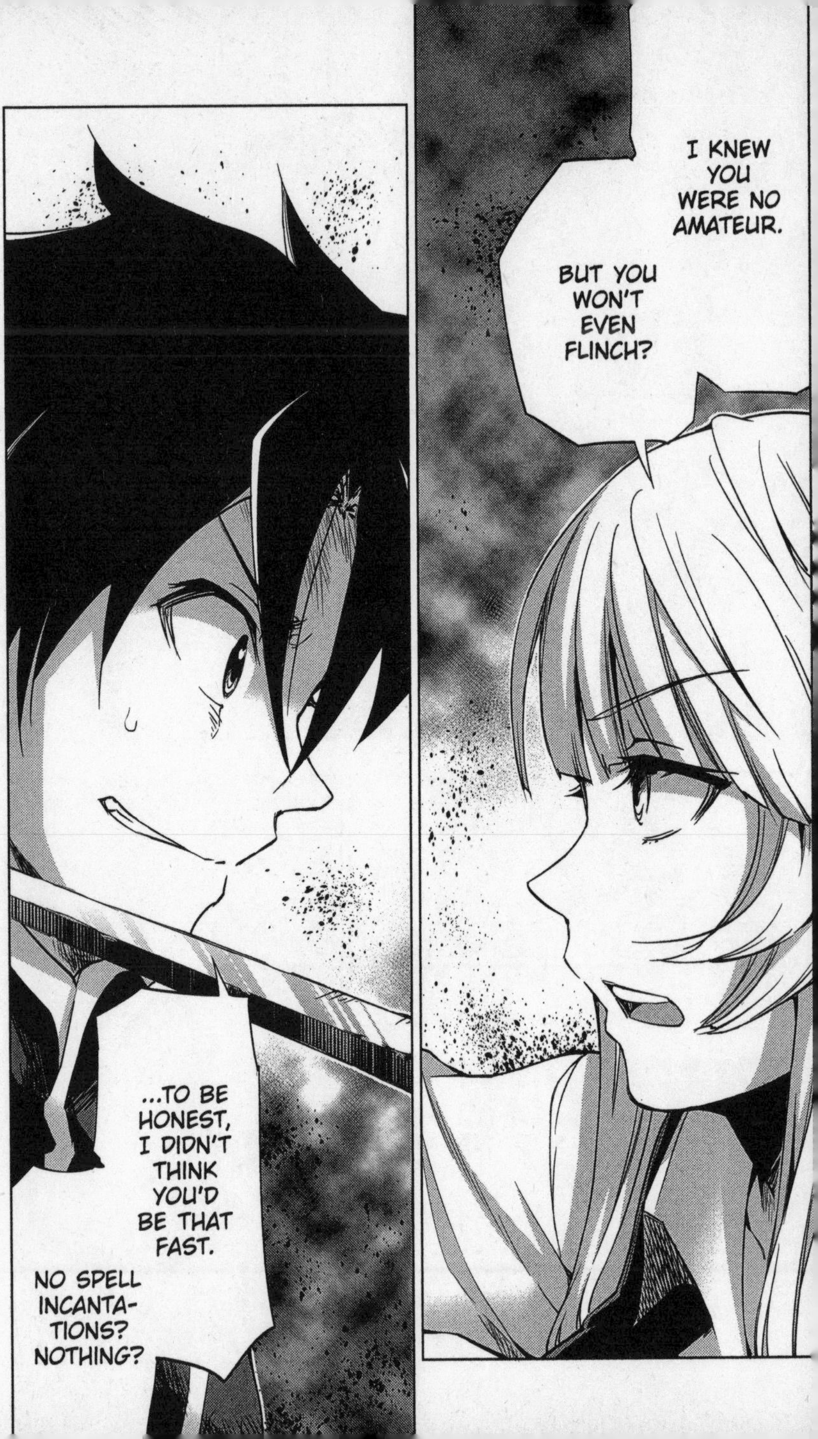
I KNEW YOU WERE NO AMATEUR.
BUT YOU WON'T EVEN FLINCH?
...TO BE HONEST, I DIDN'T THINK YOU'D BE THAT FAST.
NO SPELL INCANTA-TIONS? NOTHING?

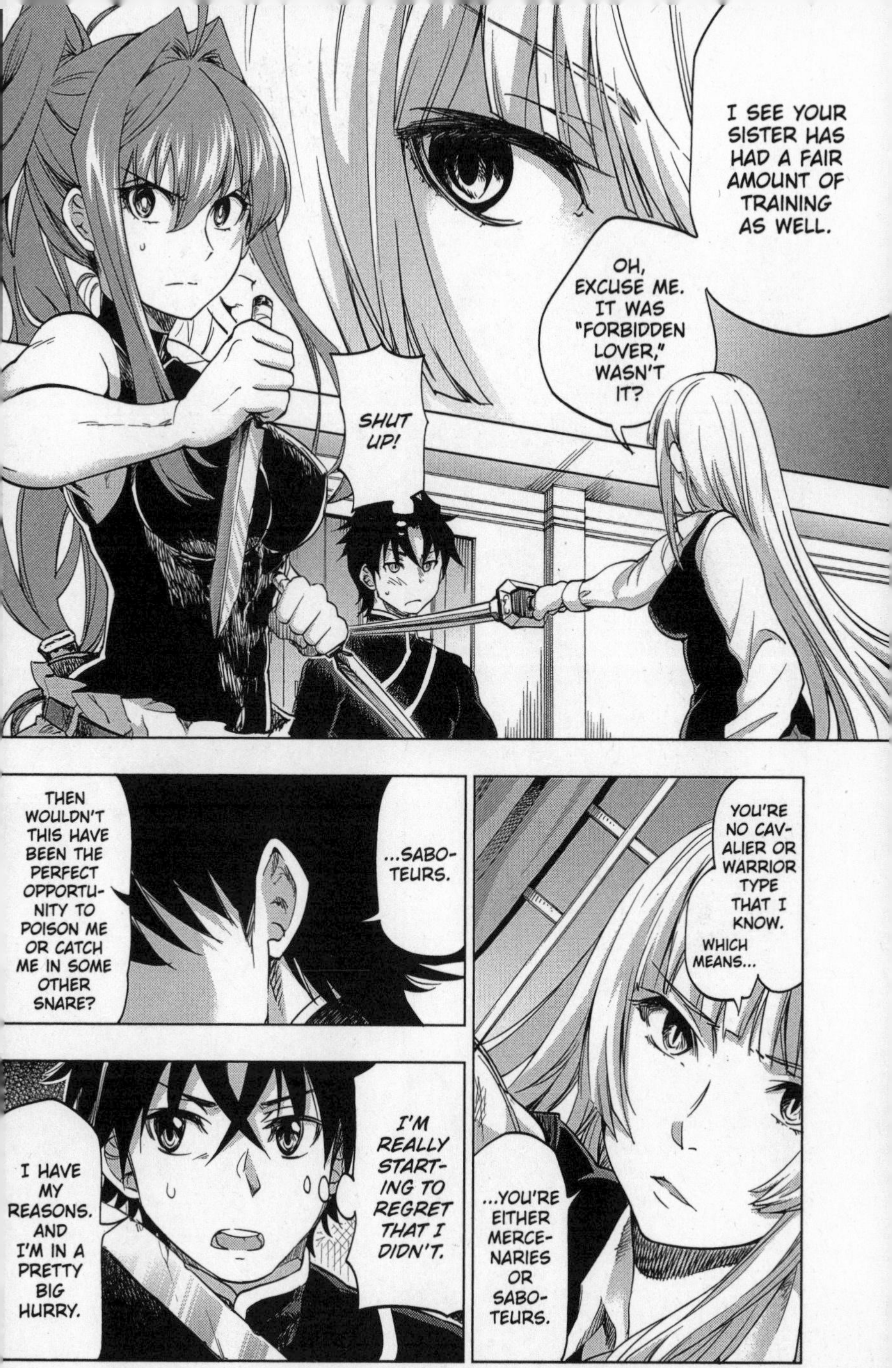
I SEE YOUR SISTER HAS HAD A FAIR AMOUNT OF TRAINING AS WELL.
OH, EXCUSE ME. IT WAS "FORBIDDEN LOVER," WASN'T IT?
SHUT UP!
YOU'RE NO CAVALIER OR WARRIOR TYPE THAT I KNOW.
WHICH MEANS...
...YOU'RE EITHER MERCENARIES OR SABOTEURS.
...SABOTEURS.
THEN WOULDN'T THIS HAVE BEEN THE PERFECT OPPORTUNITY TO POISON ME OR CATCH ME IN SOME OTHER SNARE?
I'M REALLY STARTING TO REGRET THAT I DIDN'T.
I HAVE MY REASONS. AND I'M IN A PRETTY BIG HURRY.

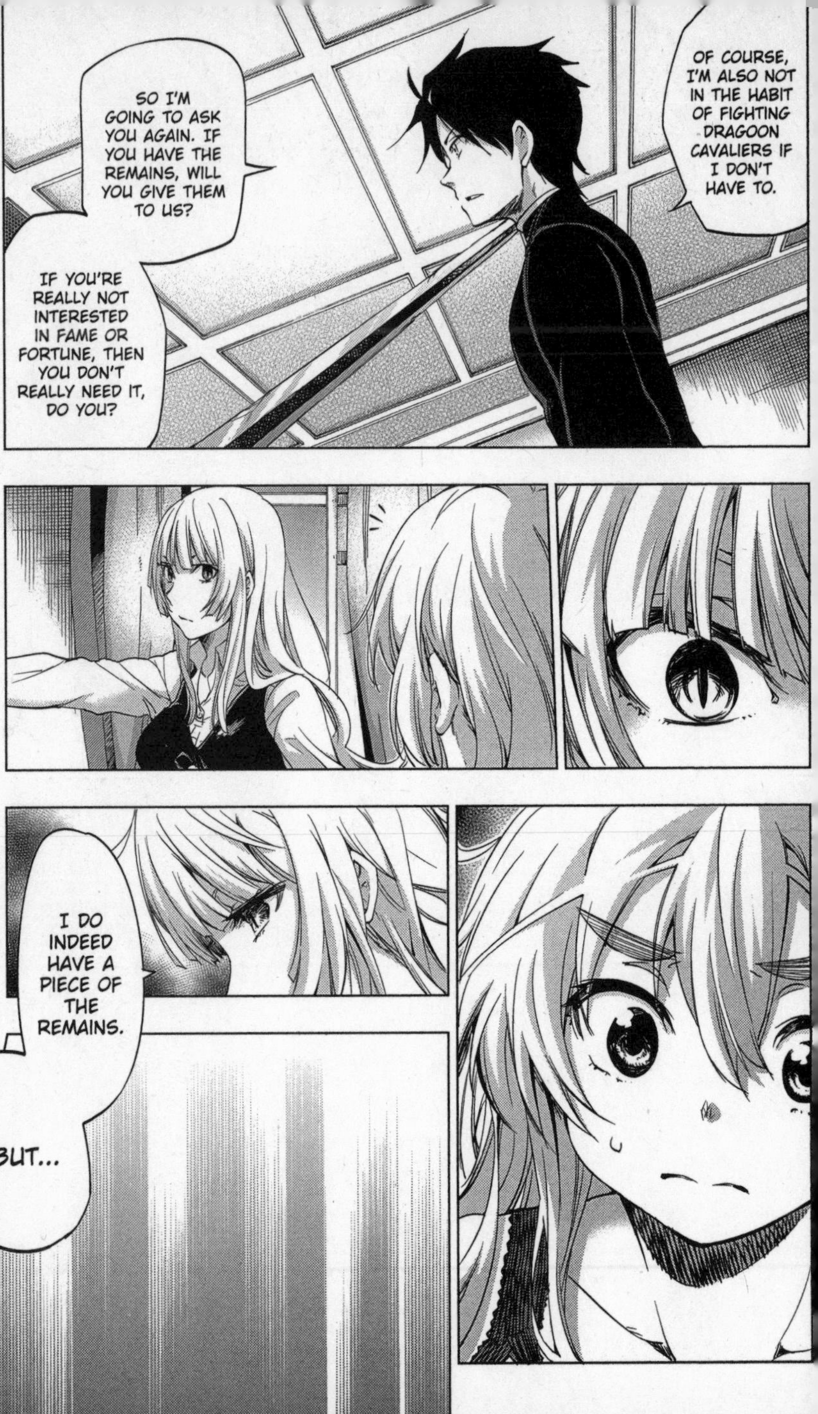
OF COURSE, I'M ALSO NOT IN THE HABIT OF FIGHTING DRAGOON CAVALIERS IF I DON'T HAVE TO.
SO I'M GOING TO ASK YOU AGAIN. IF YOU HAVE THE REMAINS, WILL YOU GIVE THEM TO US?
IF YOU'RE REALLY NOT INTERESTED IN FAME OR FORTUNE, THEN YOU DON'T REALLY NEED IT, DO YOU?
I DO INDEED HAVE A PIECE OF THE REMAINS.
BUT...

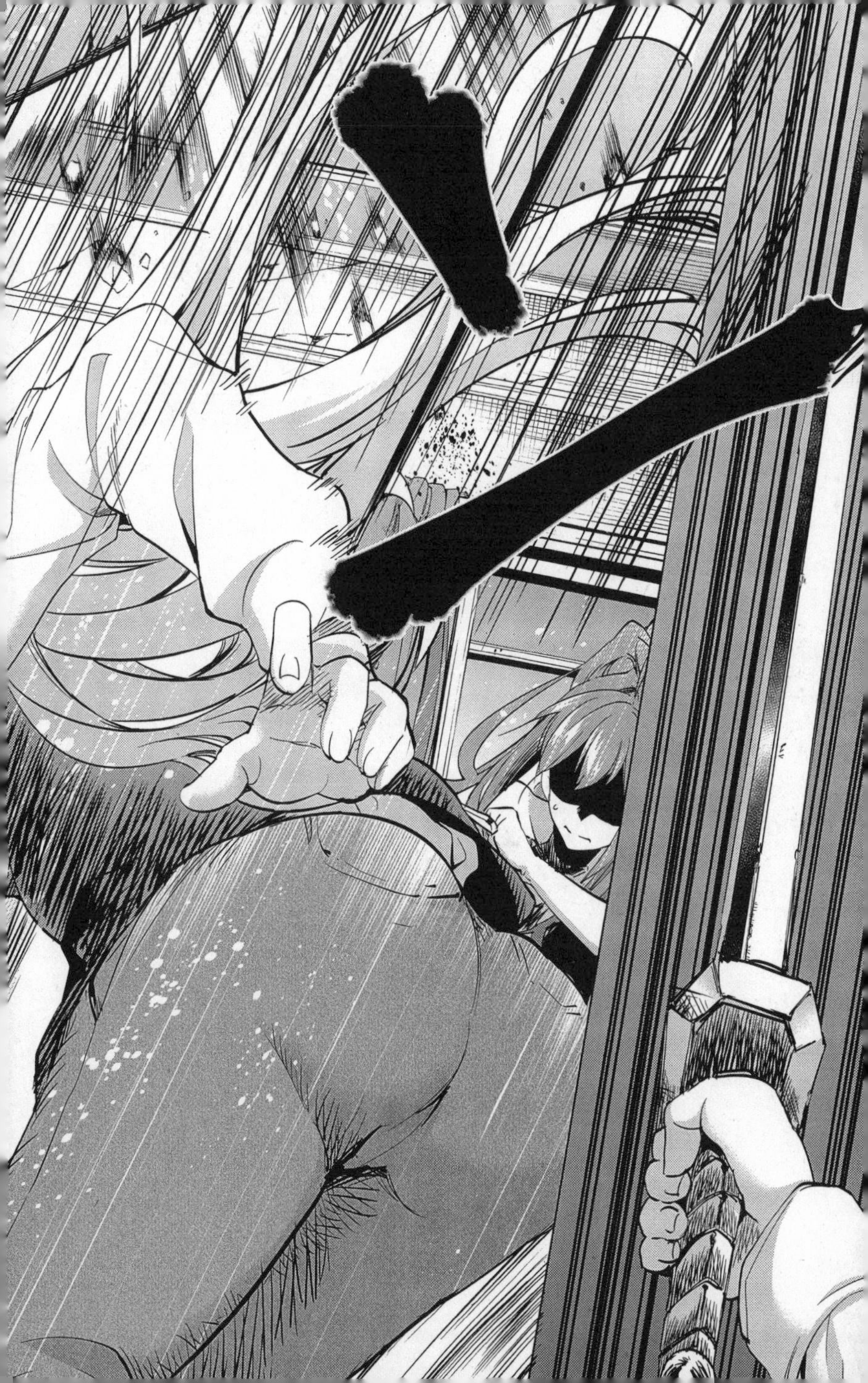

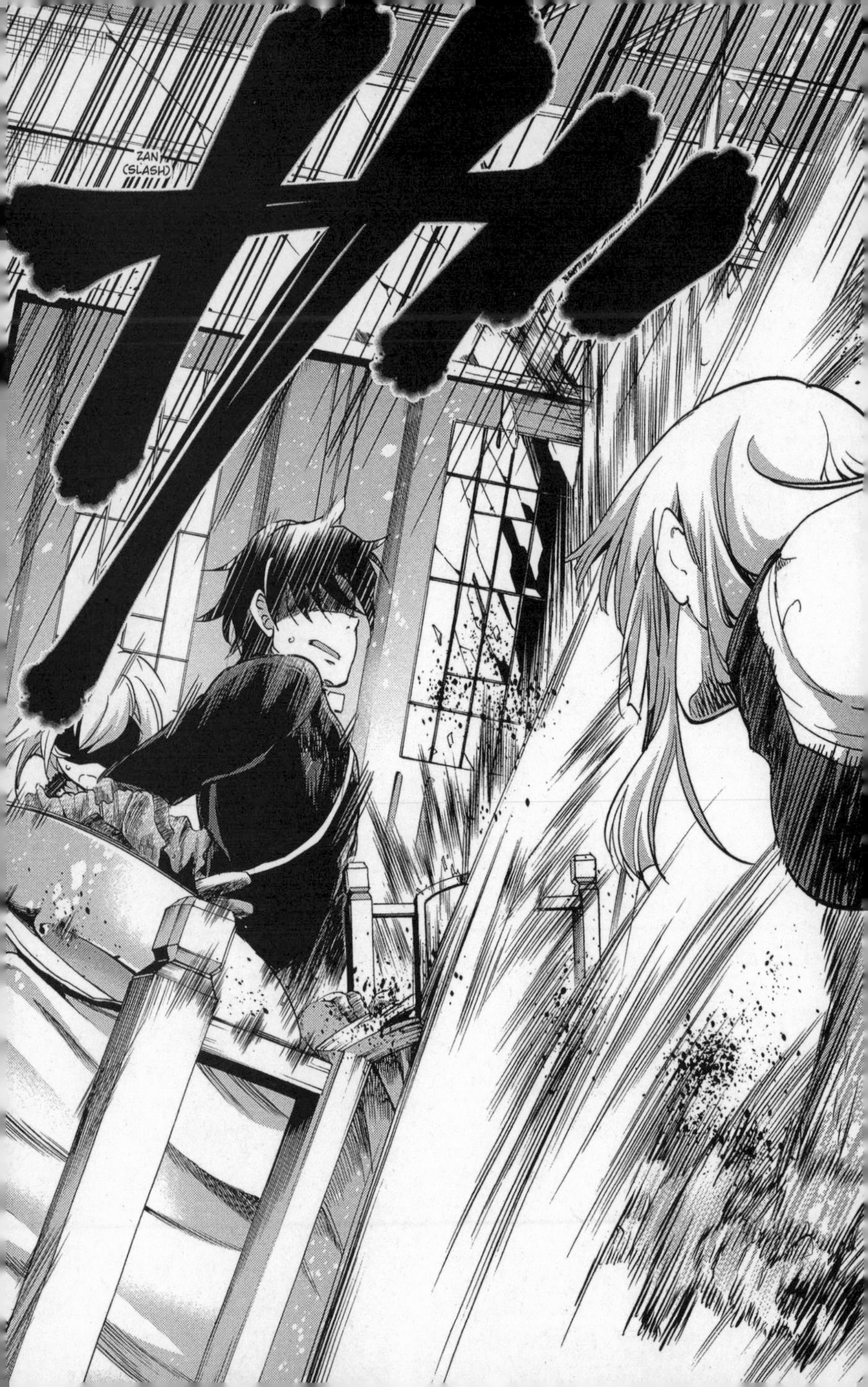
ZAN (SLASH)

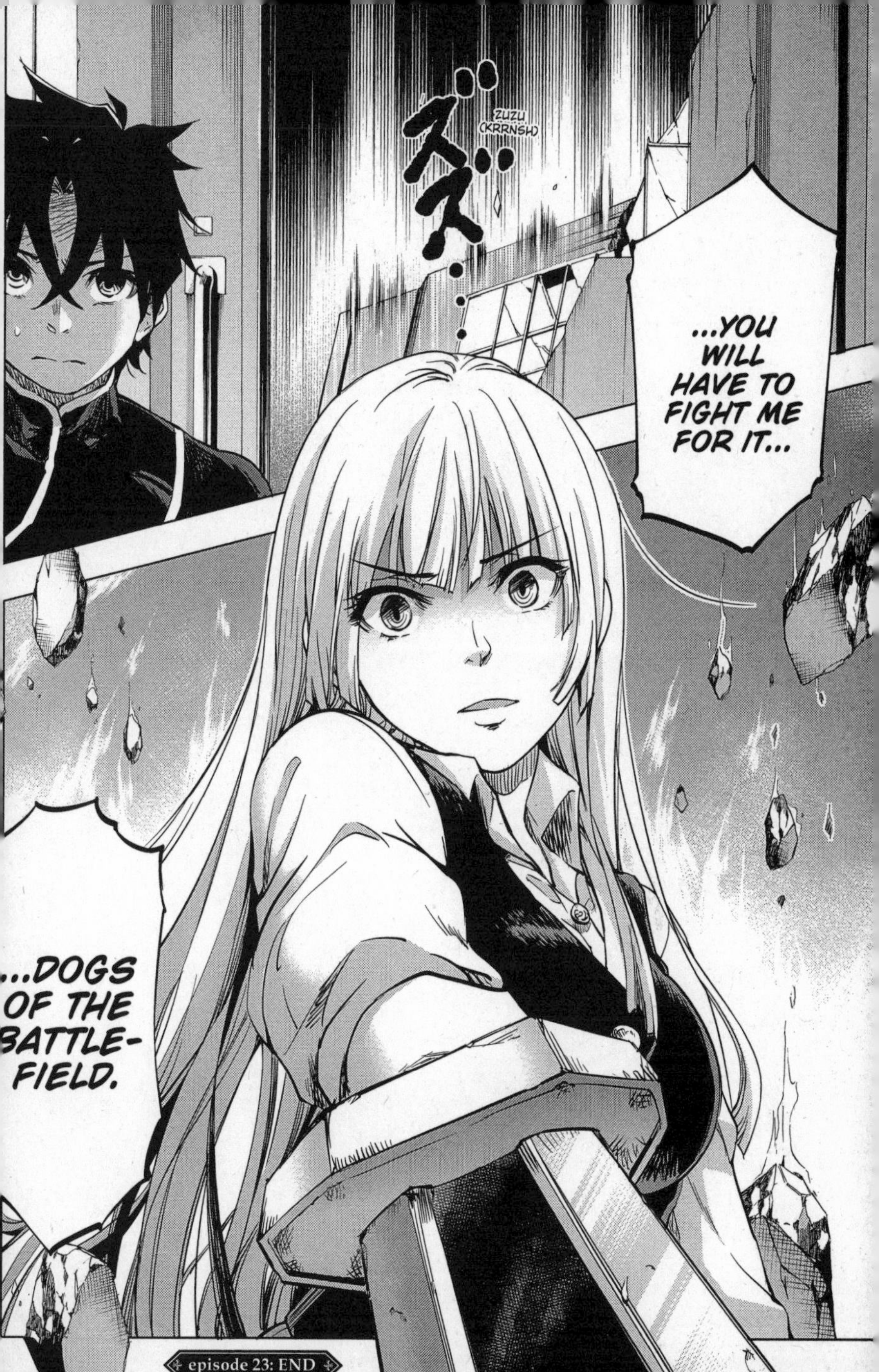
ZUZU
(KRRNSH)
...YOU WILL HAVE TO FIGHT ME FOR IT...
...DOGS OF THE BATTLE-FIELD.

episode 23: END

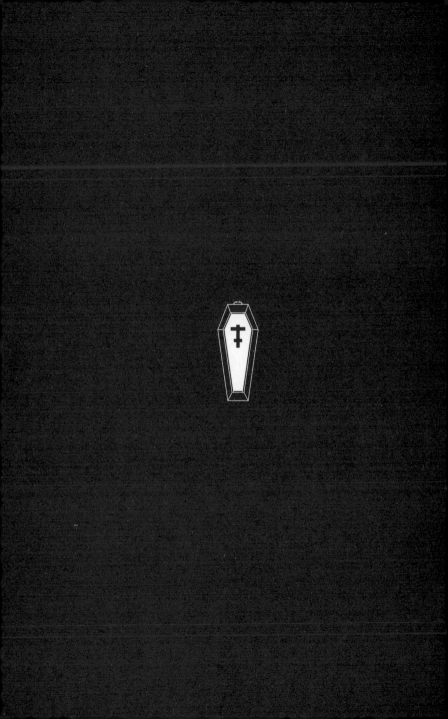

CHAIKA: THE COFFIN PRINCESS

episode 24: Remembering the Lost

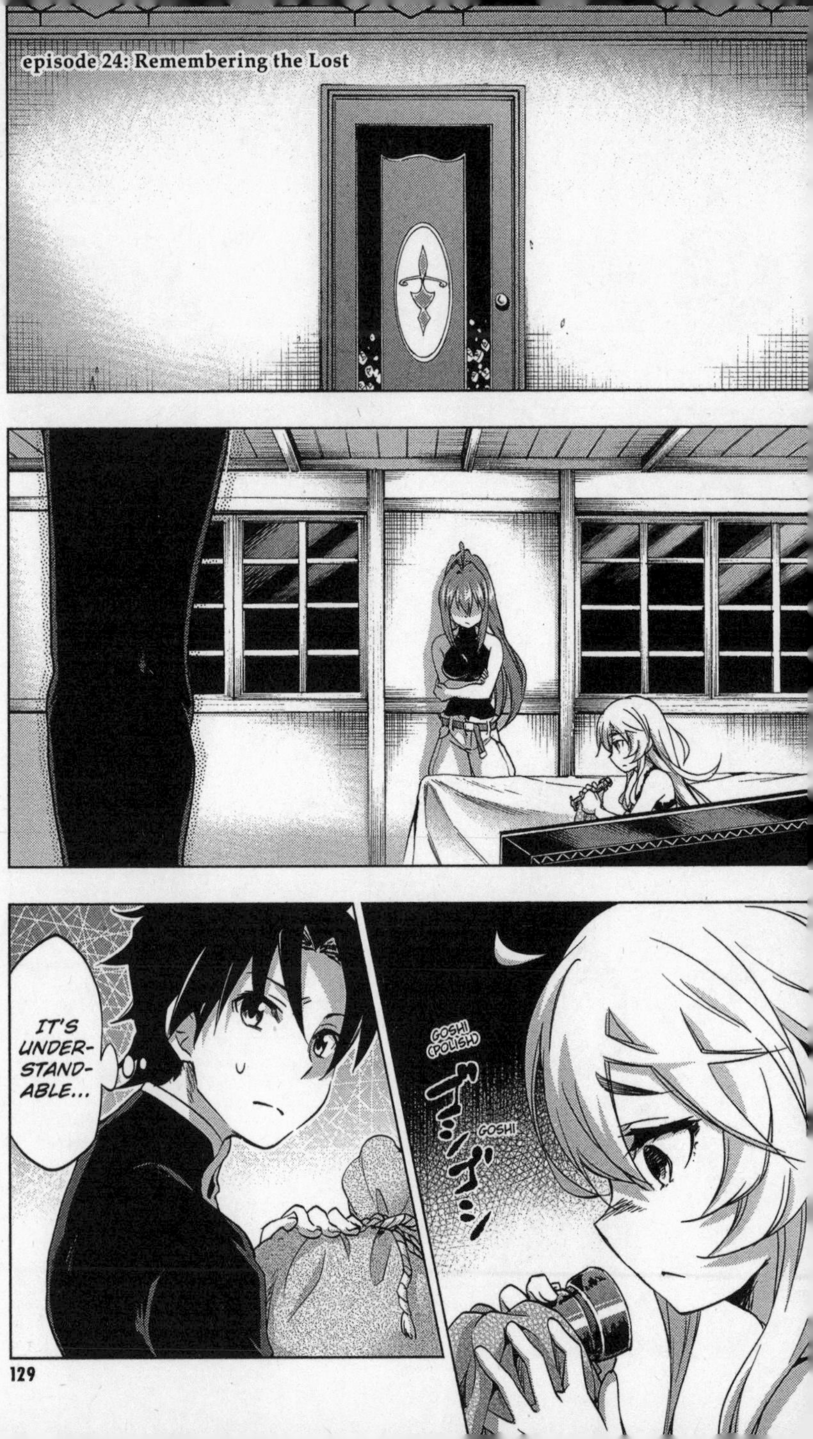
GOSHI (POLISH)
GOSHI
IT'S UNDER-STAND-ABLE...

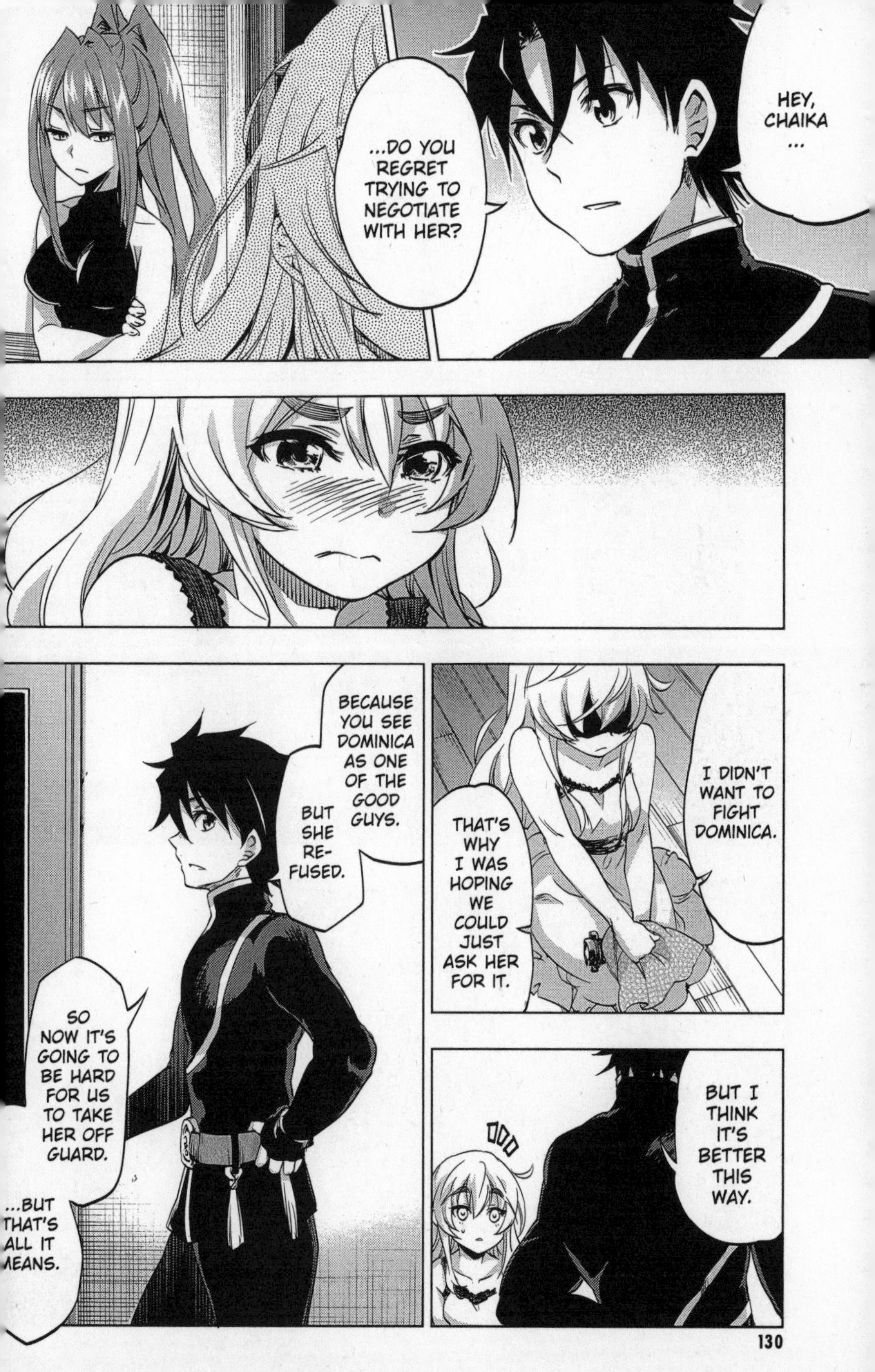
HEY, CHAIKA...
...DO YOU REGRET TRYING TO NEGOTIATE WITH HER?
I DIDN'T WANT TO FIGHT DOMINICA.
THAT'S WHY I WAS HOPING WE COULD JUST ASK HER FOR IT.
BUT I THINK IT'S BETTER THIS WAY.
BECAUSE YOU SEE DOMINICA AS ONE OF THE GOOD GUYS.
BUT SHE RE-FUSED.
SO NOW IT'S GOING TO BE HARD FOR US TO TAKE HER OFF GUARD.
...BUT THAT'S ALL IT MEANS.

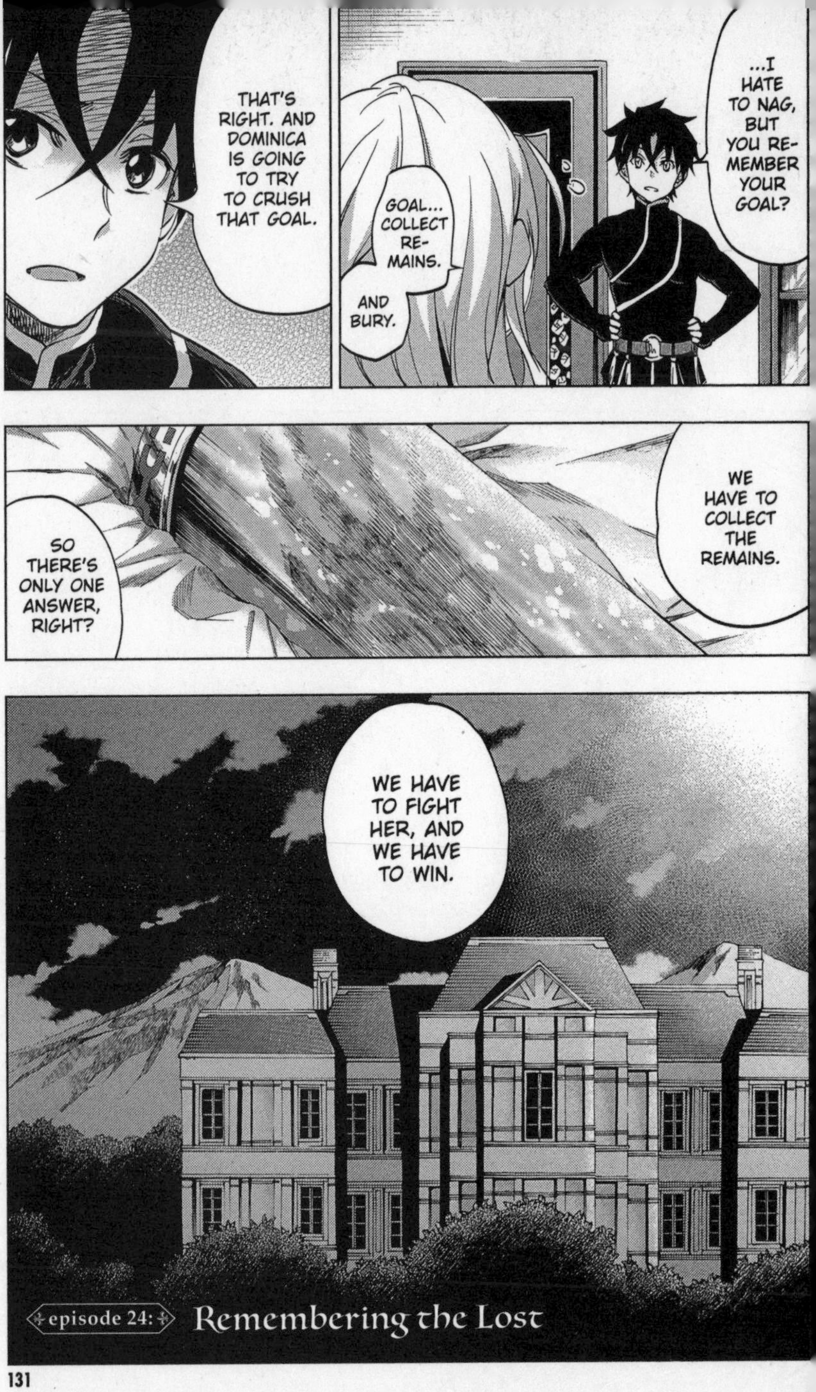
...I HATE TO NAG, BUT YOU RE-MEMBER YOUR GOAL?
GOAL... COLLECT RE-MAINS.
AND BURY.
THAT'S RIGHT. AND DOMINICA IS GOING TO TRY TO CRUSH THAT GOAL.
WE HAVE TO COLLECT THE REMAINS.
SO THERE'S ONLY ONE ANSWER, RIGHT?
WE HAVE TO FIGHT HER, AND WE HAVE TO WIN.
episode 24: Remembering the Lost

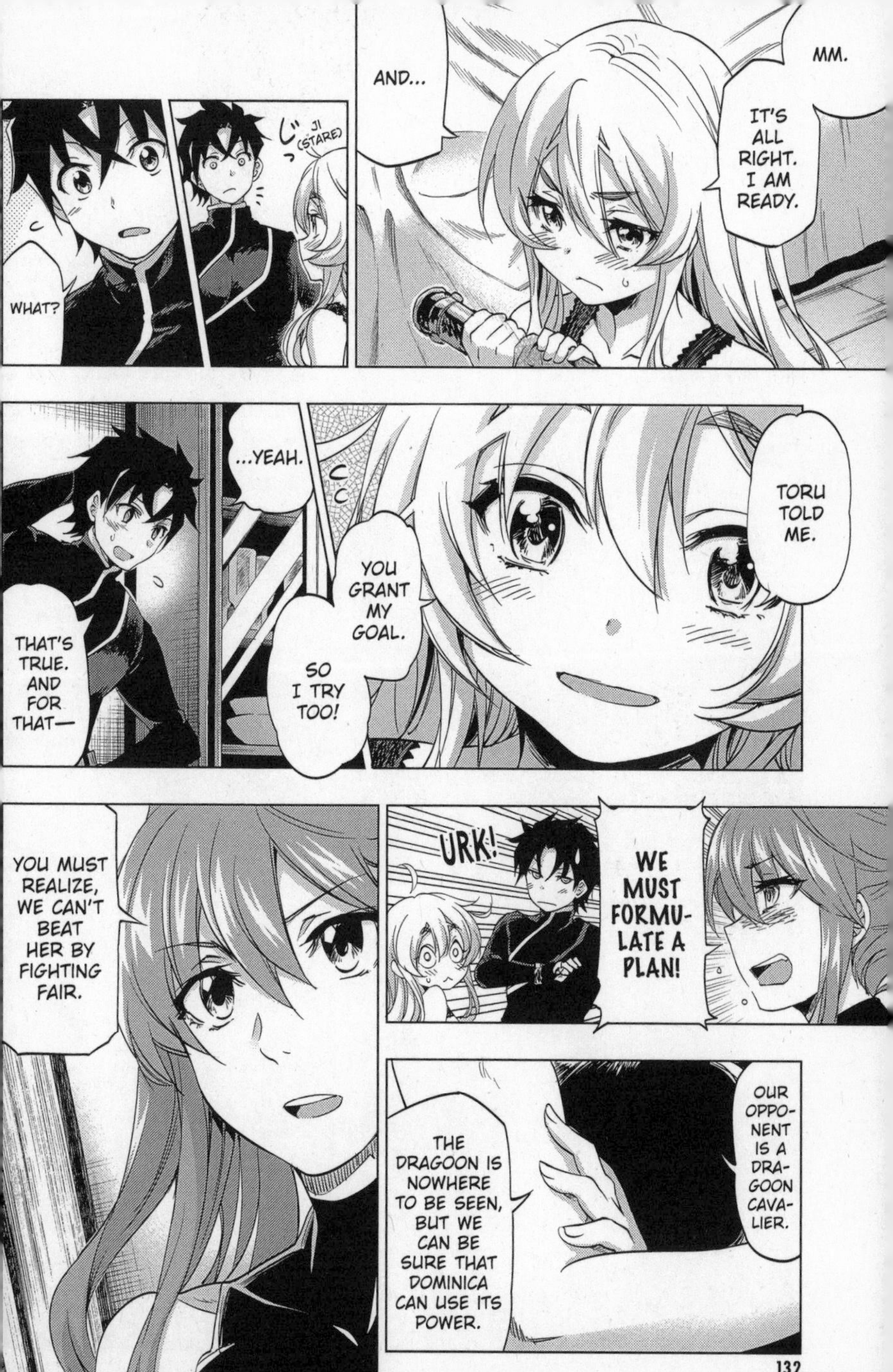
MM.
IT'S ALL RIGHT. I AM READY.
AND...
じ JI (STARE)
WHAT?
TORU TOLD ME.
YOU GRANT MY GOAL.
SO I TRY TOO!
...YEAH.
THAT'S TRUE. AND FOR THAT—
WE MUST FORMULATE A PLAN!
URK!
OUR OPPONENT IS A DRAGOON CAVALIER.
THE DRAGOON IS NOWHERE TO BE SEEN, BUT WE CAN BE SURE THAT DOMINICA CAN USE ITS POWER.
YOU MUST REALIZE, WE CAN'T BEAT HER BY FIGHTING FAIR.

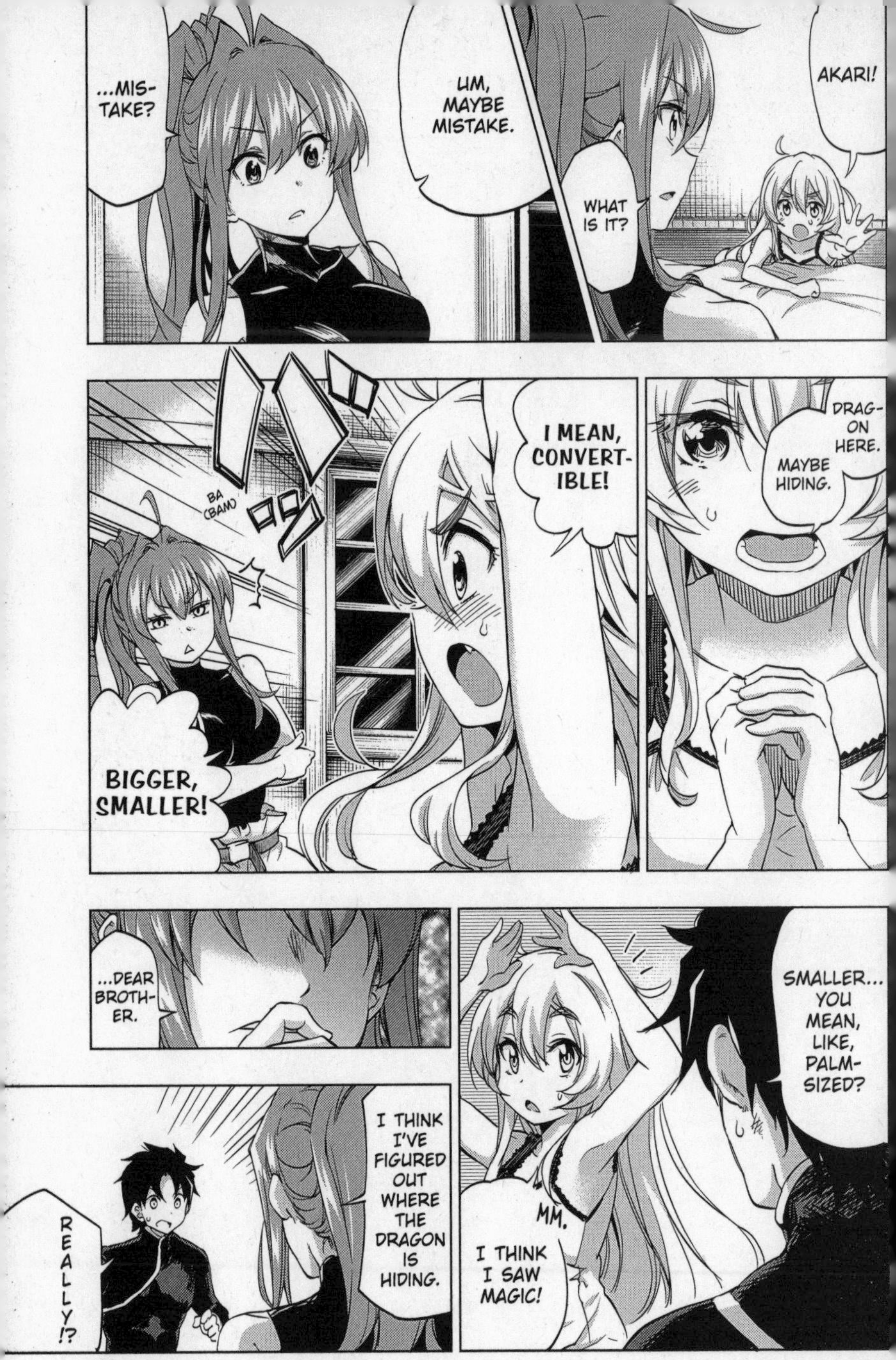
AKARI!
WHAT IS IT?
UM, MAYBE MISTAKE.
...MIS-TAKE?
DRAG-ON HERE. MAYBE HIDING.
I MEAN, CONVERT-IBLE!
BA (BAM)
BIGGER, SMALLER!
SMALLER... YOU MEAN, LIKE, PALM-SIZED?
MM.
I THINK I SAW MAGIC!
...DEAR BROTH-ER.
I THINK I'VE FIGURED OUT WHERE THE DRAGON IS HIDING.
REALLY!?

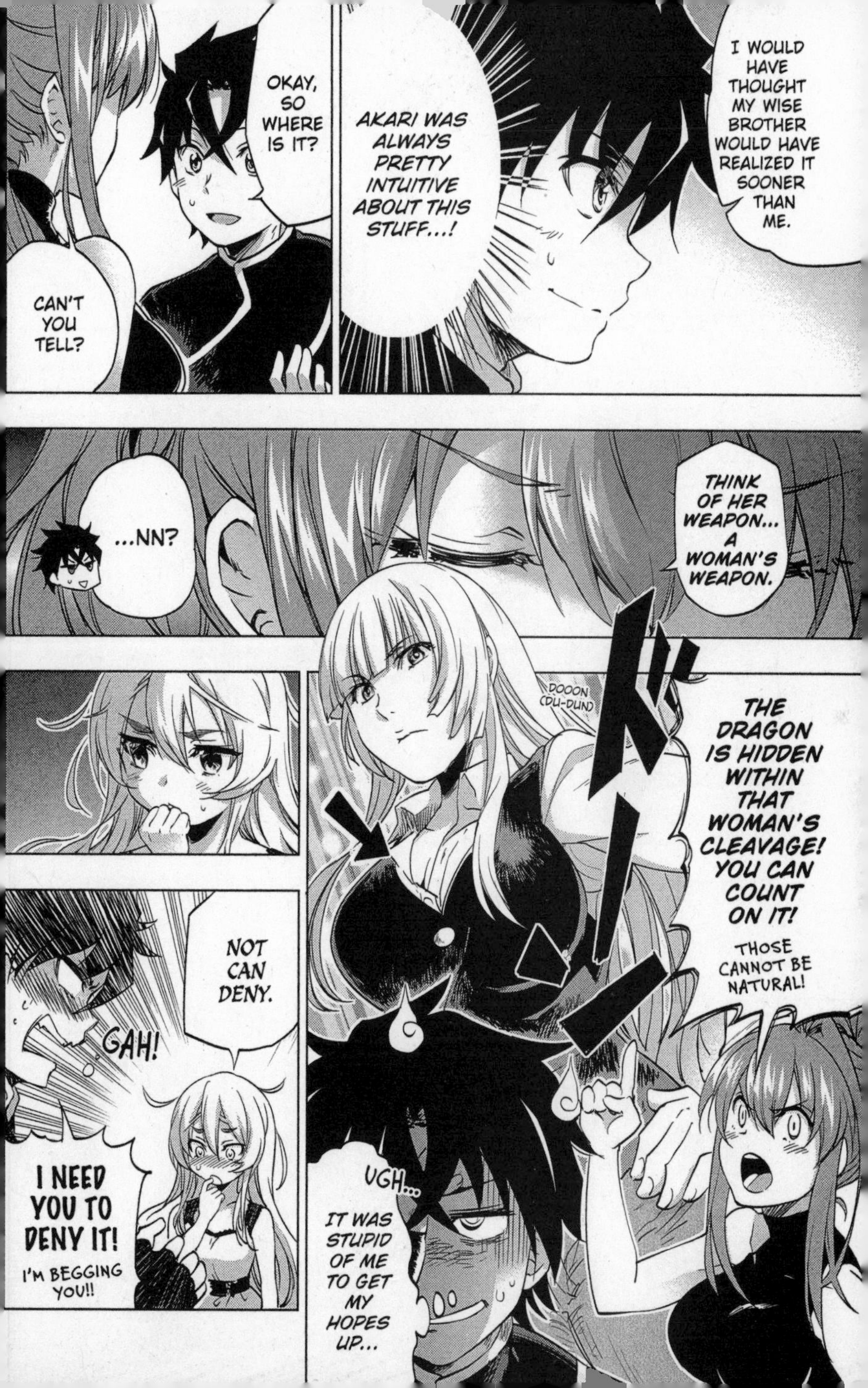
I WOULD HAVE THOUGHT MY WISE BROTHER WOULD HAVE REALIZED IT SOONER THAN ME.
AKARI WAS ALWAYS PRETTY INTUITIVE ABOUT THIS STUFF...!
OKAY, SO WHERE IS IT?
CAN'T YOU TELL?
THINK OF HER WEAPON... A WOMAN'S WEAPON.
...NN?
THE DRAGON IS HIDDEN WITHIN THAT WOMAN'S CLEAVAGE! YOU CAN COUNT ON IT!
THOSE CANNOT BE NATURAL!
DOOON (DU-DUN)
UGH...
IT WAS STUPID OF ME TO GET MY HOPES UP...
NOT CAN DENY.
GAH!
I NEED YOU TO DENY IT!
I'M BEGGING YOU!!

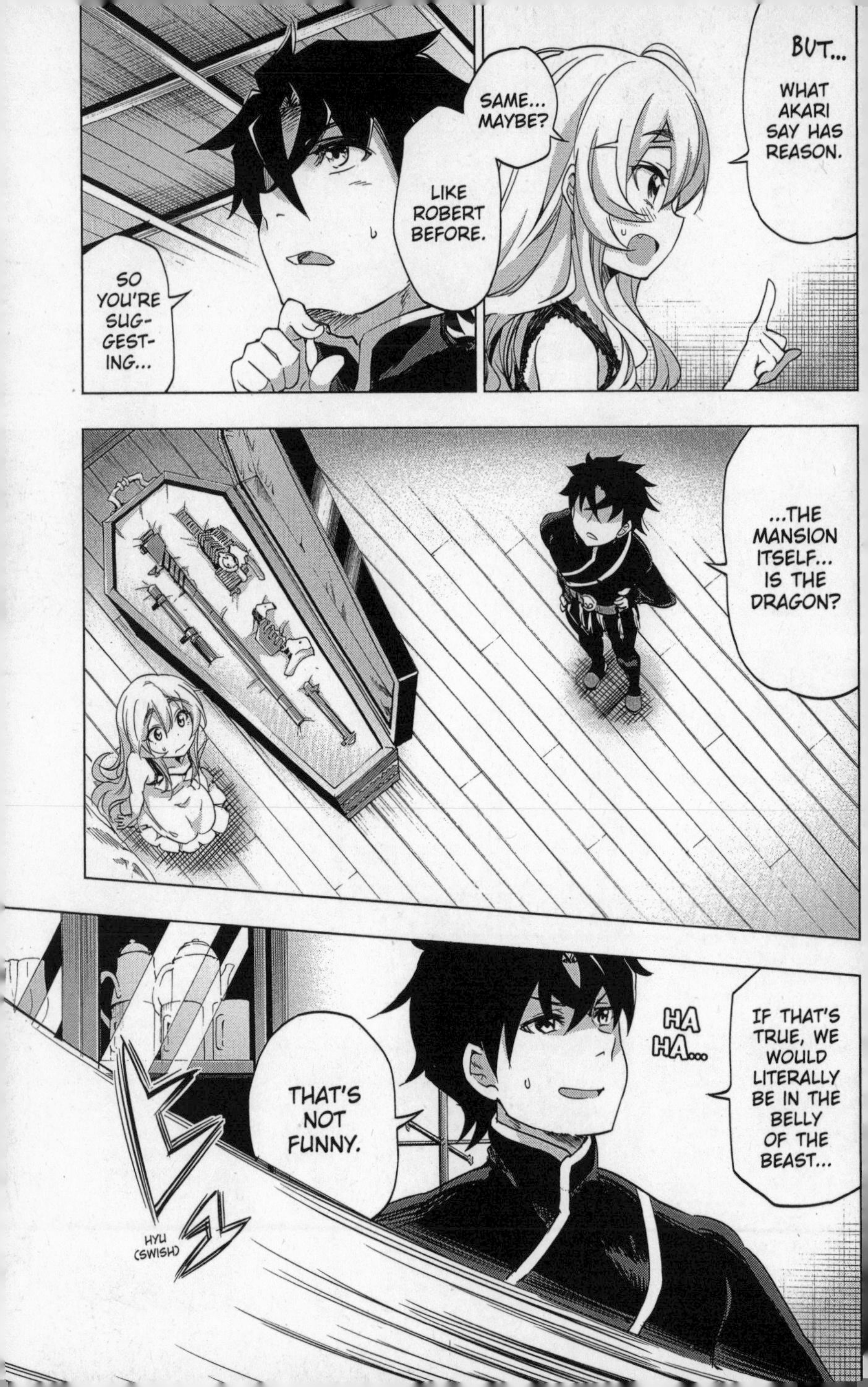
BUT...
WHAT AKARI SAY HAS REASON.
SAME... MAYBE?
LIKE ROBERT BEFORE.
SO YOU'RE SUG-GEST-ING...
...THE MANSION ITSELF... IS THE DRAGON?
IF THAT'S TRUE, WE WOULD LITERALLY BE IN THE BELLY OF THE BEAST...
HA HA...
THAT'S NOT FUNNY.
HYU (SWISH)

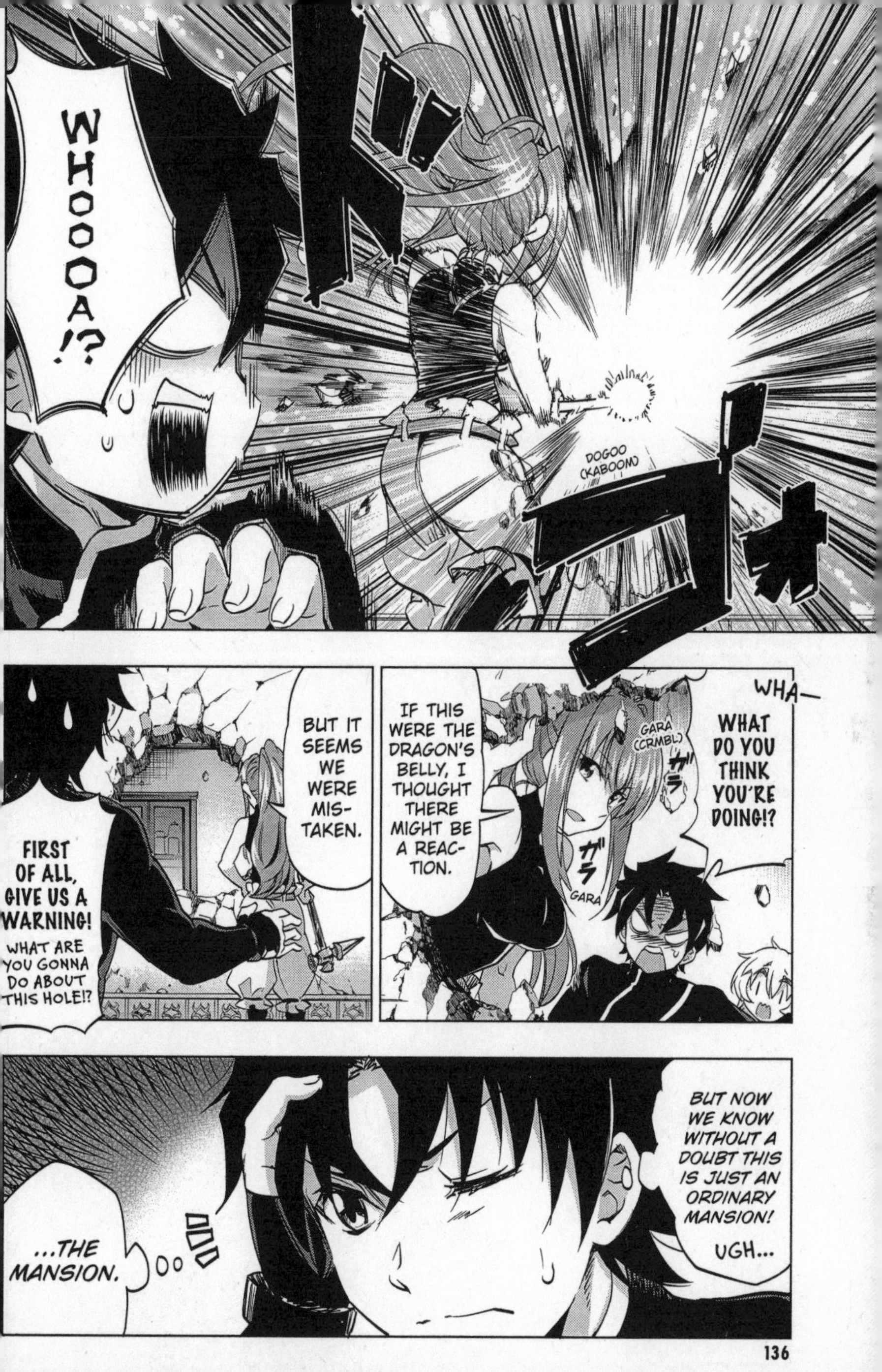
DOGOO (KABOOM)
WHOOOOA!?
WHA—
WHAT DO YOU THINK YOU'RE DOING!?
GARA (CRMBL)
GARA
IF THIS WERE THE DRAGON'S BELLY, I THOUGHT THERE MIGHT BE A REACTION.
BUT IT SEEMS WE WERE MISTAKEN.
FIRST OF ALL, GIVE US A WARNING!
WHAT ARE YOU GONNA DO ABOUT THIS HOLE!?
BUT NOW WE KNOW WITHOUT A DOUBT THIS IS JUST AN ORDINARY MANSION!
UGH...
...THE MANSION.

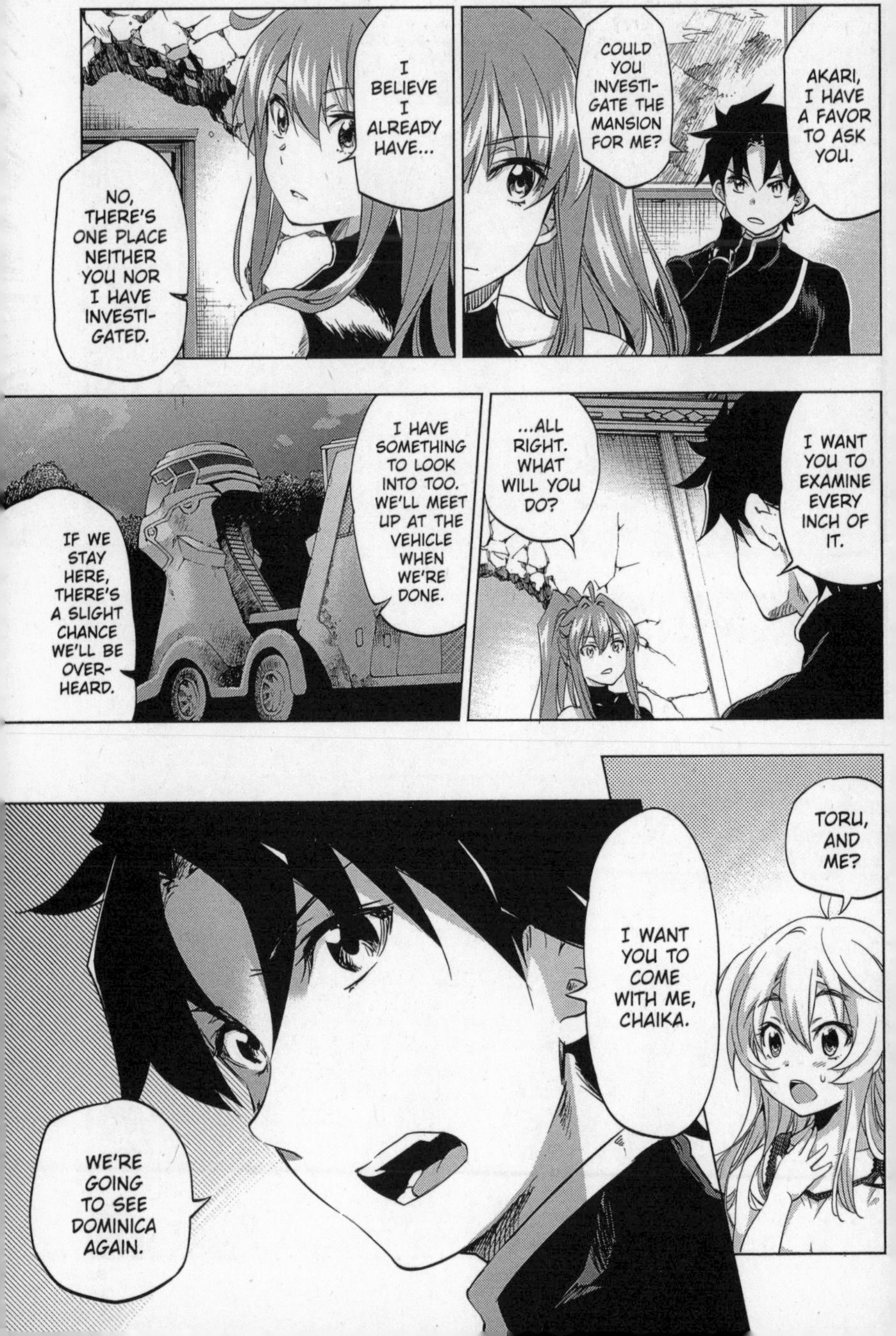
AKARI, I HAVE A FAVOR TO ASK YOU.
COULD YOU INVESTIGATE THE MANSION FOR ME?
I BELIEVE I ALREADY HAVE...
NO, THERE'S ONE PLACE NEITHER YOU NOR I HAVE INVESTIGATED.
I WANT YOU TO EXAMINE EVERY INCH OF IT.
...ALL RIGHT. WHAT WILL YOU DO?
I HAVE SOMETHING TO LOOK INTO TOO. WE'LL MEET UP AT THE VEHICLE WHEN WE'RE DONE.
IF WE STAY HERE, THERE'S A SLIGHT CHANCE WE'LL BE OVERHEARD.
I WANT YOU TO COME WITH ME, CHAIKA.
TORU, AND ME?
WE'RE GOING TO SEE DOMINICA AGAIN.

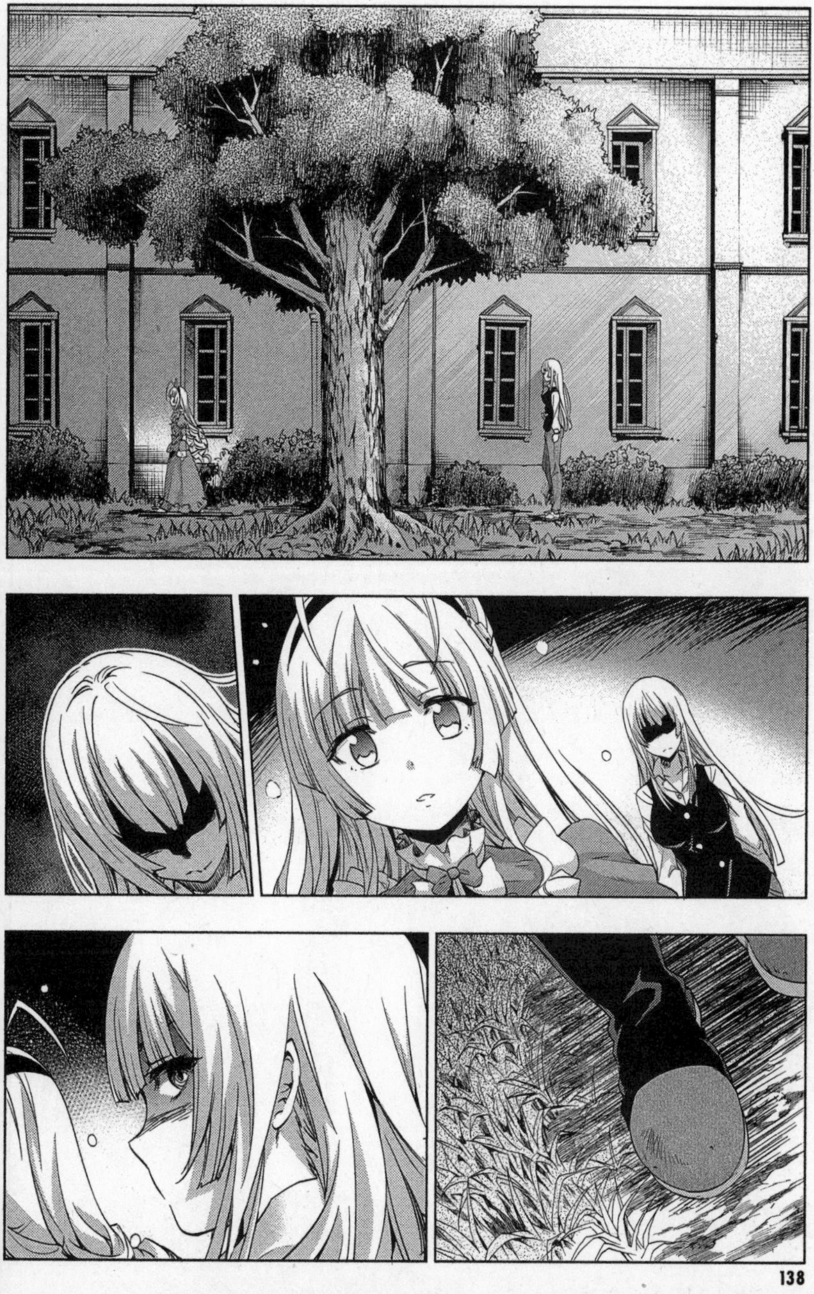

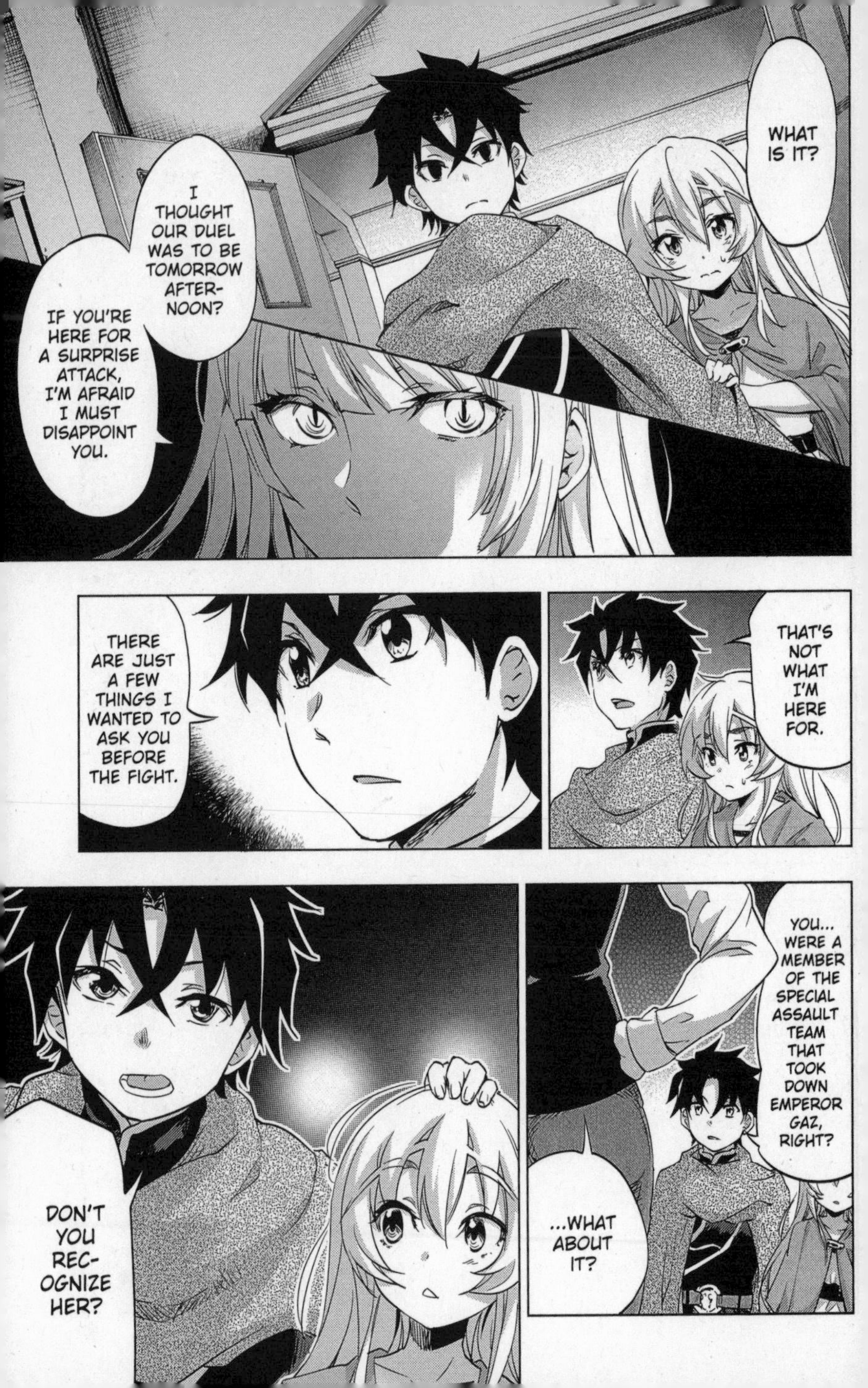
WHAT IS IT?
I THOUGHT OUR DUEL WAS TO BE TOMORROW AFTERNOON?
IF YOU'RE HERE FOR A SURPRISE ATTACK, I'M AFRAID I MUST DISAPPOINT YOU.
THAT'S NOT WHAT I'M HERE FOR.
THERE ARE JUST A FEW THINGS I WANTED TO ASK YOU BEFORE THE FIGHT.
YOU... WERE A MEMBER OF THE SPECIAL ASSAULT TEAM THAT TOOK DOWN EMPEROR GAZ, RIGHT?
...WHAT ABOUT IT?
DON'T YOU RECOGNIZE HER?

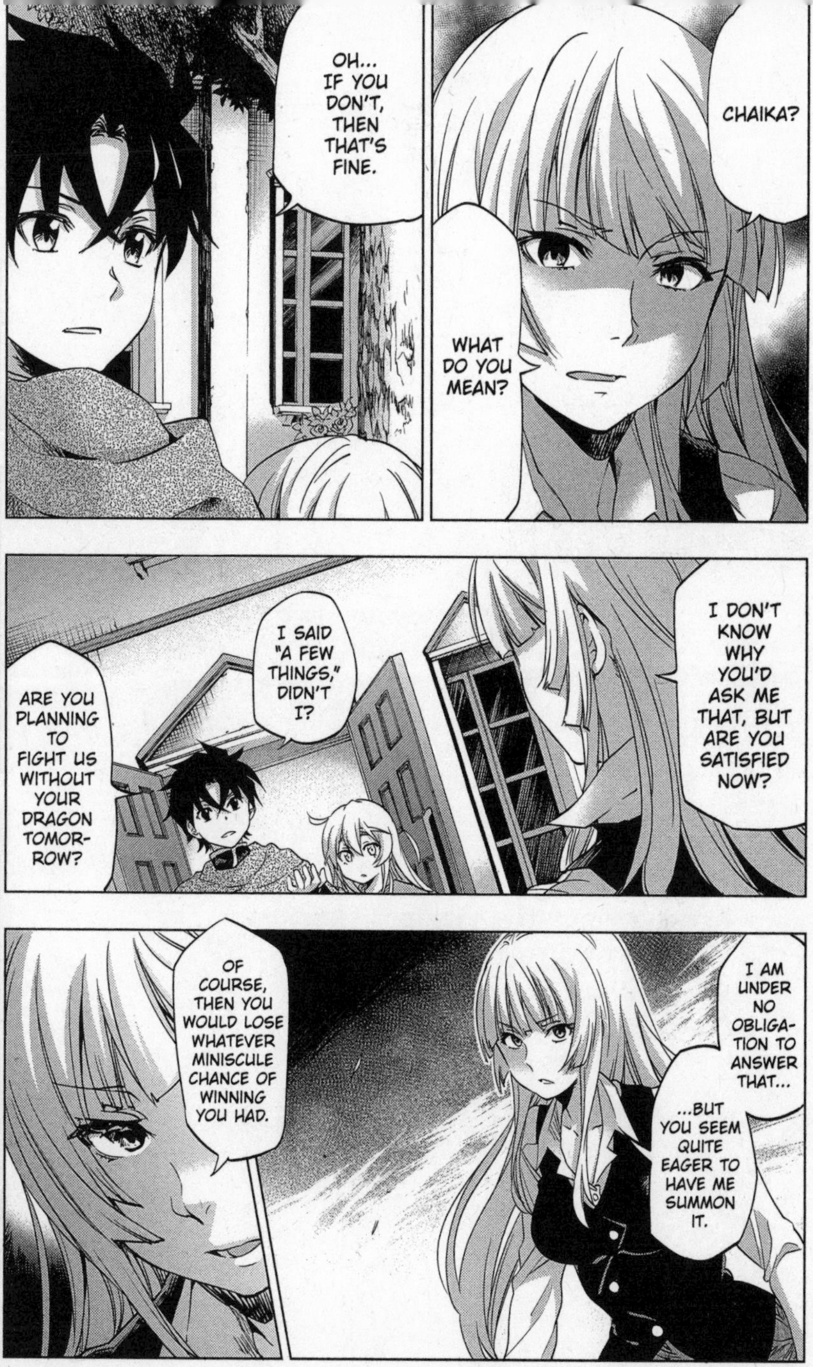
CHAIKA?
WHAT DO YOU MEAN?
OH... IF YOU DON'T, THEN THAT'S FINE.
I DON'T KNOW WHY YOU'D ASK ME THAT, BUT ARE YOU SATISFIED NOW?
I SAID "A FEW THINGS," DIDN'T I?
ARE YOU PLANNING TO FIGHT US WITHOUT YOUR DRAGON TOMOR-ROW?
I AM UNDER NO OBLIGA-TION TO ANSWER THAT...
...BUT YOU SEEM QUITE EAGER TO HAVE ME SUMMON IT.
OF COURSE, THEN YOU WOULD LOSE WHATEVER MINISCULE CHANCE OF WINNING YOU HAD.

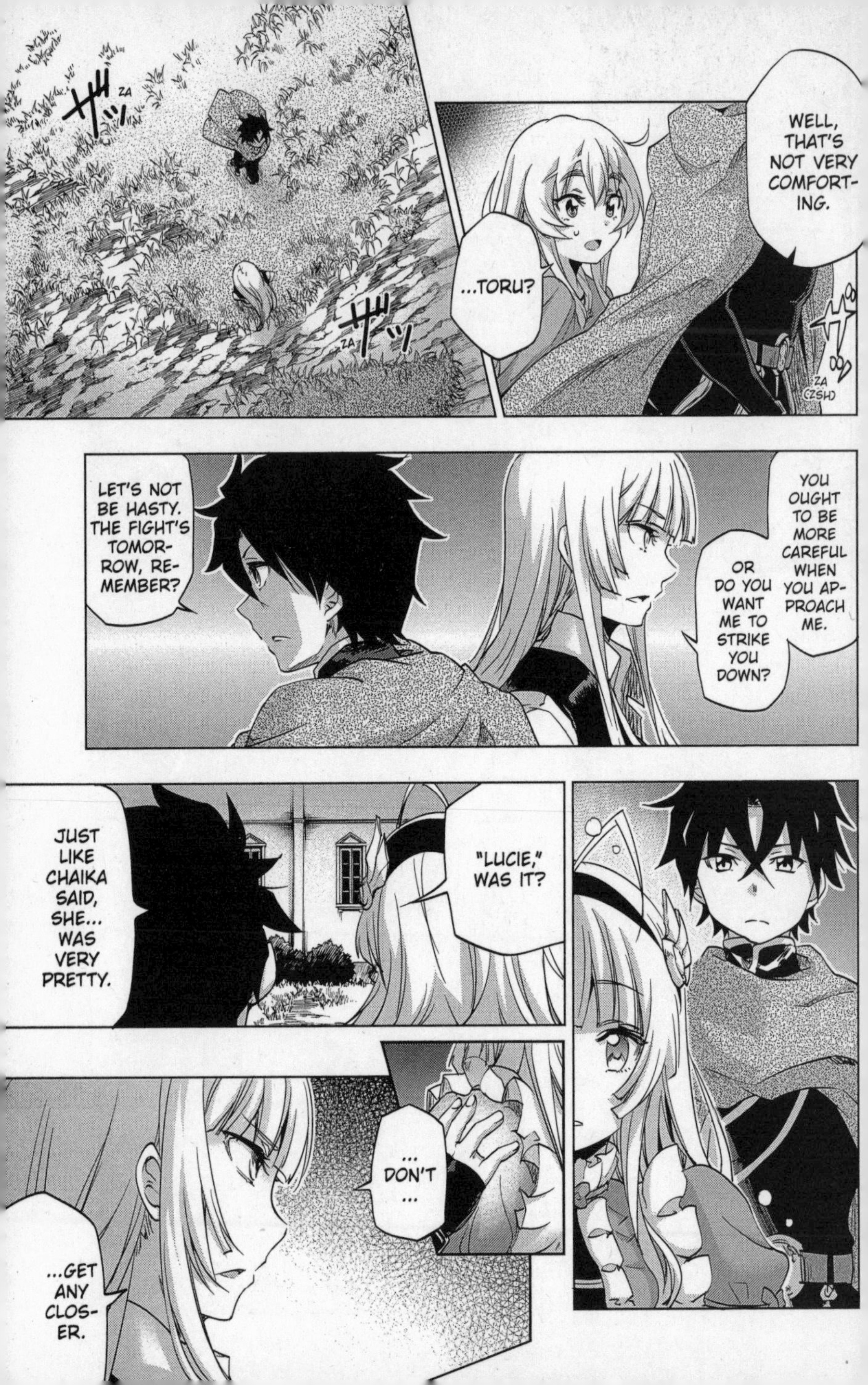
WELL, THAT'S NOT VERY COMFORT-ING.
...TORU?
ZA (ZSH)
ザッ ZA
ザッ ZA
YOU OUGHT TO BE MORE CAREFUL WHEN YOU AP-PROACH ME.
OR DO YOU WANT ME TO STRIKE YOU DOWN?
LET'S NOT BE HASTY. THE FIGHT'S TOMOR-ROW, RE-MEMBER?
"LUCIE," WAS IT?
JUST LIKE CHAIKA SAID, SHE... WAS VERY PRETTY.
... DON'T ...
...GET ANY CLOS-ER.

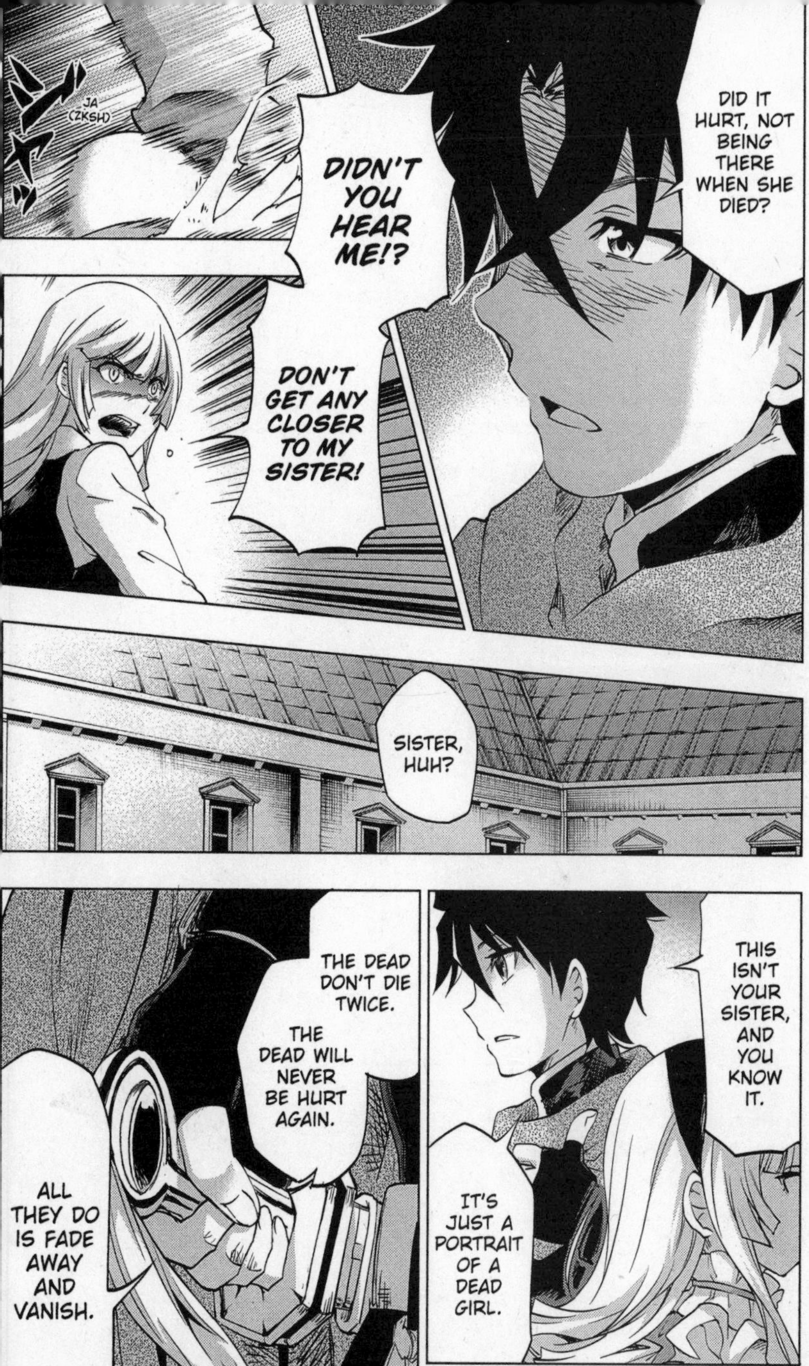
DID IT HURT, NOT BEING THERE WHEN SHE DIED?
JA (ZKSH)
DIDN'T YOU HEAR ME!?
DON'T GET ANY CLOSER TO MY SISTER!
SISTER, HUH?
THIS ISN'T YOUR SISTER, AND YOU KNOW IT.
IT'S JUST A PORTRAIT OF A DEAD GIRL.
THE DEAD DON'T DIE TWICE.
THE DEAD WILL NEVER BE HURT AGAIN.
ALL THEY DO IS FADE AWAY AND VANISH.

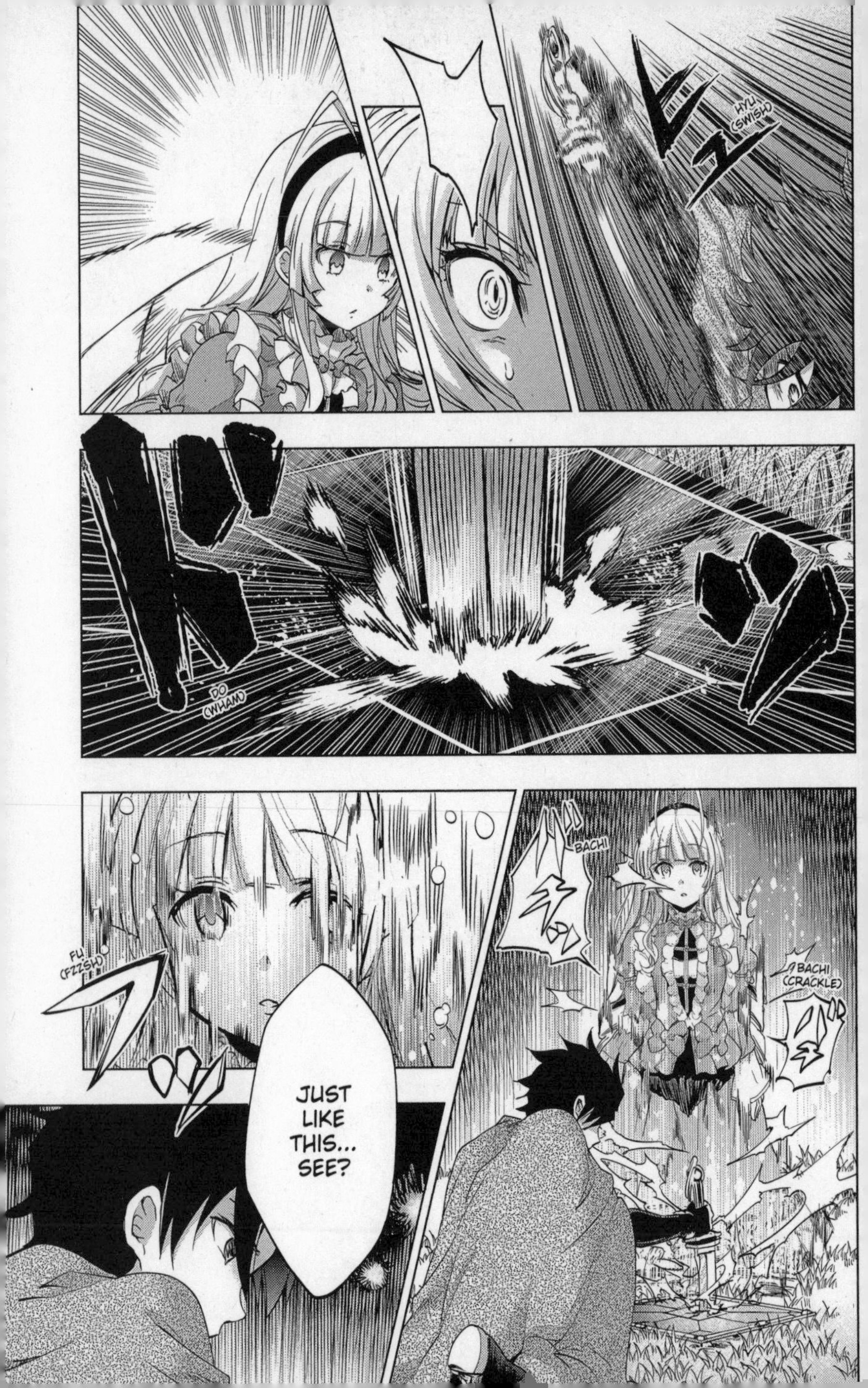
HYU (SWISH)
DO (WHAM)
BACHI
BACHI (CRACKLE)
FU (FZZSH)
JUST LIKE THIS... SEE?

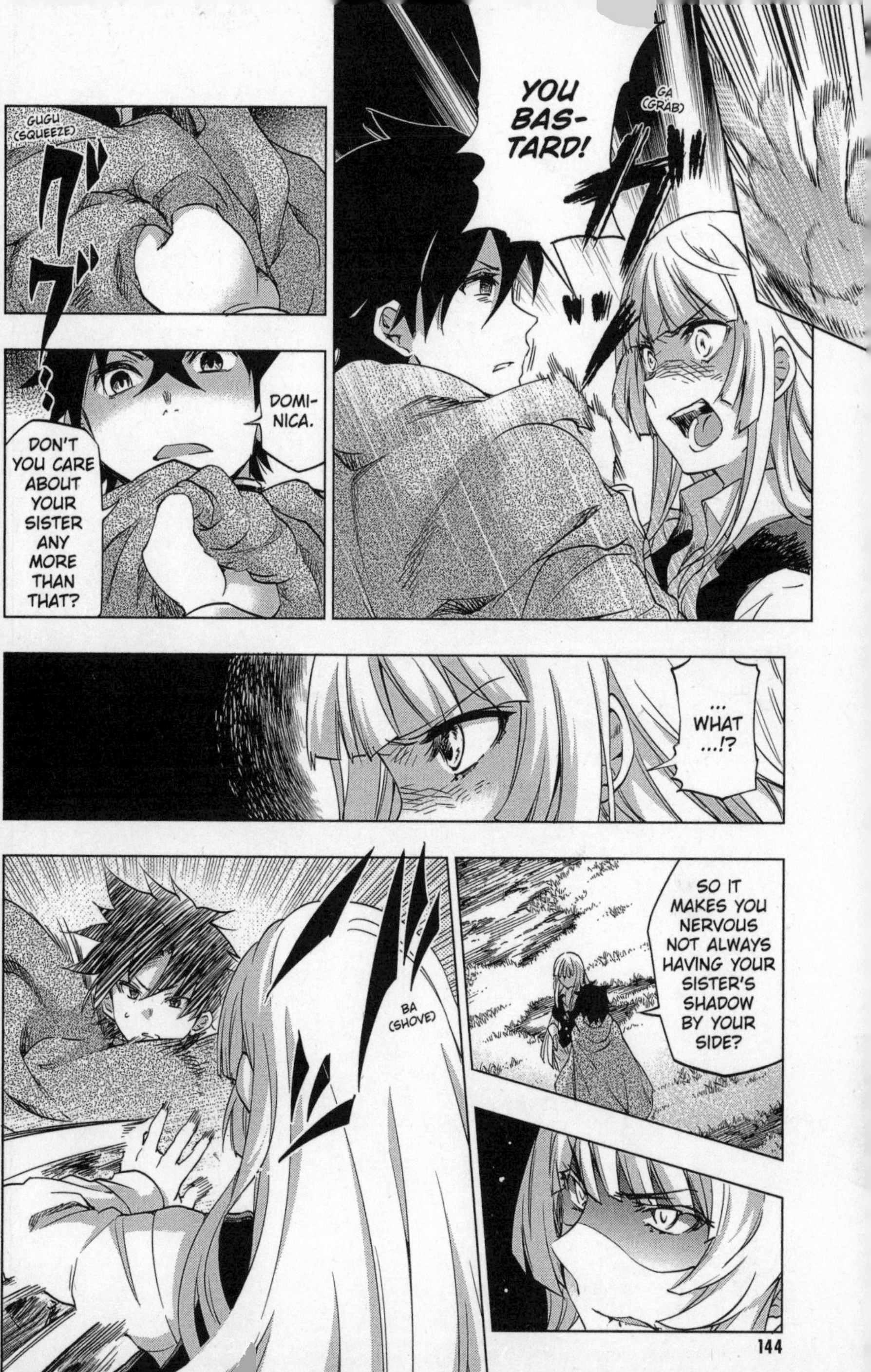
GA (GRAB)
YOU BAS-TARD!
GUGU (SQUEEZE)
DOMI-NICA.
DON'T YOU CARE ABOUT YOUR SISTER ANY MORE THAN THAT?
... WHAT ...!?
SO IT MAKES YOU NERVOUS NOT ALWAYS HAVING YOUR SISTER'S SHADOW BY YOUR SIDE?
BA (SHOVE)

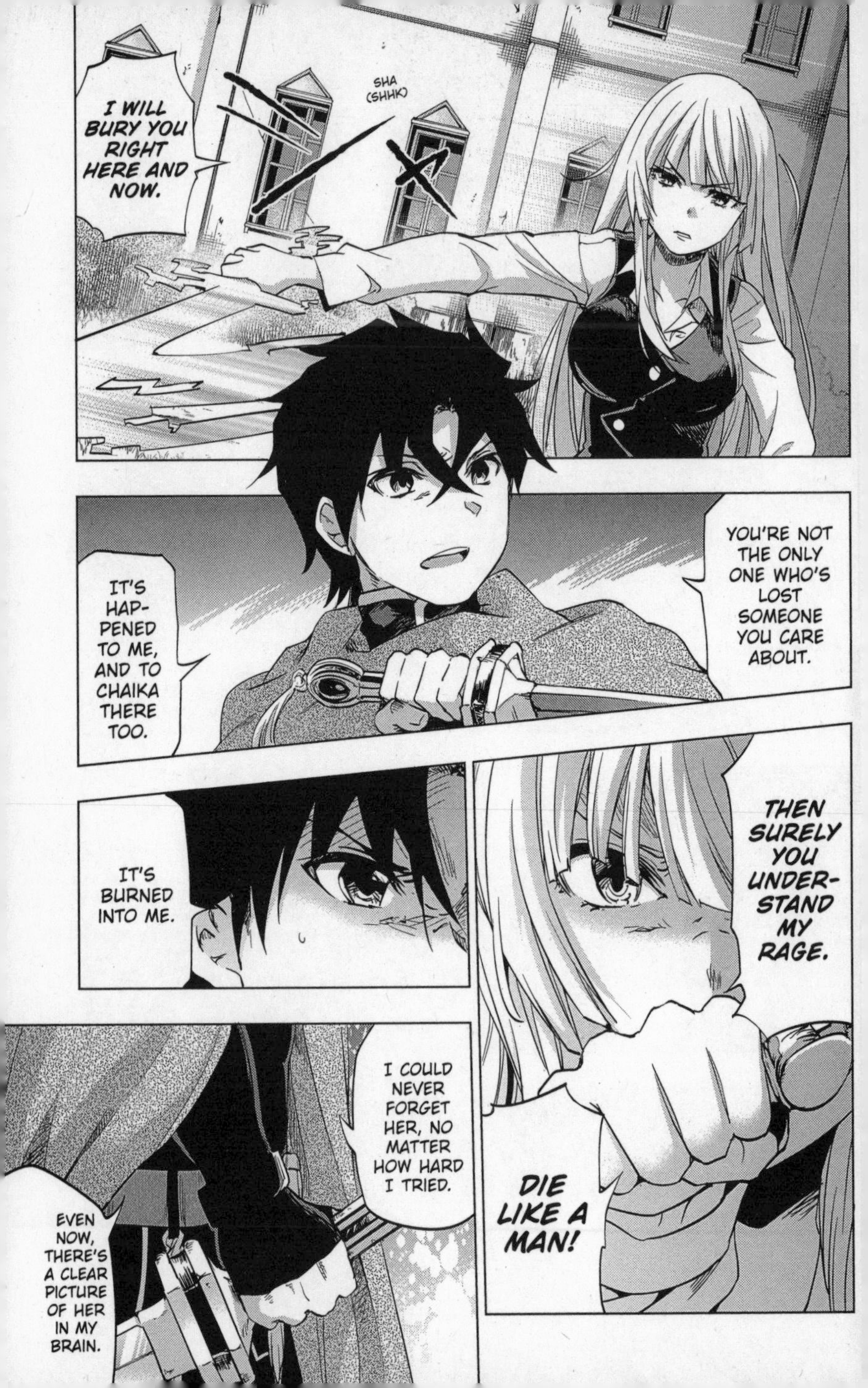
SHA (SHHK)
I WILL BURY YOU RIGHT HERE AND NOW.
YOU'RE NOT THE ONLY ONE WHO'S LOST SOMEONE YOU CARE ABOUT.
IT'S HAP-PENED TO ME, AND TO CHAIKA THERE TOO.
THEN SURELY YOU UNDER-STAND MY RAGE.
DIE LIKE A MAN!
IT'S BURNED INTO ME.
I COULD NEVER FORGET HER, NO MATTER HOW HARD I TRIED.
EVEN NOW, THERE'S A CLEAR PICTURE OF HER IN MY BRAIN.

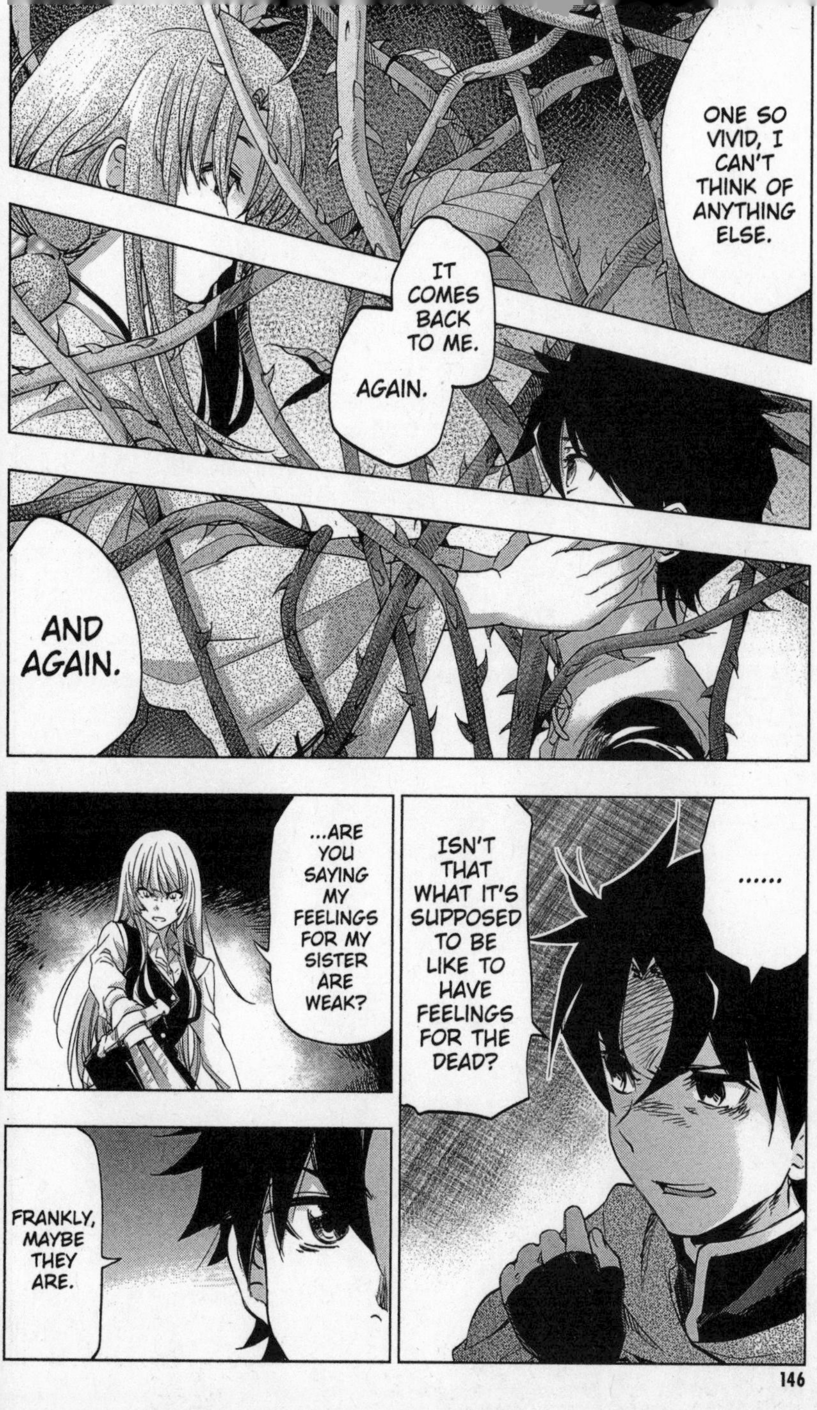

ONE SO VIVID, I CAN'T THINK OF ANYTHING ELSE.
IT COMES BACK TO ME.
AGAIN.
AND AGAIN.
......
ISN'T THAT WHAT IT'S SUPPOSED TO BE LIKE TO HAVE FEELINGS FOR THE DEAD?
...ARE YOU SAYING MY FEELINGS FOR MY SISTER ARE WEAK?
FRANKLY, MAYBE THEY ARE.

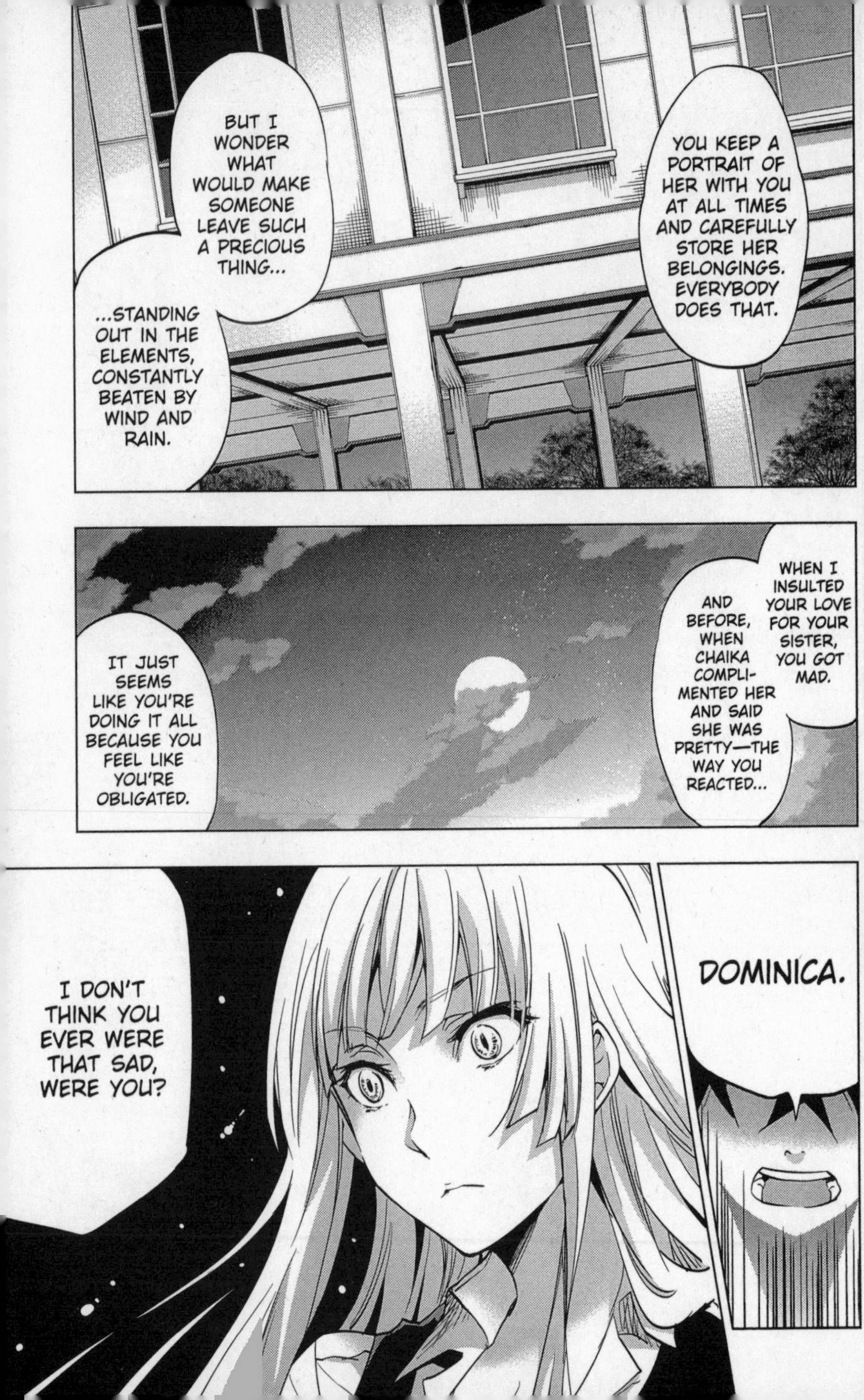
YOU KEEP A PORTRAIT OF HER WITH YOU AT ALL TIMES AND CAREFULLY STORE HER BELONGINGS. EVERYBODY DOES THAT.
BUT I WONDER WHAT WOULD MAKE SOMEONE LEAVE SUCH A PRECIOUS THING...
...STANDING OUT IN THE ELEMENTS, CONSTANTLY BEATEN BY WIND AND RAIN.
WHEN I INSULTED YOUR LOVE FOR YOUR SISTER, YOU GOT MAD.
AND BEFORE, WHEN CHAIKA COMPLIMENTED HER AND SAID SHE WAS PRETTY—THE WAY YOU REACTED...
IT JUST SEEMS LIKE YOU'RE DOING IT ALL BECAUSE YOU FEEL LIKE YOU'RE OBLIGATED.
DOMINICA.
I DON'T THINK YOU EVER WERE THAT SAD, WERE YOU?

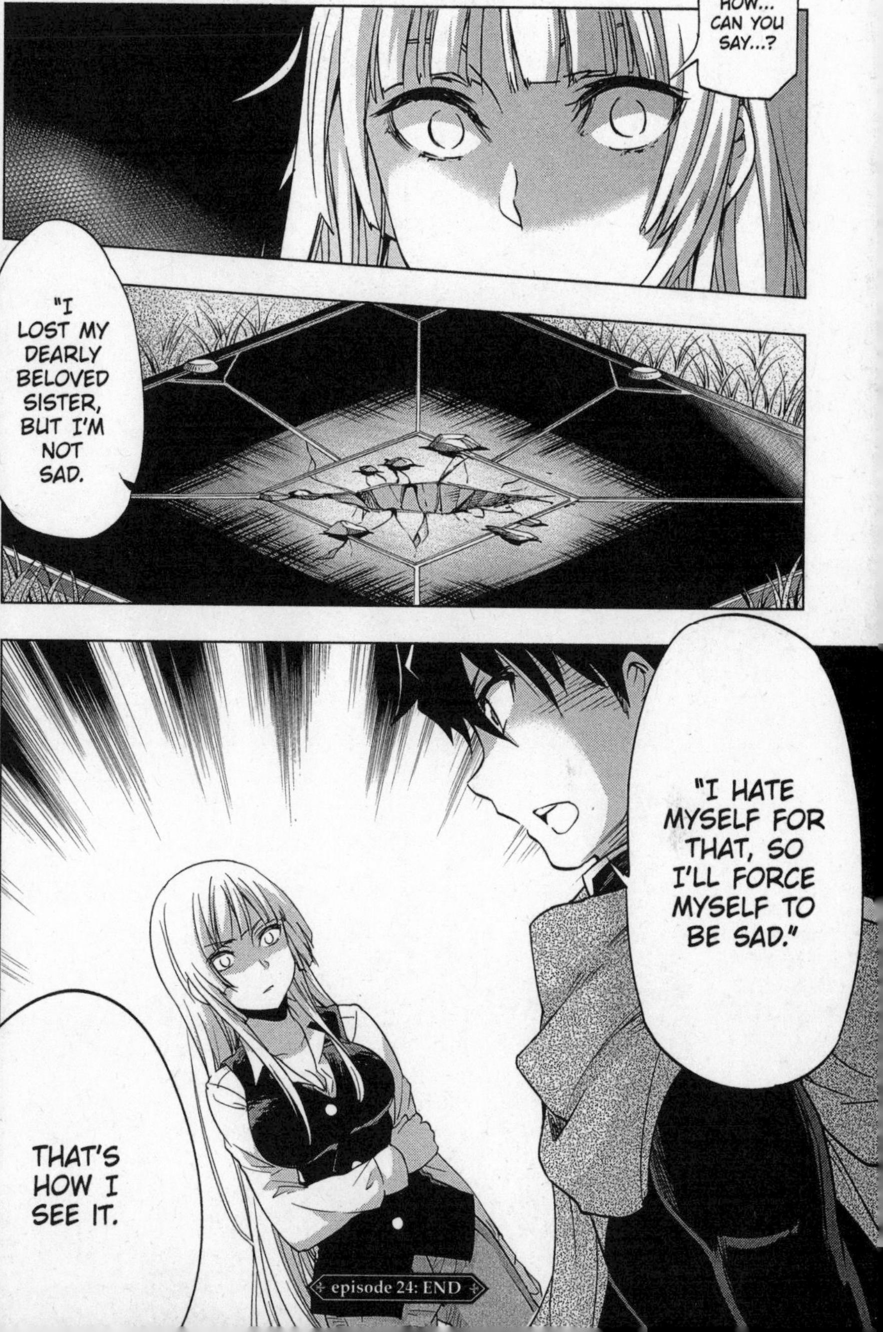
HOW... CAN YOU SAY...?
"I LOST MY DEARLY BELOVED SISTER, BUT I'M NOT SAD.
"I HATE MYSELF FOR THAT, SO I'LL FORCE MYSELF TO BE SAD."
THAT'S HOW I SEE IT.
episode 24: END

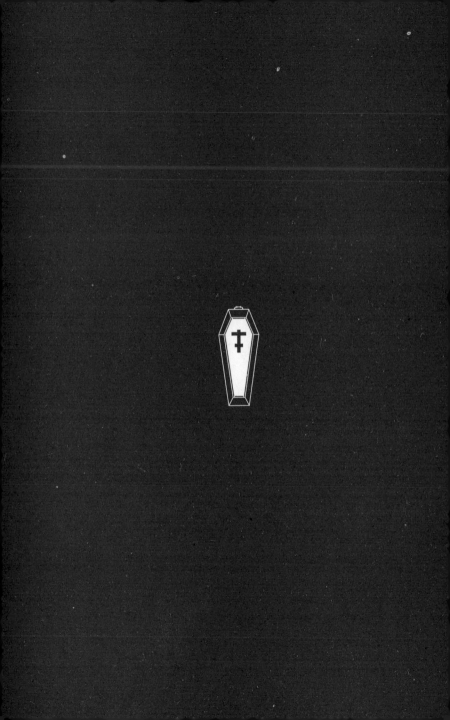

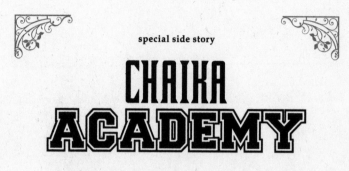

special side story

CHAIKA ACADEMY

The following story, "Chaika Academy," is a side story originally released in "Chaika If," a booklet that was produced as part of a free-gift promotion commemorating the sale of the novel and manga in 2012. Take a look at another version of *Chaika* quite unlike the one you read in the original novels or the manga proper. ♪

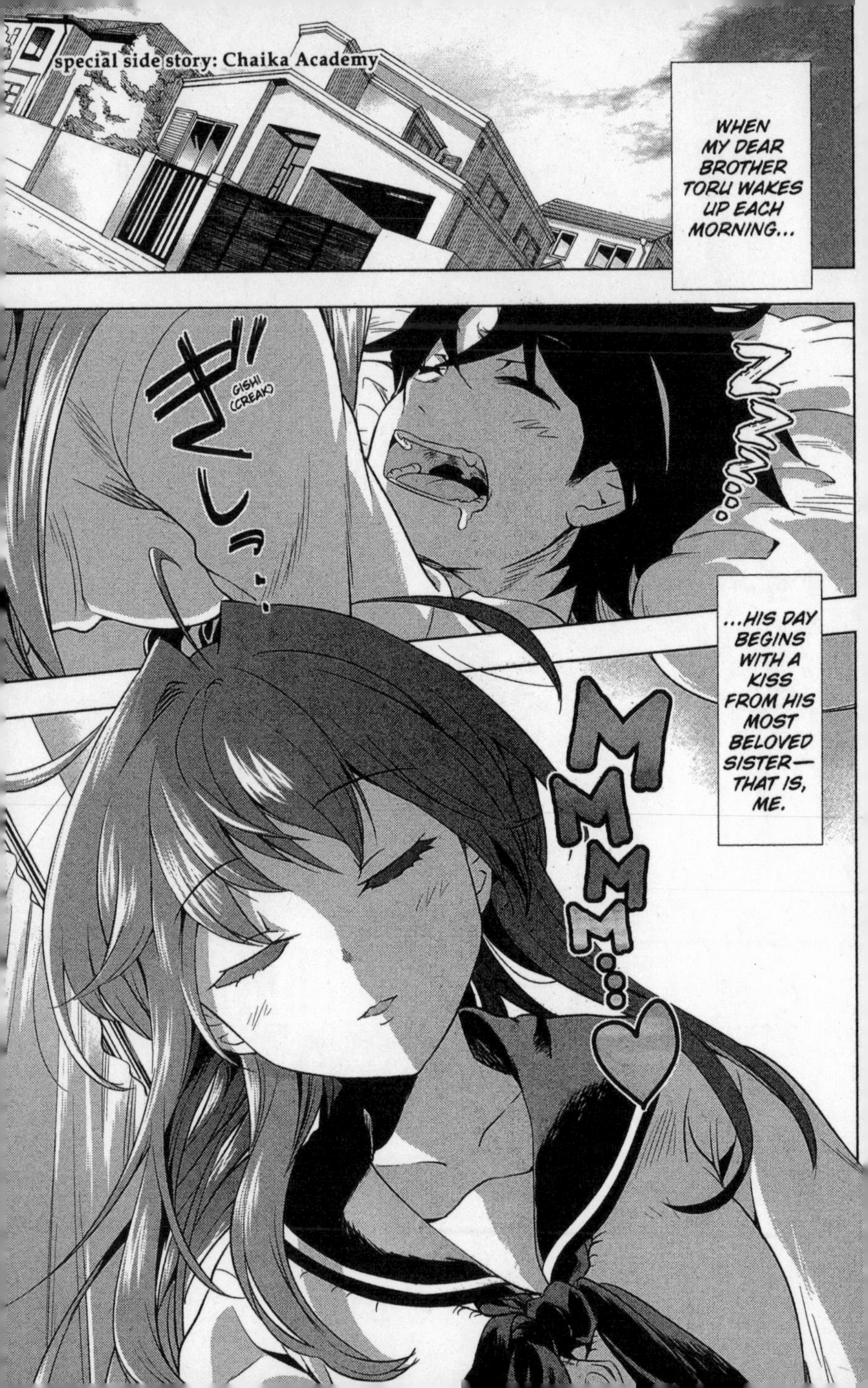
special side story: Chaika Academy
WHEN MY DEAR BROTHER TORU WAKES UP EACH MORNING...
ZZZZ...
ぎしっ
GISHI (CREAK)
...HIS DAY BEGINS WITH A KISS FROM HIS MOST BELOVED SISTER—THAT IS, ME.
MMMM...

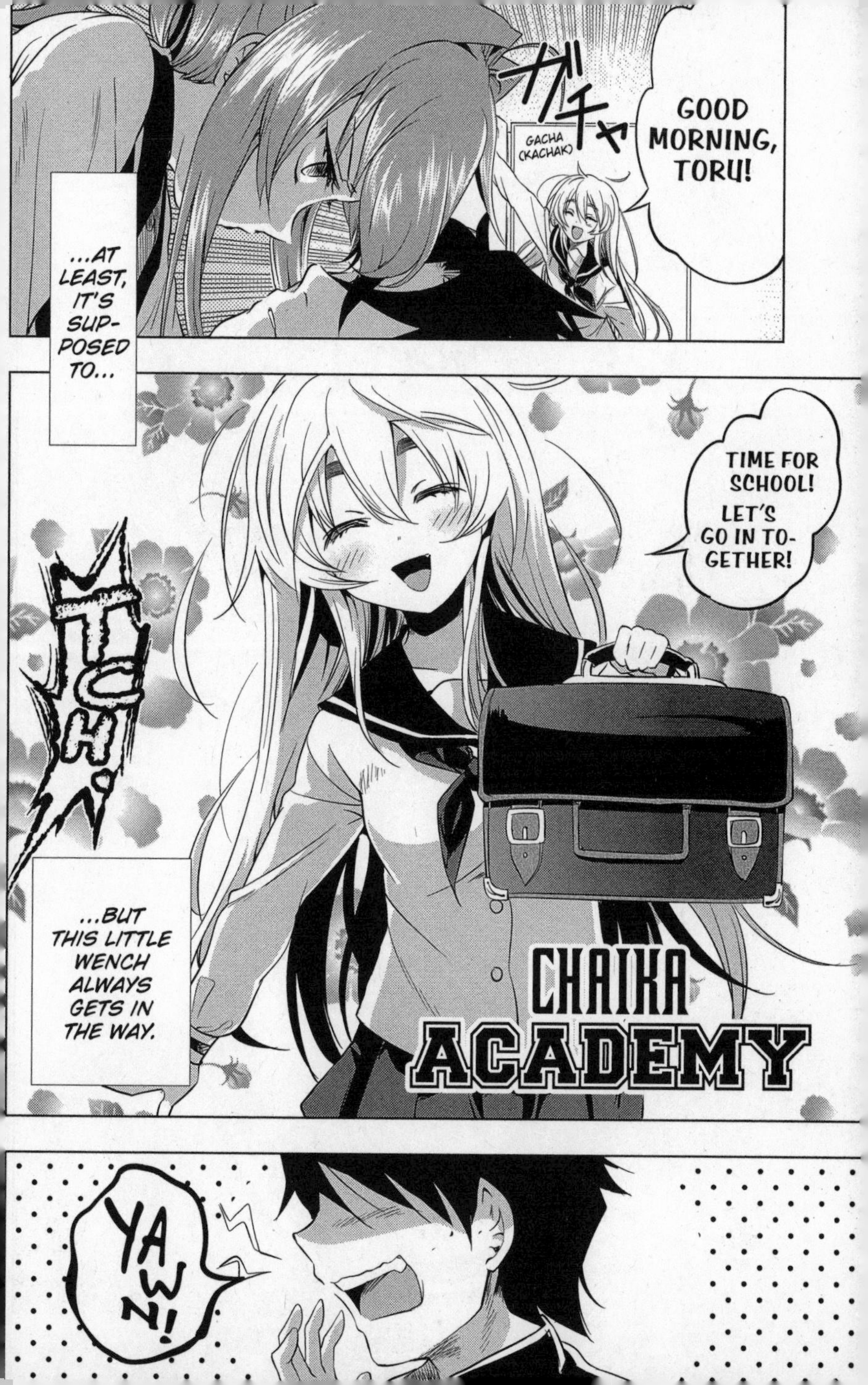
ガチャ
GACHA (KACHAK)
GOOD MORNING, TORU!
...AT LEAST, IT'S SUP-POSED TO...
TIME FOR SCHOOL!
LET'S GO IN TO-GETHER!
TWITCH
...BUT THIS LITTLE WENCH ALWAYS GETS IN THE WAY.
CHAIKA ACADEMY
YAWN!

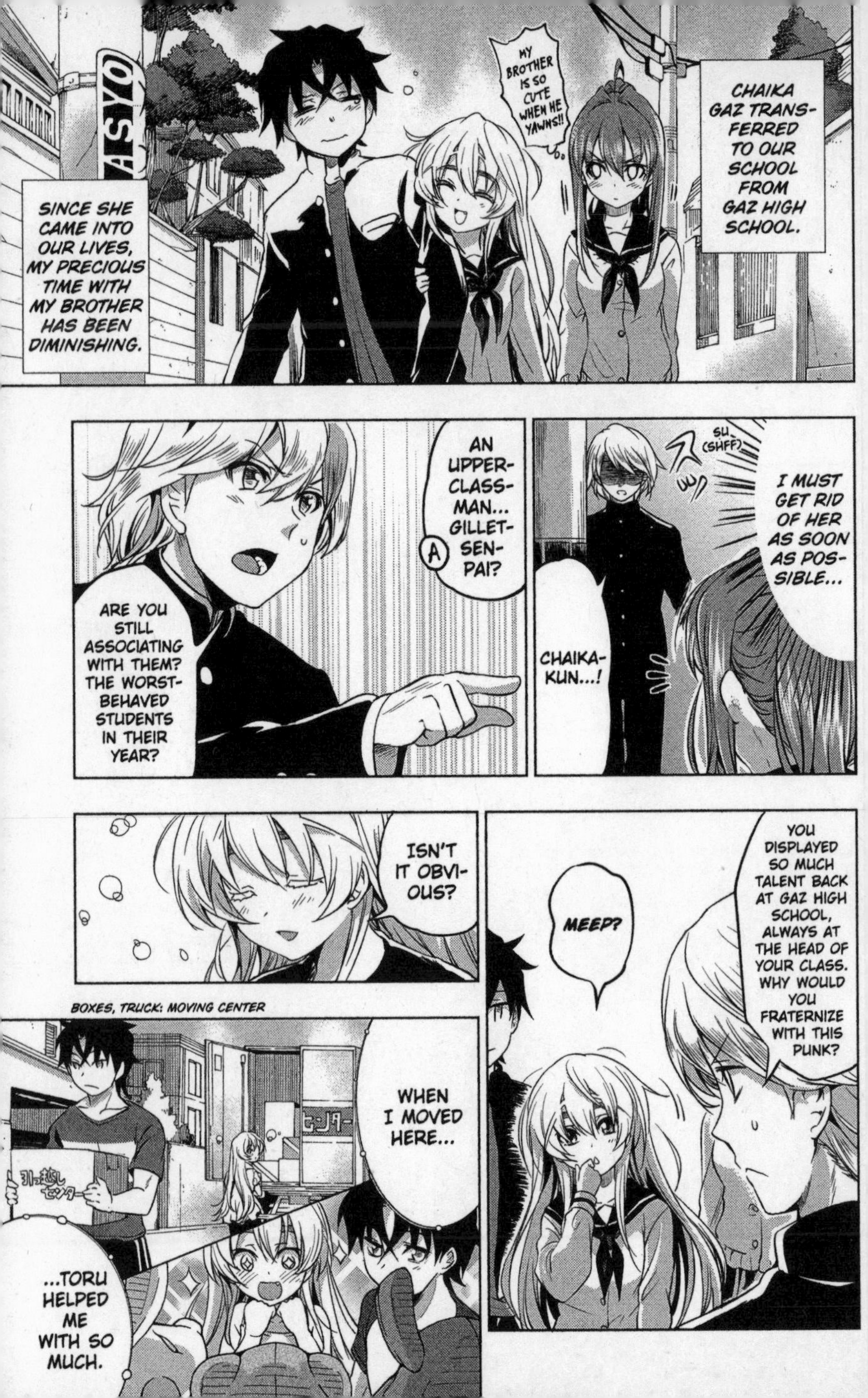
CHAIKA GAZ TRANSFERRED TO OUR SCHOOL FROM GAZ HIGH SCHOOL.
MY BROTHER IS SO CUTE WHEN HE YAWNS!!
SINCE SHE CAME INTO OUR LIVES, MY PRECIOUS TIME WITH MY BROTHER HAS BEEN DIMINISHING.
SU (SHFF)
I MUST GET RID OF HER AS SOON AS POSSIBLE...
CHAIKA-KUN...!
AN UPPERCLASSMAN... GILLET-SENPAI?
ARE YOU STILL ASSOCIATING WITH THEM? THE WORST-BEHAVED STUDENTS IN THEIR YEAR?
YOU DISPLAYED SO MUCH TALENT BACK AT GAZ HIGH SCHOOL, ALWAYS AT THE HEAD OF YOUR CLASS. WHY WOULD YOU FRATERNIZE WITH THIS PUNK?
MEEP?
ISN'T IT OBVIOUS?
BOXES, TRUCK: MOVING CENTER
WHEN I MOVED HERE...
...TORU HELPED ME WITH SO MUCH.

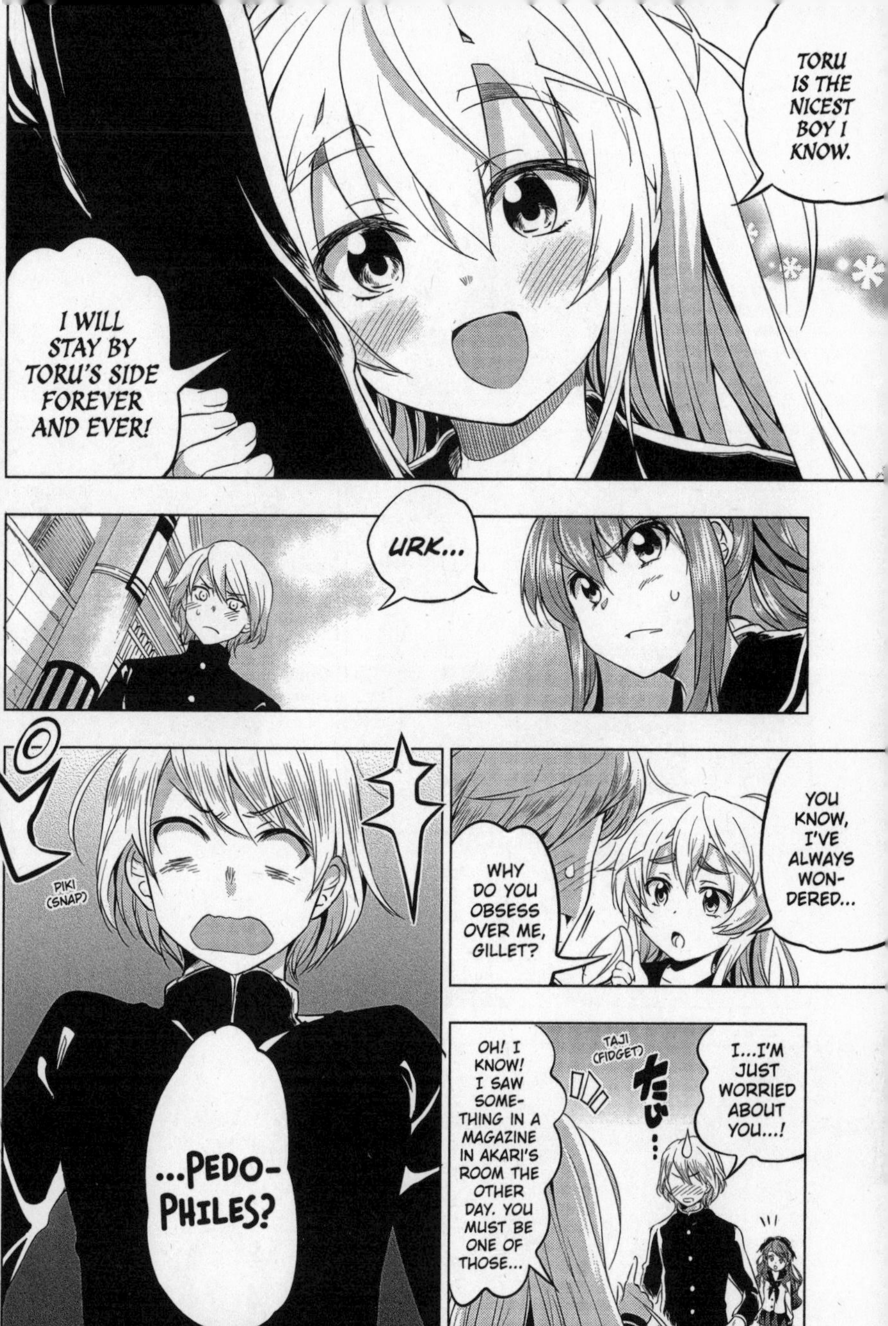
TORU IS THE NICEST BOY I KNOW.
I WILL STAY BY TORU'S SIDE FOREVER AND EVER!
URK...
YOU KNOW, I'VE ALWAYS WON-DERED...
WHY DO YOU OBSESS OVER ME, GILLET?
I...I'M JUST WORRIED ABOUT YOU...!
TAJI (FIDGET)
OH! I KNOW! I SAW SOME-THING IN A MAGAZINE IN AKARI'S ROOM THE OTHER DAY. YOU MUST BE ONE OF THOSE...
PIKI (SNAP)
...PEDO-PHILES?

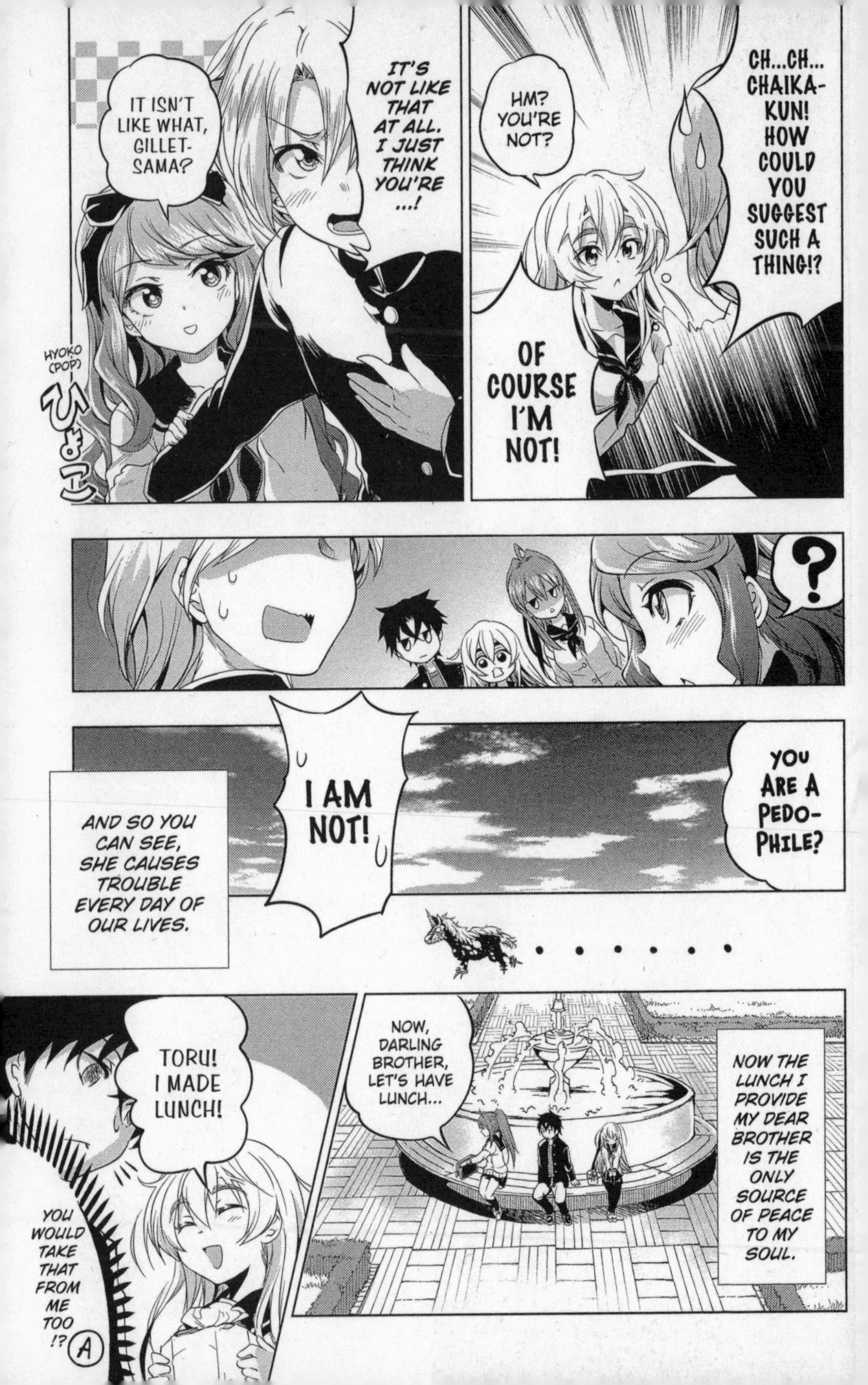
CH...CH... CHAIKA-KUN! HOW COULD YOU SUGGEST SUCH A THING!?
HM? YOU'RE NOT?
OF COURSE I'M NOT!
IT'S NOT LIKE THAT AT ALL. I JUST THINK YOU'RE ...!
IT ISN'T LIKE WHAT, GILLET-SAMA?
HYOKO (POP)
ひょこ
?
YOU ARE A PEDO-PHILE?
I AM NOT!
AND SO YOU CAN SEE, SHE CAUSES TROUBLE EVERY DAY OF OUR LIVES.
......
NOW THE LUNCH I PROVIDE MY DEAR BROTHER IS THE ONLY SOURCE OF PEACE TO MY SOUL.
NOW, DARLING BROTHER, LET'S HAVE LUNCH...
TORU! I MADE LUNCH!
YOU WOULD TAKE THAT FROM ME TOO!?
A

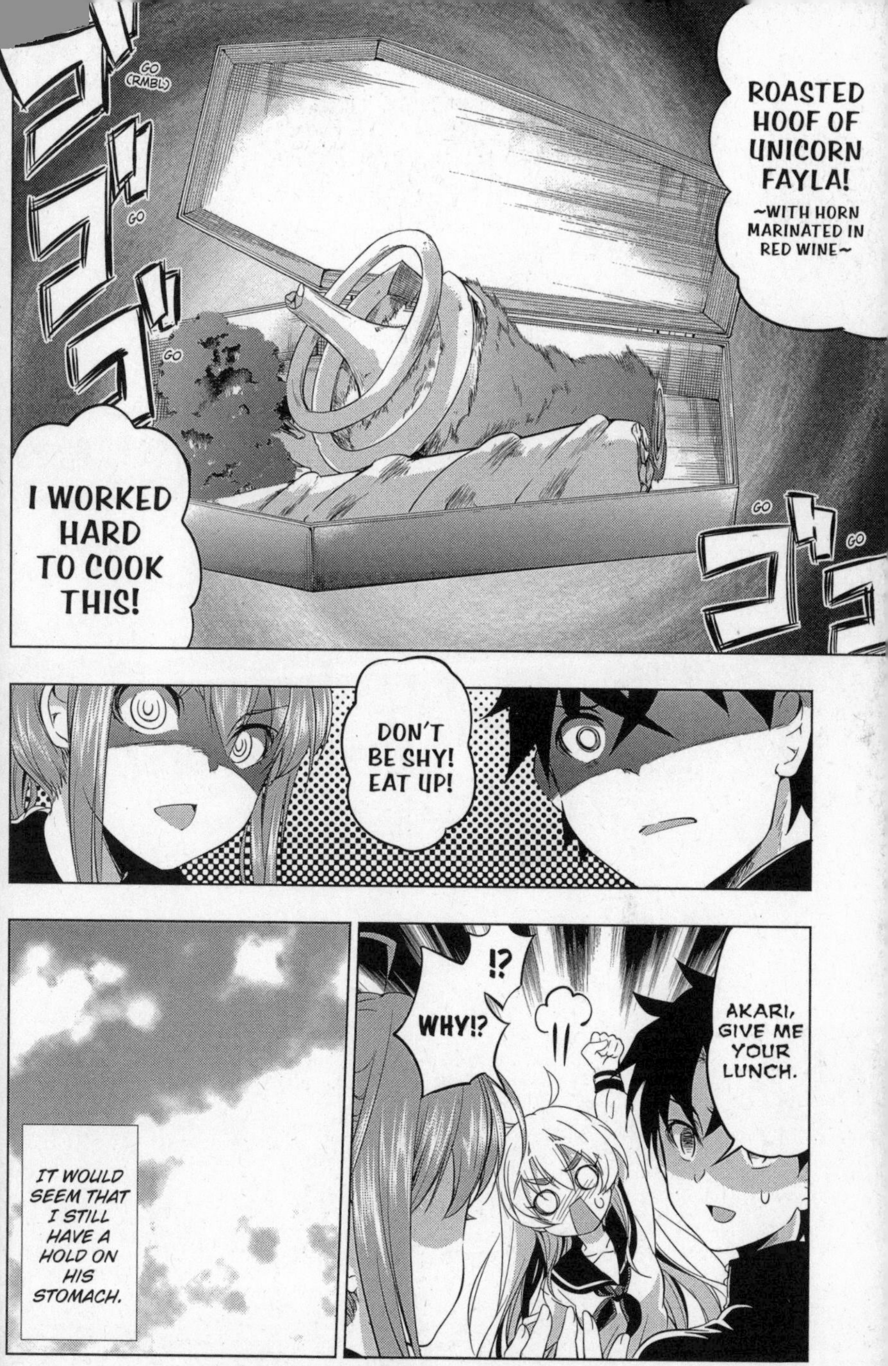
ROASTED HOOF OF UNICORN FAYLA!
~WITH HORN MARINATED IN RED WINE~
GO (RMBL)
GO
GO
I WORKED HARD TO COOK THIS!
GO
GO
DON'T BE SHY! EAT UP!
AKARI, GIVE ME YOUR LUNCH.
!?
WHY!?
IT WOULD SEEM THAT I STILL HAVE A HOLD ON HIS STOMACH.

special side story: Chaika Academy ✤ END

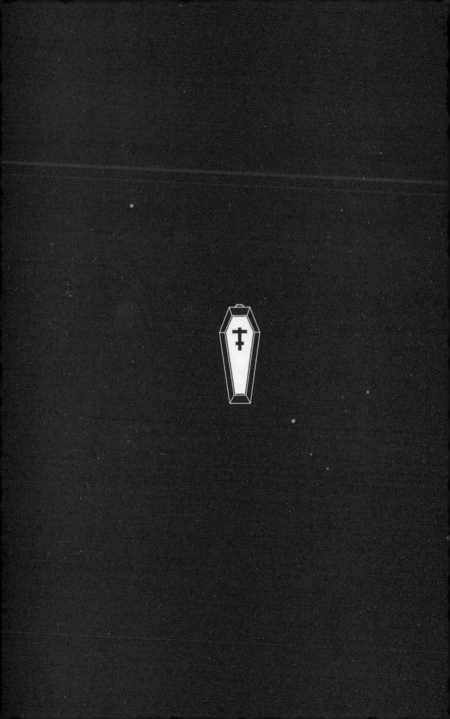

from Ichirou Sakaki

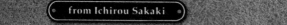

THE MANGA VERSION OF *CHAIKA* HAS NOW REACHED ITS FOURTH VOLUME. THIS IS THE DRAGOON CAVALIER DOMINICA ARC.

EVEN THE PARTS THAT I JUST CHARGE THROUGH WHEN WRITING THE NOVELS ARE HARD TO DO IN MANGA, WHICH HAS SUCH A WEALTH OF INFORMATION. IN THE VISUAL SENSE, IT'S LIKE AN ANIME—NO, ACTUALLY, ANIME HAS VOICES, BACKGROUND MUSIC, AND REAL-TIME MOVEMENTS, SO IT HAS EVEN MORE INFORMATION THAN A MANGA—BUT A MANGA IS BASICALLY PRODUCED BY ONE PERSON (EVEN IF THEY USE ASSISTANTS SOMETIMES), SO IN THAT SENSE, THE AMOUNT OF LABOR THAT GOES INTO IT IS RIDICULOUSLY HIGH.

WHILE HE FOLLOWS THE ORIGINAL FAITHFULLY, SAKAYAMA-SAN INSERTS HIS OWN UNIQUE INTERPRETATIONS EVERYWHERE, AND HE CONTINUES TO EXPAND THE WORLD AS MUCH AS EVER. THE DELIVERY OF AKARI'S LINES IS ESPECIALLY FUNNY, AND THE AUTHOR IS KEEPING THEM FOR REFERENCE. (HA-HA!)

ICHIROU SAKAKI

from Namaniku ATK

AFTERWORD
WORKING AWAY FROM HOME
CONGRATULATIONS ON RELEASING VOLUME 4! THE ANIME'S STARTED TOO, SO IT'S EVEN HARDER TO TAKE MY EYES OFF OF CHAIKA: THE COFFIN PRINCESS! PLEASE TREAT IT WELL!!
AKARI AT NIGHTTIME
2014

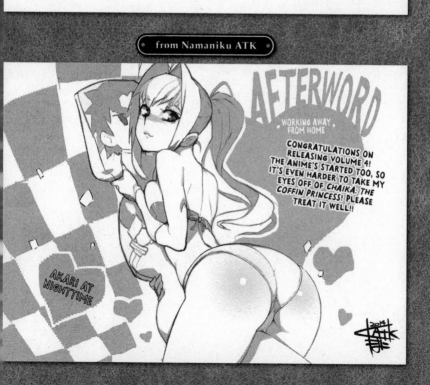

Congratulations on releasing Volume 4! I always enjoy reading the *Chaika: The Coffin Princess* manga. I love how the facial expressions ooze out of Chaika! And *Chaikakka* is on sale now too!

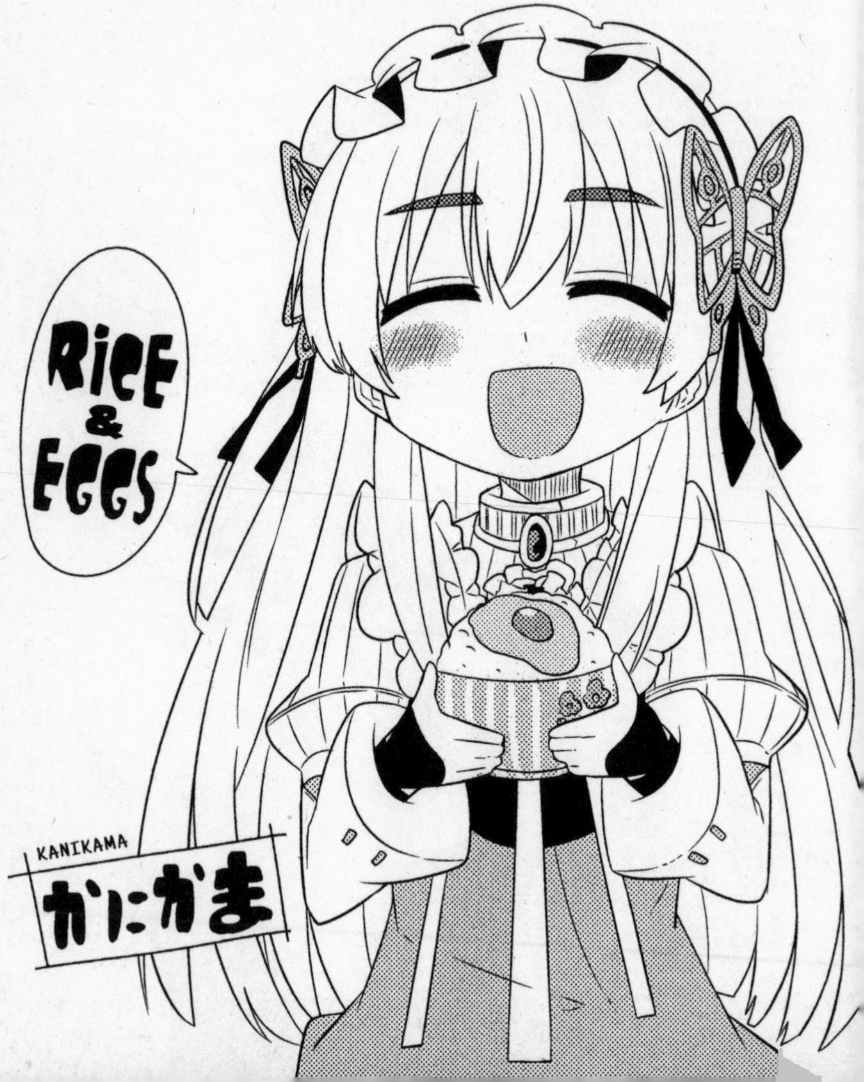
RICE & EGGS
KANIKAMA
かにかま

THANK YOU FOR BUYING VOLUME FOUR OF CHAIKA: THE COFFIN PRINCESS.

THIS IS CHAIKA: THE COFFIN PRINCESS VOLUME FOUR. I'M VERY SORRY THAT SO MUCH TIME PASSED BETWEEN THE RELEASES OF VOLUME THREE AND VOLUME FOUR. THE REASON THIS HAPPENED IS THAT I EXPERIENCED MY FIRST HOSPITAL STAY. IT REALLY SLOWED DOWN MY WORK, AND I'M VERY SORRY FOR THE INCONVENIENCE I CAUSED TO THE READERS AND THOSE INVOLVED IN THE PUBLICATION. IT WAS A REALLY POWERFUL LESSON IN HOW YOUR HEALTH SHOULD COME FIRST. AND WHILE I WAS IN THE HOSPITAL, THEY ANNOUNCED THAT THERE WOULD BE A CHAIKA ANIME, SO THERE I GO CAUSING PROBLEMS FOR EVERYONE...

THE ANIME WILL FINALLY BE STARTING IN APRIL, AND AS THE PERSON RESPONSIBLE FOR THE MANGA VERSION, I'M HOPING TO DO WHATEVER I CAN, EVEN IF IT'S NOT MUCH, TO GET YOU EXCITED ABOUT IT.

ANYWAY, I HOPE YOU FANS WILL ALL CONTINUE TO ENJOY THE NOVELS, THE ANIME, AND THE MANGA.

AND ONCE AGAIN, I WOULD LIKE TO THANK SAKAKI-SENSEI, NAMANIKU-SENSEI, AND KANIKAMA-SENSEI FOR THEIR CONTRIBUTIONS!

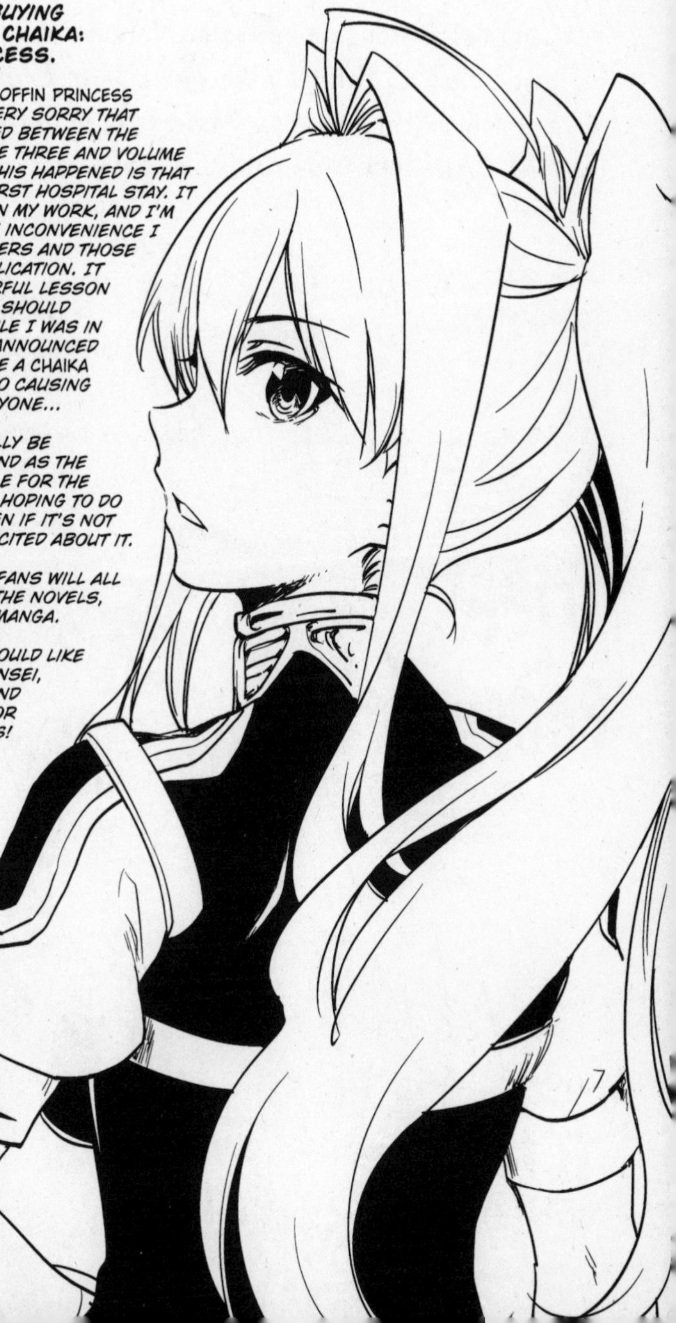

SHINTA SAKAYAMA

2014.3

CHAIKA: THE COFFIN PRINCESS

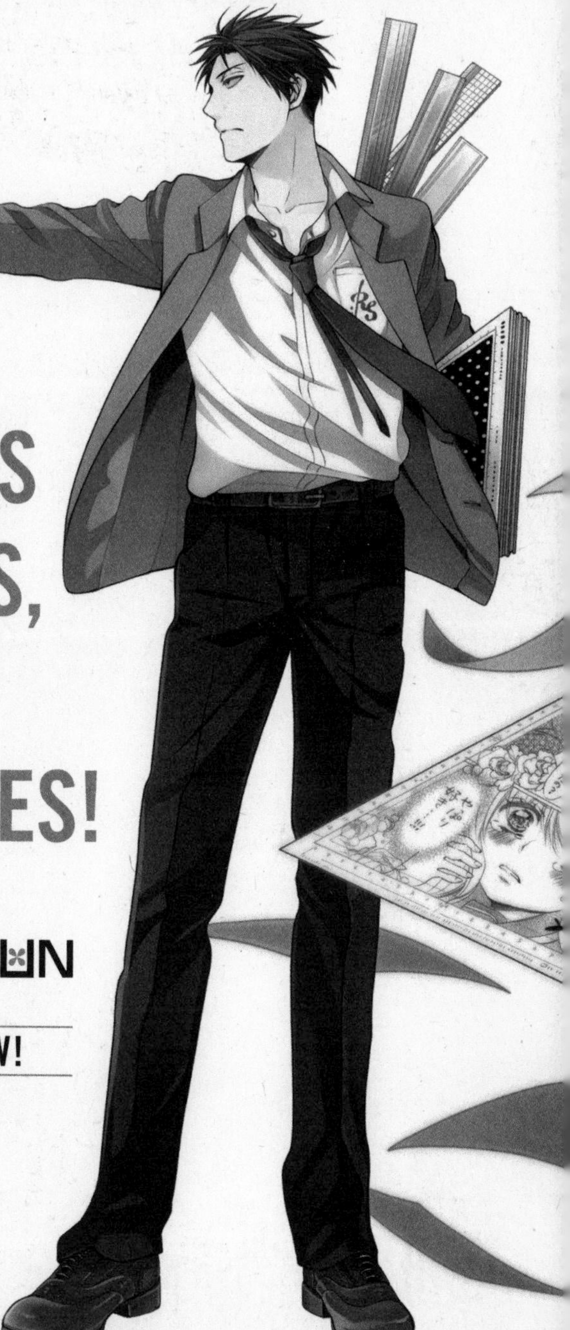

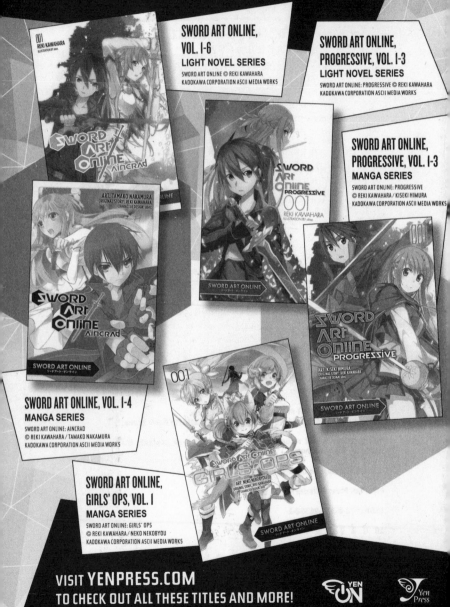

CHAIKA:
THE COFFIN PR

Original Story By: ICHIROU SA
Manga: SHINTA SAKAYAMA
Character Design: Namaniku ATK (Nitroplus)

Translation: Athena and Alethea Nibley
Lettering: Abigail Blackman

HITSUGI NO CHAIKA Volume 4
©Ichirou Sakaki, Nitroplus 2014
©Shinta SAKAYAMA 2014
Edited by KADOKAWA SHOTEN. First published in Japan in 2014 by KADOKAWA CORPORATION, Tokyo. English translation rights arranged with KADOKAWA CORPORATION, Tokyo through TUTTLE-MORI AGENCY, INC., Tokyo.

Translation © 2016 by Hachette Book Group, Inc.

Yen Press
Hachette Book Group
1290 Avenue of the Americas
New York, NY 10104

www.hachettebookgroup.com † www.yenpress.com

BVG

Printed in the United States of America